A Singing Ambivalence

A Singing Ambivalence

*American Immigrants
between Old World and New,
1830–1930*

Victor Greene

The Kent State University Press
KENT AND LONDON

© 2004 by The Kent State University Press, Kent, Ohio 44242
ALL RIGHTS RESERVED
Library of Congress Catalog Card Number 2003022253
ISBN 0-87338-794-5
Manufactured in the United States of America

08 07 06 05 04   5 4 3 2 1

Library of Congress Cataloging-in-Publication Data
Greene, Victor R.
  A singing ambivalence : American immigrants between old world and new,
1830–1930 / Victor Greene.
    p.   cm.
  Includes bibliographical references (p.) and index.
  ISBN 0-87338-794-5 (pbk. : alk. paper)
  1. Immigrants—United States—Songs and music—History and criticism.
2. United States—Emigration and immigration—Songs and music—History
and criticism.   I. Title.
  ML3551.G697   2004
  782.42'086'9120973—dc22

                                                    2003022253

British Library Cataloging-in-Publication data are available.

To John Higham, distinguished historian, colleague, and friend.

Contents

Preface and Acknowledgments

With a lifelong interest in music and song, I came to discover more recently that these art forms were much more important than simply forms of entertainment. They can also function as communication, providing a valuable method for not only composers and performers to express points of view but also more importantly for scholars to learn the sentiments of ordinary people. Music then offers an entrée into the minds of less articulate people, whose opinions are normally difficult to discern. The masses, too, I found can "speak" to the world through their attachment to song, especially to those musical works that are well-known and popular. They, too, then have the means to express themselves emotionally. The most obvious proof of this latter property of musical communication having an emotional property is its use by filmmakers, who wish to enhance public sentiment or extend a mood, whether it be joy, melancholy, or a state of apprehension or ambivalence.

Since almost every ethnic group has a musical heritage, often a rich one, scholars are likely to find public feelings and attitudes about important events in their past. The assumption of this work is that the song repertoire can discern how suppressed minorities and migrating peoples felt about their circumstances, such as treatment by the majority or their movement from their traditional home and family to an unfamiliar destination. As I indicate throughout the text, this extended study of a part of musical history, while possibly unusual, is not a pioneering work in exploiting music and song; as a number of scholars, folklorists, ethnomusicologists, and a few historians have examined the musical heritage seeking popular feeling.

The major feature of this study is that through the examination of the lyrics of selected songs, one can identify the range of emotions as hope, insecurity, and homesickness that our immigrant groups had about coming to and settling in America. In addition, through their group songs, one can make comparisons between those groups. This work concludes that while the pervasive attitude among all immigrants was mixed, on balance it was chiefly one of ambivalence tinged with unhappiness.

The wide range of groups covered and the distinctive, extended repertoire of the nearly dozen immigrant groups here obviously had to rest heavily on the help of the few theoretical publications on the subject and many colleagues who were experts in the various group musics. The major inspiration for this work was Leonard Levine's classic *Black Culture and Black Consciousness* (1977) and his sensitive use of music and song to learn the feelings of slaves. Added to this was the encouragement and substantial criticisms of my project provided by James Leary, Judith McCulloh, Philip Bohlman, Bill Malone, the students of the 1994 NEH summer seminar in popular nineteenth-century American music, and especially its directors, Ronald Walters of the Johns Hopkins University and John Spitzer of the Peabody Conservatory.

I am grateful, too, to others who either responded at length to questions I asked or their comments on sections of the work, such as John Jentz, Anne-Charlotte Harvey, Roger Daniels, Him Mark Lai, Su de San Zheng, Emily Hill, Xiaohong Shi, Susan Cheng of Music of China, Philip Sonnichsen, William H. A. Williams, James Dorman, Nancy Carnevale, Stephen Whitfield, and colleagues at the University of Wisconsin-Milwaukee: Ron Ross, Michael Gordon, Joseph Rodriguez, Lawrence Baldassaro, and Edith Moravsik. I had to call on many, of course, to assist in translations. They are all listed in the notes, but a few added more substantial help, such as Karen Majewski and Thaddeus Gromada of the Polish American Historical Association, Juha Niemela of Finland, Luisa Del Guidice of UCLA, Paul Melrood of Milwaukee, Ulf Beijbom of the Swedish Emigrant Institute, Chana (Eleanor) Mlotek of Yivo Institute, and Joel Wurl and the staff of the Immigration History Research Center, University of Minnesota. I also wish to express my thanks to the archives staff at the Milwaukee County Historical Center, the Lilly Library at Indiana University, and the Enoch Pratt Free Library and Maryland Historical Society, both in Baltimore, for their kind assistance.

Timely grants enabled me to hasten the completion of the work. I am grateful to the NEH summer seminar program, the Milwaukee Society for Jewish Learning, and a sabbatical leave provided me by the University of Wisconsin-Milwaukee.

My greatest debts for this work especially are to my esteemed colleague, the late John Higham of the Johns Hopkins University, whose distinguished scholarship, creative intellect, and elegant writings were a model for me throughout the years, and my wife, Laura, whose skill at writing has helped my own prose immeasurably.

Finally I am exceedingly grateful to Joanna Hildebrand Craig and Kathy Method of the Kent University Press, who along with Dr. McCulloh had more faith than I that this manuscript would appear in print.

Grateful acknowledgement for permission to reproduce from the following:

"A Brivele Der Mamen" ("A Letter to Mother"); words and music by Solomon Small; copyright © 1933 (renewed) Music Sales Corp. (ASCAP); international copyright secured; all rights reserved.

"Barndomshemmet"; translation from *Swedish Emigrant Ballads*, ed. Richard L. Wright; copyright ©1965 University of Nebraska Press; copyright © renewed 1993 University of Nebraska Press.

"Bröder vi har langt att gå" (traditional); courtesy House of Emigrants, Växjö, Sweden.

"A Conversation between Two Ranchers"; from P. Taylor, "Songs of the Mexican Migration," in *Puro Mexicano*, ed. J. Frank Dobie (Austin: Encino, 1935); courtesy Publications of the Texas Folklore Society; PTFS 12.

"Corrido de Robstown"; from Paul S. Taylor, *An American Mexican Frontier*; copyright ©1934 University of North Carolina Press.

"Defense of the Emigrant"; from P. Taylor, "Songs of the Mexican Migration," in *Puro Mexicano*, ed. J. Frank Dobie (Austin: Encino, 1935); courtesy Publications of the Texas Folklore Society; PTFS 12.

"The Disillusioned Immigrant"; from J. Leary and R. March, "Farm, Forestry, and Factory," in *Songs about Work: Essays in Occupational Culture for Richard A. Reuss,* ed. Archie Green; courtesy Special Publications of Folklore Institute, Indiana University, Bloomington.

"An Emigrant's Farewell"; from P. Taylor, "Songs of the Mexican Migration," in *Puro Mexicano*, ed. J. Frank Dobie (Austin: Encino, 1935); courtesy Publications of the Texas Folklore Society; PTFS 12.

"The Emigrant's Farewell"; courtesy Lilly Library, Indiana University, Bloomington, Indiana.

"Farewell, Mother Norway"; from *Norwegian Emigrant Songs and Ballads,* ed. and trans. Theodore C. Blegent and Martin R. Ruud (Minneapolis: Univ. of Minnesota Press, 1936); copyright ©1936 University of Minnesota Press.

"Farewell Song for German Emigrants Going to America"; from *Eagle in the New World,* ed. Theodore Gish and Richard Spuler (College Station: Texas A&M Univ. Press, 1986); courtesy Texas A&M University Press.

"Farewell to Slieve Gallon"; from *Thousands Are Sailing,* comp. John Moulden (1994); courtesy Ulstersongs, Northern Ireland.

"Farväl, O moder Svea"; courtesy House of Emigrants, Växjö, Sweden.

"Give an Irish Lad a Chance"; courtesy Lilly Library, Indiana University, Bloomington.

"The Green Fields of America"; from John Moulden, *Thousands Are Sailing* (1994); courtesy Ulstersongs, Northern Ireland.

"Hail to Thee, Columbus, Be Praised!"; from *Eagle in the New World,* ed. Theodore Gish and Richard Spuler (College Station: Texas A&M Univ. Press, 1986); courtesy Texas A&M University Press.

"Hälsa dem därhemma"; courtesy House of Emigrants, Växjö, Sweden.

"The Happy Shamrock Shore"; courtesy W. A. Craig, Coleraine, Northern Ireland.

"I'm Sitting on the Stile, Mary"; from *Irish Emigrant Ballads,* ed. Richard L. Wright; copyright © 1975 Popular Press; courtesy University of Wisconsin Press.

"In America"; from *The Two Rosetos,* ed. Carla Bianco (Bloomington: Indiana Univ. Press, 1974); courtesy Indiana University Press.

"In a Steel Mill"; from J. Leary and R. March, "Farm, Forestry, and Factory," in *Songs about Work: Essays in Occupational Culture for Richard A. Reuss,* ed. Archie Green; courtesy Special Publications of Folklore Institute, Indiana University, Bloomington.

"Joaquin Murrieta"; from P. Sonnichsen, liner notes to *Corridos y Tragedias de la Frontera,* Arhoolie CD 7019/20 (1994), Arhoolie Records, El Cerrito, California; www.arhoolie.com.

Lyric segment from Samuel Gompers, *Seventy Years of Life and Labor,* vol. 1; courtesy Augustus M. Kelley, Publishers.

"Mamma, Mamma, Mamma, Damme Cendo Lire"; from *Italian Traditional Song,* 2d. ed. (1995), trans. Luisa del Guidice; courtesy Luisa del Guidice.

"Mayn Yingele" ("My Little Boy"); trans. Frederick Rzewski; from Pete Seeger and Bob Reiser, comps., *Carry It On!: A History in Sound and Picture of the Working Men and Women of America* (New York: Simon and Schuster, 1985); courtesy Frederick Rzewski and the European Public Relations Consulting.

"McKee's Farewell to Ireland"; from *Thousands Are Sailing,* comp. John Moulden; courtesy Belfast Public Libraries, Northern Ireland.

"My Girl from Donegal"; courtesy W. A. Craig, Coleraine, Northern Ireland.

"Oleana"; from *Studies and Records,* vol. 2, ed. Martin R. Ruud (1927); courtesy Norwegian American Historical Association, Northfield, Minnesota.

"Paddy's Farewell"; from *Irish Emigrant Ballads,* ed. Richard L. Wright; copyright © 1975 Popular Press; courtesy University of Wisconsin Press.

"Persecution of Pancho Villa"; from G. Hernandez, liner notes to *The Mexican Revolution,* Arhoolie CD 7041/4 (1996), Arhoolie Records, El Cerrito, California; www.arhoolie.com.

"A Pole Was Journeying"; from *Merrily We Sing: 105 Polish Folksongs*, ed. H. Pawlowska; copyright ©1983 Wayne State University Press.

"The Renegade"; from Manuel Gamio, *Mexican Immigration to the United States: A Study of Human Migration and Adjustment* (Chicago: Univ. of Chicago Press, 1930); courtesy University of Chicago Press.

"Rich Amerikay"; from *Irish Emigrant Ballads*, ed. Richard L. Wright; copyright © 1975 Popular Press; courtesy University of Wisconsin Press.

"Riley to Ameriky"; from *Ballads and Sea Songs of Newfoundland*, ed. Elisabeth Bristol Greenleaf and Grace Yarrow Mansfield (Cambridge, Mass.: Harvard Univ. Press, 1933); copyright © 1933 Harvard University Press.

"St. Patrick's Day in New York"; courtesy Lilly Library, Indiana University, Bloomington, Indiana.

"The Swedish Girl"; from *America's Ethnic Music*, ed. Theodore Grame (Tarpon Springs, Fla.: Cultural Maintenance Associates, 1976); courtesy Theodore Grame.

"Thousands Are Sailing to America"; from *Thousands Are Sailing*, comp. John Moulden (1994); courtesy Ulstersongs, Northern Ireland.

Untitled song from Marlon Hom, "Some Cantonese Folksongs of the American Experience," *Western Folklore* 42 (1983); copyright © California Folklore Society, Long Beach, California.

Untitled song from *Norwegian Emigrant Songs and Ballads*, ed. and trans. Theodore C. Blegent and Martin R. Ruud (Minneapolis: Univ. of Minnesota Press, 1936); copyright ©1936 University of Minnesota Press.

Untitled song from *Studies and Records*, vol. 2, ed. Martin R. Ruud (1927); courtesy Norwegian American Historical Association, Northfield, Minnesota.

Untitled song from *The Two Rosetos*, ed. Carla Bianco (Bloomington: Indiana Univ. Press, 1974); courtesy Indiana University Press.

"We Sold Our Homesteads"; from A. Widen, "Scandinavian Folklore," *Bulletin of the American Institute of Swedish Arts, Literature, and Science* 2 (Jan.–Mar. 1947); courtesy American-Swedish Institute, Minneapolis, Minnesota.

"What We Can Find in America": from *The Two Rosetos*, ed. Carla Bianco (Bloomington: Indiana Univ. Press, 1974); courtesy Indiana University Press.

"A Young Bride Calls across the Hills"; from *The Sandalwood Mountains*, comp. Tin Yuke Char (1975); copyright ©1975 University of Hawai'i Press.

Introduction

While one historian may have claimed too much by defining American immigration history as synonymous with all of our national history, certainly many in the recent past wish to learn more about what was on the minds of our foreign ancestors when they arrived on these shores over the last three centuries. Did America turn out to be for them the haven of "milk and honey," or was it a place of much discomfort, a land that dashed their hopes of a better life, where they encountered misery, shock, and alienation? Or was their early experience a mixture of hope and sorrow? My answer is that it was likely the latter, more unhappy for nonwhites than others.

The question of their feelings about the new land, raised now at the start of the twenty-first century, has particular relevance since the immigration issue remains on people's minds due to with the heavy influx of minorities over the last half century. In fact the public concern over the place of ethnic and racial groups in American society has clearly intensified. A sizable part of the flood of newcomers, being illegal, has caused profound worry about "controlling our borders" and securing our national welfare in the face of subversives and terrorists. Particularly since the mid-1960s, with the liberalization of the nation's formerly discriminatory immigration policy and the ensuing influx of particularly nonwhite arrivals, the issue of whether to tighten restrictions or to continue our policy of multiculturalism has produced a new nativism willing to debate the dangers of America as culturally diverse.[1]

Those issues, along with an increased interest in the lives of ordinary Americans, have influenced academics to reexamine the process of Americanization. The question is how, to what extent, or even whether our disparate racial and ethnic groups assimilated into one people or remained separate and fragmented, retaining their minority cultures. A recent historian's foray into the question of

Americanization—that is, whether the formation of that national identity among the various ethnic communities was coercive or free—has continued the controversy over "e pluribus unum" and is evidence of the ongoing scholarly effort being applied to the topic.[2]

Whatever the disagreements over how and even whether immigrants became Americans, the post-1960s generation of historians all would agree that the process was neither as simple nor as linear as previous observers had thought. Becoming American was a complex transformation.

The new social historians conceded that the older, elitist, ethnocentric, and outsider perspectives on these incoming peoples needed to be revised in favor of more sophisticated studies from within the groups and from the masses, those at the lower ends of the socioeconomic scale. The clarion call for many of this post-1960s generation of academics was for an immigrant and ethnic history that was "from the inside out" or "from the bottom up." Those "poor and huddled masses" described in Emma Lazarus's poem at the base of the Statue of Liberty were no longer viewed as passive objects of social forces but as subjects, individual actors, who, whether successfully or not, confronted middle-class Anglo-American culture on their own terms, constructing their own institutions.[3]

Yet while the more recent historians have responded to that appeal with more-comprehensive and more-complex profiles of the many previously neglected or ignored groups, that revisionist scholarship itself remains incomplete. On the whole it still offers, for example, a more generalized outline of these minority cultures rather than an individualized one. The concentration on discreet collectivities, such as the Polish, Mexican, and Hmong communities, seems to have obscured the complexity of the personal, individual bonds within those cultures. The connection with one's group and national heritage was and is not uniform and homogeneous, of course, but very possibly composed of various elements, even those that might be contradictory. The entire process of identity development is again certainly not a simple one that can be generalized easily; it was one that entailed considerable internal differentiation. Even from a group rather than an individual perspective, that the ethnic collectivity was not monolithic is a widely accepted proposition.[4]

The concentration here on the psychological nature of ethnic, racial, and national affiliation is neither original nor new. Immigration historiography has always included numerous sources from an individual level. Autobiographical accounts, the many published collections of immigrant letters, and the rich, creative ethnic literature all refer to the personal experience of newcomers. Still, obtaining a more complete spectrum of the psychic variation among group members in order to record their emotional makeup remains neglected.

One way to illuminate that more intimate, emotional dimension in the assimilation process may be found in studying the popular arts. A richly expressive culture emanated from within all the groups. Art, music, and drama are an entrée into and a sensitive gauge of both ethnic and individual adjustment.

American immigration historians have lagged behind their colleagues in related fields, such as ethnomusicology, anthropology, and folklore, in exploiting that ethnic aesthetic in depth, thus at least partially obscuring the psychology and popular *mentalité* of the past. That reluctance is rather surprising as most of those familiar with immigration and their subjects' thorough creativity and enjoyment of the popular arts consider them as reflective of grassroots history "from the bottom up." Historians are well acquainted with the extensive and vibrant cultural life of the groups. The arts, in fact, have always been some of the elements that actually *constituted* ethnic culture. As one writer has put it, those activities "present the essence of a group's culture. As symbolic expressions of identity, they touch directly on a group's most deeply-held values . . . [,] reinforce a feeling of belonging . . . [,] and define the communities for others . . . and themselves."[5]

If the goal then is to monitor and assess the process of cultural assimilation among immigrants, then a more sophisticated exploitation of previously neglected sources, particularly the folk and popular arts, is essential. Reviewing the expressive culture among immigrants would certainly enhance an understanding of *both* the nature of ethnic cohesion and the variety of personal ties even while they changed over time.

A few ethnic historians have at least formally recognized the existence of an immigrant aesthetic as an integral part of migration and settlement. One leading proponent has been John Bodnar, whose masterly synthesis *The Transplanted*, unlike other survey and interpretive texts, does refer to ethnic folklife in the lives of newcomers.[6] He and a few other historians found that groups held regular, festive celebrations that were examples of an inventive, malleable, and dynamic group identity. But they viewed their groups collectively, not as individuals with varied, personal ties to tradition.[7]

It has been largely nonhistorians who have recognized the full value of studying the arts in determining ethnic identity. The work of anthropologists like Clifford Geertz on culture as a symbolic system and Victor Turner on cultural performances as ritual, as well as Benedict Anderson's reference to aesthetic symbols as the source of imagined national communities, all encourage scholars of history to examine the ethnic aesthetic.[8]

This book closely examines a part of the immigrants' expressive culture, namely the popular music and song of these groups, as an intimate reflection of their concerns about their migratory experience. The ballads in particular offer a sensitive evocation of the complex emotional feeling that individuals had about both their movement to America and their ties to their ethnic tradition. Knowing the lyrical content of those songs, their social and situational context, and the circumstances under which they were sung all lead to the conclusion that immigrants generally, though not uniformly, suffered personal discomfort from and disillusionment over their transfer. For most, such psychic unease was not total, however, for these newcomers also retained in America some of the optimistic sentiments that originally propelled them to the new land. They did recognize that it was in some ways a better place for them. But as aliens in an unfamiliar society, they soon came to understand better the sacrifice they made in moving. Most did stay while some returned. More significantly here, they developed a considerable ambivalence about their migration, rendered in both music and song.

Social historians have already cited the salience of songs in their own works, but it has been largely as casual illustrations of sentiment, not as an important means of communication for all groups.[9] Concentrating on popular music and song as a research methodology will certainly enhance social-history scholarship since it aims to probe the mentality of the masses.

Over the last generation, as Anthony Seeger has stated, social scientists have rarely considered music in discussions of group formation; only a few folklorists, musical scholars, and postmodern theorists have recognized the significance of this genre.[10] Popular music to this handful was far more salient to understanding that mass mentality than just a pleasant form of entertainment and diversion. That aesthetic reflected a social reality as understood and felt emotionally by its audience, the listeners, and performers of an immigrant ethnic community.

Recent medical findings support the view that music is closely connected to the mind. They suggest that musical patterns have a special ability of enduring in listeners' consciousness. A familiar piece has such a profound retentive effect, both conscious and subconscious, that the affected individuals consider it a part of their identity. Psychological and musicological research refer to that property as "music on the brain."[11]

Postmodern theorists also have supported the revelatory character of familiar music by their criticism of the hegemony of Western civilization. These intellectuals have challenged the old canons of taste for ignoring and even suppressing the cultural expression of repressed marginal groups. Doing so, they charge, was not just a grievous oversight; postmodernists claim that by neglecting the aesthetic among minority groups, prior social critics also were deliberately ignoring evidence of the flaws in the society. Whatever the merits of their argument, certainly postmodern theory upholds ethnic music as an important expression of opinion and group sentiment.[12]

A few others in folklore, anthropology, and ethnomusicology, always sensitive to what ordinary people sang and played, have also indicated that music reflected the attitudes of both the ethnic individual and the group. They have arrayed a set of powerful reasons for studying such aesthetic activity.

Above all, they point out, popular music, whether purely folk or commercially produced, contributes to the collective sentiment of people that is the essence of ethnic tradition. That kind of music familiar to all encourages the masses "to feel they are in touch with an essential part of themselves, their emotions, and their 'community.'"[13] Musical "tones," as one musicologist put it, are themselves "associated with qualities attributed to non-aural modes of sense perception."[14]

Thus music and song are really communication and similar yet more sensitive to ordinary speech in their ability to convey the entire spectrum of emotional expression, the "variety of feelings, moods, emotions, and qualities of mind and character: emotional turbulence, exquisite tenderness, mounting excitement, [and] ecstatic release."[15] Clearly then, again, by their very nature, music and song not only offer auditory pleasure but also allow entrée into and even induce a freer mood in the psychological conditioning of the audience.[16]

That psychological property can therefore illuminate the nature of collective and group association in the individual. Again, as one of several symbols of collective life, music plays a part, if not the major role, in the very construction and persistence of an ethnic consciousness. The "power of music," a recent scholar has observed, "while elusive and difficult to analyze[,] . . . helps create . . . social bonds between people. . . . [It has] great impact on human behavior in the ways in which people organize and give meaning to their lives, individually and collectively."[17] Another leading student of the ethnic basis of nations listed music as one of those symbols of collective life, such as diet, etiquette, art, rituals, language, and religion, that are important internally as "constant reminders of a common heritage and fate."[18]

One music scholar has gone even further in broadening the social significance of musical performance as it induces a state he calls "musicking." Being involved with music, he states, is not just separate activities commanding the attention of an audience or offering pleasure; it really entails human action. People at a musical event "come together" as "players, listeners and hall staff alike—to take part in a ceremony in which their values, which is to say, their feelings about what are right and wrong proper relationships are affirmed, explored and celebrated."[19]

Other observers have stressed music's psychological power in nostalgia. Theodore Reik points out that hearing a musical composition can restore in people at least some associations with past emotions and ideas.[20] Hence by inference, he too suggests that music preserves and strengthens ethnic cohesion over time.

Compared to other cultural products, such as paintings that one views or literature that one reads, music and song provide a more intimate association of art and the individual. One is more deeply involved emotionally in the latter partly because it is often participatory. Responding to the intensifying interest in rock music in the 1950s and 1960s and its property of being social communication, sociologist Simon Frith has pointed out that while that music is aimed at a mass audience, popular music can also so affect an individual that it becomes a part of both a private and group identity. Its melody is "possessable in ways other cultural forms . . . are not," and familiar folk music "mark[s] the boundaries of ethnic identity."[21] In both composition and performance, by its timing, aural dynamics, rhythm, and other dynamics, music certainly generates considerable emotion.

Additionally, in a succinct summation of music's distinctive role in human communication as stated by the distinguished ethnomusicologist John Blacking, one of his colleagues observed that that art form had both intellectual and emotional properties: "Music is . . . *felt* as well as made and heard; it induces and invokes the participation of the whole person, body and soul, not just the processes of intellectual reason"; and he reiterated Blacking's theme that "the human capacity to send and receive messages through tone, melody, and rhythm is . . . a biological phenomenon as well as a cognitive one."[22]

Another observer has stressed the extraordinary effect of music on children. They are so deeply engaged in music that adults do not recognize that involvement. It "is on their minds and in their bodies. . . . [It] appears everywhere in [their] lives . . . ," especially as it involves their participation. And she concludes that "embedded within the melodies and rhythms are messages . . . , expressions of ideas that are both concrete and abstract," that tell of "important sentiments . . . understood as well by children as by adults."[23]

If individuals retain music as deeply affective, it follows that song added to melody also represents and even further contributes to a person's emotional state. One observer who has related the folksong to individual consciousness has cited one of its properties as revealing ordinary people's *mentalité*. Drawing from Hans Kohn's idea of social communication, he points out that the "poetic character of song underlines its function as a highly effective medium of secondary-symbol formation. . . . From this angle, light may also be thrown on the . . . problem of historically differential forms of common people's consciousness, or . . . mentalities."[24]

Another psychiatrist, following the idea of Freud and Reik of the haunting melody, found after examining over two thousand hit tunes of the nineteenth and twentieth centuries that the lyric as well as the music can be a vehicle of the unconscious.[25] In noting the importance of language in the emerging sense of nationalism, Benedict Anderson stresses that patriotic airs were particular formative. Singing, he adds notably, in the form of poetry and song helped create community. "Anthems such as the 'Marseillaise,' 'Waltzing Matilda,' and 'Indonesia Raya' provide occasions for unisonality, for the echoed physical realization of the 'imagined community.'"[26]

Certainly then lyrics, more than just music alone, provide direct and immediate contact between performer and listener. Sociologists since the 1950s have always recognized the value of content analysis of lyrics to discern popular social attitudes, and the more recent efforts in doing so have grown in sophistication. So the method remains of value. As Frith has pointed out, folk-type songs (those popular within the groups as distinct from those of the mainstream culture) "are significant [social sources] because they have a 'real closeness' with their consumers."[27]

Several properties of popular songs make for this special closeness to their audience. First, the familiar ballads have an authentic origin in the past in at least two ways. Whether or not accurate historically, they are based on well-known past events or the exploits of a familiar hero or heroine. Also, as folklorists point out, as a part of an oral tradition these songs can be the true voice of the masses, especially of the least articulate lower classes, who are the more difficult group to reach in the historical record.

A second property of songs is that lyrics convey emotions more pointedly and express attitudes more directly than music alone or either written or oral testimony. Music and song have a wide range of dynamics, soft and loud, and in major and minor keys. Finally, song lyrics are a less inhibited form of expressing sentiment than other types of communication. They can be free messages, less restricted or monitored than other cultural forms (as indicated below). So lyrics as music help symbolize and hence bond the group.

Widely sung ballads are, of course, popular internally. Whether folk, and thus handed down through generations, or composed for profit, they provide a means of expression for people who otherwise would not be heard speaking about their lives. Thus they are indeed important historical sources.

Two observers of the English song tradition, for example, have identified that type of aesthetic source as significant for historians. They view popular ballads as being valuable evidence of public memory and opinion on social conditions and problems, in their case the results of industrialization. These particular songs, they state, reveal the difficult adjustment workers had to make in their move from a rural to urban society, all expressed in a "truthful and sympathetic manner." Hence the songs are, in fact, "lyrical statements of the emotional and practical problems of the bearers," and while music scholars have neglected them for their mediocre quality, when "properly organized . . . , they could produce valuable material for historians, social scientists [and others]."[28]

As to the problematic character of some of these ballads, that they are the voice of only the balladeers, profit-seeking performers, or composers rather than that of their audience, writers point to the popularity of those works. They have responded to that charge by asserting that since these songs were so well known, they can lead to historical truth. To be popular means that there had to exist a "close and affectionate relationship between . . . [the] song-writers and their audience." To be successful the balladeers had to be "extraordinarily skillful in capturing the ear of the public and appealing to the popular taste." They conclude, therefore, that broadside sheets "tell . . . what was felt and what was believed by [both] those who wrote ballads and those who bought them[; they] show how public opinion was formed and help to explain the growth of popular traditions."[29]

Besides song lyrics contributing to an accurate picture of the popular consciousness, they also provide another type of authenticity. This is the deeper meaning of sentiment with expressions that convey meaning through metaphors, humor, and satire. Song allows oppressed minorities and marginal groups to broadcast their innermost feelings and emotions through a code language unintelligible to outsiders. Where powerful hegemonic majorities have placed and enforced restrictions on the free speech and private conversations of minority groups, they also tend not to scrutinize song texts that, from their comprehension, appear as innocuous entertainment. Grievance and protest are then open to minority song makers without the risk of suffering penalties from the authorities. One can extend the comments in a recent historical work on political songs to all popular tunes: they can "embody symbolisms, both literary and musical, that often reveal more about the emotional and intellectual texture of a movement than political speeches, newspaper articles, or party platforms."[30]

Alan P. Merriam, an anthropologist, has noted certain qualities of song texts that one could apply to immigrant minorities in particular and the oppressed generally. Lyrics, he points out from evidence obtained from native peoples, can express their "psychological set or 'ethos' . . . and the deep-lying values and sanctions as well as the problems of a given group of people." How texts and lyrics do so is clear. Songs "provide psychological release for participants" and thus provide individuals with a way to alleviate their frustrations and problems. Hence they encourage participation in song. Singing also allows for a freedom of expression, a circumstance uninhibited by normal restrictions that characterize ordinary conversation. As Merriam states, "In song the individual . . . can apparently express deep-seated feelings not permissibly verbalized in other contexts."[31]

The value of music and song lyrics in conveying the historical and psychological makeup of groups and the individual's differing ties to them is clear. It is not only in the expression of group identity but also in the variety of themes that songs convey the patriotic, romantic, and historic cultural bonds that constitute the individuals' declared attachments to group tradition.[32]

There is still another beneficial property of American ethnic ballads and of songs in particular. They reflect the continual modification of group ties, showing that ethnic tradition is not static but changeable and dynamic. In fact, the continual composition of ethnic songs not only may have been a sensitive recorder of the American immigrant experience, but it also shows the process of assimilation, which itself may have been a cause for that transformation and the creativity that went into composing the song.

Ethnic scholars now understand that group memory and tradition are not simply based on the primordial corpus of cultural bonds such as historical events, epic literature, art, music, and song. Recent observers have stressed that especially for American ethnic groups who have been coming to the New World over time, ethnic identity is continually being remade. In fact, it is that very migratory experience, the ensuing disengagement from and hence weakened connection to place (according to Eric Erickson and others), that is the identifying mark of Americans.[33] The national characteristics of a peripatetic people ever moving and changing, along with the rootedness of the ritual celebration of American immigrant communities, have encouraged artists to express the nature of their own group connection and that of their people.

If there is a model for this work, it is the classic study of the African American secular song in Lawrence Levine's *Black Culture and Black Consciousness* (1977). By bringing to life the vibrant and expressive musical culture of that oppressed minority, Levine has provided a method for uncovering how all marginal peoples might have employed their songs. These tunes were not a political defense or mere protest against discrimination, they were thoughtful reflections of African Americans about their daily lives. This work, then, will aim at analyzing not just the tunes opposing oppression but also, like Levine's examples, the musical expressions of marginal peoples about their general immigration experience.

While I will follow Levine's goals, my methodology of song selection will differ. This study will be of immigrants, mostly people who came to America voluntarily, whatever economic or social forces pushed them out. Thus the characteristics of the lyrics run the broad spectrum of sentiment, from contentment to dissatisfaction with their settlement in America.

While the aim of this book is to offer new and neglected evidence about assimilation, the means for uncovering it is certainly problematic. It is obvious that all ethnic groups have a sizeable musical culture, so a major difficulty is the immense number and variety of popular vocal works among the many groups who have come to these shores. The ballads and songs refer to the many facets of lived experience, home, family, work, religion, patriotism, customs, and the human sentiments of love, hope, success, failure, and the like. Besides the overwhelming number of works, an added challenge for the investigator is the accessibility and recovery of those pieces that were popular and familiar. They range from the most informal tunes sung spontaneously by singers, to folksongs altered to fit new conditions, to the many commercialized and published tunes about life. The aim of revealing the immigrant *mentalité* through song must include the criteria of selection.

One restriction is that the study is confined to just one century in the years after the early 1800s. That period, extending to the era of immigration restriction around 1930, was the time of the largest mass movement to America, including many culturally differing peoples, from white Europeans to nonwhite Asians and Latin Americans. The pre-nineteenth-century sources are much less accessible and fragmentary.

In addition to the limited time coverage, the focus is also restricted largely (though not entirely) to the repertoires of eight major groups who constituted the largest immigrant populations during that period. These will be three groups from the "old immigrants," the Irish, Germans, and Scandinavians; three "new" ones, Poles, East European Jews, and Italians; and two nonwhite peoples, Chinese and Mexican immigrants. The work also alludes to examples from a few other important groups, such as the English, Hungarians, and Japanese.[34]

Since this study highlights those tunes that refer to the everyday life of immigrants, it deals with topics that were common to and therefore on the minds of group members. Universal in these repertoires was musical commentary on such themes as home and homesickness, work and employment, and nationalist matters and concerns about group identity in the face of differing and threatening social and cultural values of and discrimination by the dominant Anglo-American majority. Rather than try to cover the huge lists of songs from all of these groups, to the greatest extent possible this analysis will cite only those that were most popular, and if not commanding a wide audience themselves, the pieces are representative of a genre of works that were. Thus the number cited in each ethnic culture need not be large.

Another restriction in the selection is that most of the examples will be secular rather than religious works. Hymns and liturgical music were of significance to immigrant lives as an integral part of their ethnic bond, but most were brought over with little change, and these and others did not comment whatsoever on the immigration experience. As this study deals with the movement to and life in a new land, it is limited to those pieces that reflect that shift, a quality not obviously evident in traditional church music. While the text does include some old-country patriotic pieces, they are offered to show the struggle over groups' ethnic identity in America. Ethnic nationalism did grow for some groups on the western side of the Atlantic.

Still another standard for selection may also seem questionable. That is the inclusion of some works that popular comic entertainers performed in theaters. These were commercialized presentations, hardly folk, and were composed by entertainers, not by ordinary group members. But while the personal creations of a particular comedian, these pieces taken from ethnic vaudeville are still relevant to an understanding of the immigrant *mentalité*. Certain gifted group performers produced skits and songs that sensitively expressed the needs and desires of their audience, which was indeed the reason they were enormously popular. Critics stated that these entertainers had an uncanny ability to articulate the sentiments of the rank and file.

A final consideration in understanding the ubiquitous nature of immigrant songs is to know the variety of other venues of musical performance, particularly those of a spontaneous nature and those by amateurs. I address in detail the performing environment in the various chapters devoted to particular groups. But some general comment on place is possible and necessary. They varied greatly, from the most intimate of settings in the homeland and in America to semipublic and public group gatherings, that is, from home to community to organizational and festive meetings of group associations. In this regard the transatlantic ship and the saloon were two important sites.

The many accounts of those on Atlantic boats emphasize the value of music, song, and dance on board, particularly in the early years of the nineteenth century around the 1840s, when passage took two to three months compared to the last years of the 1800s, when the crossing by steam was less than two weeks. Music offered an outlet for the primary emotion of steerage passengers, who even late in the period feared for their safety. The poor conditions in the early years did improve, of course, in time as later ships were built specifically for emigrant traffic and other minimum standards were mandated. But complaints about conditions continued. Often put in cramped quarters, such passengers suffered also from poor ventilation, inadequate water supply, bad food, epidemics, abuse by the crew, a lack of privacy, seasickness, ship disasters, and storms and bad weather. Thus typhus, cholera, dysentery, and measles were not uncommon occurrences in the early years.[35]

Emigrants' earnest wish was to find psychic relief from these dangers. They found some solace and comfort in the music-and-dance sessions that were common in steerage. Throughout the period immigrants frequently brought musical instruments on board so fiddlers, accordionists, harmonica performers, and

Dancing between the Decks. Mid-nineteenth-century woodcut, probably of Irish emigrants in steerage. From *Illustrated London News,* July 5, 1850.

others could play familiar ethnic tunes for their co-passengers. Robert Louis Stevenson's comment about his 1879 ship passage to America was representative of other observers. The songs, he said, were "inexhaustible . . . , [for] singing was their refuge from [uncomfortable] thoughts and sensations."[37]

Another vitally important setting for many groups to cultivate their musical tradition and the songs about immigrant life was the well-known place for socialization, the saloon or cafe. Here, at ordinary unplanned occasions or organized family and community gatherings such as weddings, seasonal observances, funerals, and fraternal meetings, musical entertainment was common. Along with playing cards and drinking beer or wine, visitors at ethnic taverns and cafes found much pleasure at the end of a workday, or especially on payday, in joining with group members at the neighborhood waterhole. Since these were places where one could relax with friends and where music was participatory, tavern-goers offered songs that expressed their innermost hopes and disappointments. These sites then provided an emotional safety valve for the hard life of foreigner workers. The overall effect was also to enhance new ethnic bonds by homeland regional interaction, thus promoting a more homogeneous immigrant subculture in America than in the Old World.[37]

The ship crossing and the saloon or cafe, then, were venues that immigrants commonly experienced and settings that offered places for song performance. But they also provided differing, in fact opposing, functions in immigrant life; one threatened their lives and the other made their difficulties more bearable. So while the various groups had similar experiences coming to America, afterward one can view them in more distinctive detail, for as the songs suggest, the groups had both similar and differing emotions and experiences.

Finally, readers will note that a good part of my selection of immigrant songs has come from secondary works. But since they contain song lyrics, I would consider them primary sources. It would have been impossible to locate all the songs of ten immigrant groups in the original; some were entirely oral and never in print.

1

The Irish

Exploited Exiles

The Irish were the largest group of English-speaking immigrants (some also spoke Gaelic) and came to America in massive numbers over a very long period of time, three centuries to the present. These features of their coming, along with their extraordinary success in political activity in the New World, probably made them more familiar to Americans than any other minority group. As important as the Irish urban political machines in providing the group's image to outsiders were their popularity, prominence, and their lively involvement in public entertainment, particularly musical performance.

For much of the late nineteenth century, they so dominated American vaudeville that even the most hostile public stereotype of the Irish was also connected with music. The familiar image was a simian Irishman with a caubeen hat, dancing a jig, and clutching the well-known artifacts of that culture, a shillelagh, clay pipe, and a whiskey bottle or jug.[1] Certainly, at least as much as any other immigrant group, Americans of many different origins know that the Irish possessed a richly expressive musical culture.

Song reflected almost every part of their daily lives. To the delight of contemporary Irish and the pleasure of all Americans, the popularity of and indeed the fascination with that rich repertoire of ballads and dance continue down to the present. Thus it is no wonder that Irish song has clearly conveyed emotional feelings about the various aspects of the group's immigrant experience. Whether lyrics describe the traumatic departure from home, family, and loved ones simultaneously with the need for leaving; the physical and psychological ordeal of crossing the Atlantic; or the hardships of settling in the United States, another potentially hostile Anglo-Protestant society, the Irish vocalized about it in song. Or better put in succinct terms, they provided listeners with their *feelings* about their migratory experience.

This kind of communication in music, then, is valuable to any historical observer. One authority has asserted directly that this type of group expression was an ideal indication of the most intimate sentiments of the masses. The songs of the Irish emigration, he has pointed out, are "closer in spirit to the feelings and expression of ordinary people who endured the experience than any other kind of historical document. When an emigrant song is sung," he concludes, "it imparts not only the facts but emotion, and in an especially memorable way."[2]

It is important to remember the ways that Irish ballads were disseminated, those about emigration and otherwise. Most were readily available to people of any station for most of the nineteenth century because they were printed cheaply and heard widely. Normally most were composed and sung by street singers at any time in the open, and many appeared printed on broadsheets sold throughout the country at a penny per sheet.[3]

While the various topics of the songs are similar to those of other American arrivals and refer to feelings about departure, homesickness, and the lure of and disappointment in the new land, making for a general pattern, still a distinctive character of this Irish musical genre is also clear. The songs had strong political overtones, for overall they suggest that emigrants were generally not voluntary travelers but considered themselves as unfortunate exiles, forced from their home by the oppressive British majority.[4] Even when they expressed the advantages of America (which was a common feature of the songs of other immigrant groups), the greater freedoms it offered the newcomers, and the potential for economic opportunity, they still considered themselves reluctant emigrants, expecting one day to return to a free homeland.

But again, a distinctive feature of the Irish emigrant ballads throughout the century was its heavy emphasis on politics. Most, but not all, of this musical expression told about the dissatisfaction and objection with British-Protestant exploitation and mistreatment. This placing of the responsibility for the forced diaspora on the English did not mean that all who considered emigration saw departure as a solution. Many tunes stated that moving across the Atlantic was too much of a sacrifice to the families and that the dangers of going west far outweighed the benefits. It was, in fact, the rare piece that was totally optimistic about the move to America. While it may have been a better place to live in peace and get a better income, it still was not entirely the paradise that other groups may have expressed in their music. Life was hard in the New World as well.

In any event only the rare statement, especially in the earliest songs brought out before the Civil War, was enthusiastic about going abroad and achieving success. America too, some lyrics reminded listeners, was dominated by an Anglo-

Protestant culture that, especially in the era of the Protestant Crusade (1830–55), was also a threat to the Irish Catholic way of life. As noted below, the leading Irish songs about work (in particular) sung in free America lamented anti-Irish economic discrimination.

The latest historical interpretations are consonant with the melancholy character of Irish emigrant music. The consensus of the best standard histories of Irish immigration is that the peasant masses left reluctantly with a feeling of banishment from their homeland; that mistreatment was always very much on their minds. As additional evidence, academic writers thus usually use the term "emigration" rather than "immigration" to describe the movement of those who left Ireland for America.[5] Thus while a review of Irish songs does not revise the standard interpretation of immigrants as exiles, it does more pointedly reveal the personal, emotional discomfort emigrants felt about their move overseas. It was a gloomy sentiment that worsened over the nineteenth century.[6]

For a full understanding of how the songs reflect that immigrant mentality and its modification over time, it is necessary to review briefly the historical context in which that musical expression occurred. The total number of nineteenth-century Irish coming to America was quite large, probably over four million. The few who appeared before 1800 were both Protestant and Catholic who often lived together in Irish communities along with a number of political refugees who fled after participating in unsuccessful insurrections.

The mass Irish exodus began just after the Napoleonic Wars, around 1820, with Catholics being the vast majority by the early 1830s. The numbers fluctuated over the entire era of mass movement, 1815–1922, rising to and falling from a high point in midcentury. About one million left up to 1845; one and one-half million just after the famine, 1845–1855; another million, 1856–1870; and a final one-half million, 1870–1922.[7] The leading demographic and economic causes were the high birth rate and the failure of the potato crop, the group's main food source, that began in the 1820s and became widespread, causing severe famine and poverty by the mid-1840s. Other causative factors were the consolidation of landed estates, the high taxes, the loss of agricultural markets due to free-trade legislation, and, of course, the ongoing hatred of British rule as a result of landlord exploitation and property foreclosures. The tradition of the peasants singing about their troubles actually predates the 1800s, particularly their bitterness directed at the many absentee landowners and Protestant-English control.

One of the earliest tunes initially popular before 1820 already spoke about themes that would be repeated later. It conveyed that welling up of conflicting emotions over whether to leave the traditional home or remain, a torment that would beset many emigrants. On the one hand was the miserable life in the Irish village caused by closed markets, while on the other, the economic and political opportunity that America offered. Hence while expressing the reluctance to leave, it also glorified the society overseas with the appropriate title, "The Green Fields of America."

> Farewell to the land of the shillelagh and shamrock,
> Where many a long day in pleasure I spent;
> Farewell to my friends whom I leave here behind me,
> To live in poor Ireland if they are content;
> Though sorry I am to leave the Green Island,
> Whose cause I support both in peace and in war,
> To live here in bondage I ne'er can be happy,
> The green fields of America are sweeter by far.
>
> I remember the time when our country did flourish,
> When tradesmen of all kinds had both work and pay,
> But our trade all has vanished across the Atlantic
> And we, boys, must follow to America.
> No longer will I stay in this land of taxation,
> No cruel master shall rule over me;
> To the sweet land of liberty, I'll bid good morrow,
> In the green fields of America we will be free.[8]

Characteristically, other emigrant songs, although not most, through the entire immigration period viewed America as a sanctuary of freedom and opportunity for the oppressed Irish. This was also true of the tone of letters sent back in the years around midcentury.[9]

Even the most optimistic hopes also expressed misgivings. "McKee's Farewell to Ireland" appeared in 1855, composed by a Bravo McKee, a schoolmaster from Belfast who also idealized the nation across the Atlantic. This song describes the conflicting thoughts of an imminent emigrant, one who also is reluctant to leave his native land. The piece reiterates the profound ambivalence that the bulk of the songs suggest, expressing mental anguish and uncertainty. The narrator's final decision to depart was thus a very painful one, for he deeply loved what he had to leave behind. Note too the political undertone of his melancholia, the signature feature of the Irish emigrant song.

> Farewell lovely Erin, the land of my fathers,
> These daisy hills I will wander no more;
> I'm now going to cross o'er the Atlantic Ocean
> My fortune to try on a far distant shore.

Yet the land of my fathers I still will remember;
The place of my birth shall be dear to my heart;
I will think of my home in a far distant nation,
I'm not reconciled with these valleys to part.

The Trade has got low and the wages are scanty
And Erin's best friend from our land has now fled
Which makes many a bold hero to venture
Across the wide ocean in search of some bread.
There's nothing in Ireland but want and starvation
The rents are so high we're scarce able to pay
With cesses [sic] and taxes they always perplex us,
There are no such impostures in Amerikay. . . .

Farewell to my country the land of my sire
Adversity drives me away from your shore
May fortune yet smile on your green daisy hills
When wide foaming billows between us do roar,
So come my brave boys we will tarry no longer
We will go to the country they call liberty
We'll leave this poor nation in so much distress
And enjoy equal rights in Amerikay.

See how many thousands are gone from this country,
And are now living in the United States.
They have no rents to oppress them nor tax to distress them
Nor no one to call at their door for Poor Rates.
There is no tyrant there to claim their habitation,
Nor find heavy burdens for to keep them down.
They have liberty stamped on the coin of the nation,
That shows they have neither landlords nor Crown.

In all this hyperbole about his better life to come, the lyricist still comes to the painful conclusion that he will never be able to return, "all these green valleys I'll see no more."[10]

The bulk of the more popular ballads return again and again to those opposing pressures on those considering departure. And time did not relieve them. On the one hand, early in the century, difficult living conditions beset the homeland only to be intensified in midcentury by the more horrendous calamity of the famine. The circumstances more forcefully encouraged emigration. Yet on the other hand

Irish Emigrants about to Leave Home—The Priest's Blessing. From *The Illustrated London News,* May 10, 1851.

were conflicting emotions to motivate them to leave, such as the guilt over deserting the family when it was in need. Departure would mean the breaking up of their home, abandoning the beauty of the countryside, and the move to a far, distant land, away from lovers, family, and friends.

One of the more personal emigrant lamentations in this regard was the widely known broadside ballad of 1809 from Ulster, "Paddy's Farewell." The first section of the piece refers to the "hard fate" at home of poverty, the loss of freedom, the distress, and the general oppression. It concludes with Paddy's uncertain hope and a rationalization for departing for the sake of his loved ones. Although "America . . . bound," he was going to seek his fortune to adequately support his "virtuous wife and children dear." His only consolation is that he would "return once more [and] enjoy the felicity with thee on the Shamrock shore."[11]

Probably the best-known and frequently performed piece that highlights another emigrant dilemma over whether to stay or leave was a conversation between a father and son. In this case it offers another rationalization for leaving: to win Irish freedom for those at home.

The youth first asks his father the embarrassing question why he fled abroad when he so loved his home and country, then under the heel of the British. To rationalize his flight and to ease his guilt, he replies that his departure would actually help Ireland. He had intended to recruit other emigrants already in America to continue to work for Irish freedom abroad. At any rate the song still reviews the psychological tug-of-war on the emotions of prospective emigrants.

This popular ballad is entitled "Skibbereen," the name of the well-known town in Cork whose people were known for their leadership in the struggle for Irish independence. The lyrics tell of a father who had suffered much at home. He not only lost his sheep and cattle to blight, had his house torched by a landlord, and endured other crises that ended his wife's life, but he ultimately was forced to flee as a political refugee after the failed 1848 insurrection. At the end the son, previously bitter at his father's going, finally not only understands and accepts the "desertion" but also views his parent as a role model. He concludes that some day he would take his father's place and lead "the gang beneath Erin's flag of green" and would "raise the cry: 'Revenge for Skibbereen!'"[12]

More familiar, historical proof of the pain felt by the Irish emigrant was the modification of a distinctive traditional ceremony when an individual died in practice long before the massive exodus. That ritual was known as a "wake" and, during the nineteenth century a similar ceremony was given for those going off across the Atlantic, the "American wake." Its meaning and tone was in the expression of family and community grief over the departure of an emigrant or emigrant group. In the eyes of relatives and the community, the leaving was considered similar to the departing one's death.

While grieving over the departure of loved ones was certainly a common experience for *all* ethnic groups, it certainly was not as formalized or as communal as among Irish family and friends. This ceremony for the emotional and physical departure (by ship) of a loved one has been well known to historical scholars and anthropologists.

The American wake was a gathering of friends and family just prior to, sometimes the evening before, departure. It included lamentations of grief, especially musical vocalizations by women, known as keening. Keening was a loud wailing sung by either the mother of the traveler or a female neighbor known for doing such performances. Essentially the singer bemoaned the forthcoming loss. Since the American wake was similar to the normal tradition of honoring the deceased, it too was like a requiem for the dead. One can imagine how difficult the event must have been for any emigrant, something like attending his or her own funeral. The tradition thus highlighted the mental anguish of the emigrant.[13]

While the American wake came out of a tradition of communal commemoration for both the deceased and those departing, it did develop into a sort of paradoxical event like other similar occasions among the Irish. Despite its generally somber character, it still was a combination of *both* melancholy and joy. Particularly after about 1830 it also became a time for festive merrymaking, with food, singing, and general entertainment. Women would prepare the meals for the participants days in advance. At the evening wake, while people were enjoying themselves, emigrants would go around to their relatives, friends, and neighbors in attendance offering their farewells.

But, as joyous as the party might be, the emigrants must have suffered emotionally. A feeling of sadness was still pervasive, according to firsthand accounts. Plausibly, the keening of women might well have included a specific sad statement of loss.

Harriet Martineau, the well-known critic of social practices both in Britain and antebellum America, reported on one probably representative wake she attended just after the famine. The crowd, she said, was in tears as a family of four was about to leave for America. The departing gestures, she recalled, "were terrible to see. . . . We saw the wringing of hands and heard the wailings . . . [and] a shrill united cry."[14]

Other evidence of the discomforting aspect of the wake was its direct effect on the emigrants. It became so upsetting that occasionally, to salve their guilty conscience, the subject individuals would steal away quietly and leave the ceremonies early. The grieving continued the next day as some of those who had attended the wake accompanied the emigrant to the place or port of departure.

Another song introduced about 1865, also one of the most popular, depicted the full period of the wake itself, both at the evening and morning-after activities. "Thousands Are Sailing to America" offered a good picture of the events and especially the distress produced among the thousands of sons and daughters deciding to leave home.

> On the night before leaving [they] bid the neighbors good-bye
> And early the next morning their hearts give a sigh
> The tears from their eyes they are falling like rain
> When the horses are starting going off for the train

At the communal meeting the departing children then must say goodbye to their mother.

> Their friends do assemble and the neighbors also
> When their trunks are packed up and fast ready to go
> They do kiss their mother and with these words do say
> Good-bye darling mother I'm going away

They finally arrived at the port, feeling like marginal figures.

They put their foot on the tender [ship] just leaving the strand [shore]
And give one look back to their dear native land
Their hearts are a-breaking for leaving the shore
Good-bye dear old Ireland will I ne'er see you no more.[15]

Interestingly, the wake was only for those going to America; the many who left for England and Scotland did not have such melancholy communal gatherings. The reason for the lack of ceremony for these more local emigrants was because their absence was much less permanent.[16] In any event, it is quite plausible to assume that some of the ballads sung at the wake were also performed on other occasions, as on board emigrant ships (which will be described later) and at social venues in America. Two such pieces were "Goodbye Johnny Dear" and "Three-Leaved Shamrock."[17] For the community, song rather than the written or spoken word was a better way to articulate feeling and a more comfortable outlet for stress.[18]

A related type of song that was popular throughout the century (and that also shows the tension in the dilemma between leaving or staying) was the "romantic" ballad. This was an expression of the feelings between lovers as husband and wife. One authority estimated that over one-half of all the Irish songs in the antebellum era were of this type. Even though they were about a universal romantic sentiment, one-third of that half did concern emigration.[19]

One example was "The Emigrant's Farewell." It is a personal testimony of a man's conversation with his beloved Mary, but it is also political in the way he has to justify his leaving. After pointing out the economic and political tyranny that forces him away, he does hope for better days. But until then, "my last embrace I'm taking now, and my lips are on your cheek / the parting hour is drawing near."[20]

Another familiar tune was that of a husband reminiscing about the courting of his deceased wife. He pours out his grief over emigrating at her grave and that of his child. His lament includes the more general motivation of other emigrants, which was the better economic opportunity in America. The well-known song has at least two titles: one was "The Emigrant's Farewell," and the other, "I'm Sitting on the Stile, Mary" (the "stile" is one step among several over a wall or fence).

Oh, I'm sitting on the stile, Mary, where we sat side by side,
On a bright May morning long ago when first you were my bride;
The corn was springing fresh and green and the lark sang loud and high,
And the red was on your lips, Mary, and the love lay in your eye. . . .

I'm bidding you a long farewell, my Mary kind and true,
But I'll not forget you darling, in that land I'm going to;

For they say there's bread and work for all and the sun shines always there
But I'll ne'er forget my Mary were it fifty times as fair.[21]

Similarly, in "My Girl from Donegal," the man says America is the place to go. "I
would be glad, but times are bad / to work on Irish soil," so " when out west I'll do
my best from morn to setting sun," where "my fortune will be won." In that case,
he will return and "wed [his] pretty Eileen . . . , My Girl from Donegal."[22]

In "The Emigrant's Farewell," again the larger economic need is a temporary
justification for the separation. "If fortune favors, to crown his labors," he will
return from the States "with [his] gold in store, and bring [his] love back to
America."[23]

Some songs offered still other obstacles to anyone considering flight from the
homeland. This genre might be termed "anti-emigration" ballads, for they stress
the disadvantages of leaving for America. Themes in this repertoire are several:
abandoning the family in dire need, generally neglecting established obligations
to loved ones, encountering the numerous perils of ocean crossing, being igno-
rant of the unfamiliar and strange customs of a Protestant American culture, and
feeling uncomfortable about the strange, natural element of the New World
wilderness and getting settled there.

One of the better-known examples of this type is "Rich Amerikay." It is the
reply of a wealthy Irish woman to her peasant lover in the New World who
wants her to join him. She balks, saying her parents need her and that she
fears going to the "savage shore . . . where savages wild do play." After meeting
her lover once again, she is finally persuaded by his eloquence and his ardor and
returns with him.[24] But while finally deciding to emigrate, the woman still highlights the obstacles of migrating and expresses the difficult choice the Irish had
to make.

Another ballad from later in the emigration era, "The Happy Shamrock Shore,"
advises its listeners to remain in Ireland for the same reasons. "Do not come unto
the lands they call America," it warns, for the narrator's experience was a difficult
one; he had to stay for some weeks in "the wild woods," where "wild beasts and
venomous insects were ready to devour." He nostalgically concludes, "Sure I could
wish to be safe back on the Happy Shamrock Shore."[25] Other negative advisories
are in "Farewell to Slieve Gallon," which refers to an emigrant who poor, disabled,
and unemployed lies in a nameless grave far from "where the blooming heather
waves."[26]

Also rather commonly expressed as another both real and psychological bar-
rier to migration was the ship passage. As the Irish emigrated throughout the
century, they experienced the worst as well as the more comfortable passages.
While they did try to ease the trip by performing entertainment in steerage with

lively music, dance, and song, many of their ballads about that crossing warn listeners about the hardships of ship conditions. These were inadequate and bad food and water, which led to sickness, disease, and death; the personal insecurity of steerage, with petty crimes; the exploitation and abuse of women by crews; and of course the vagaries of the weather. As one might imagine, bad storms causing shipwrecks and devastating fires did occur aboard the wooden vessels. These ominous conditions involving steerage victims helped contribute to the adoption of the term for such boats, "coffin ships." Obviously, shipboard conditions were worse early in the century during the famine era and in the age of sail, when crossing could take as long as three months or more. Almost all of these transportation songs remind listeners of the greater dangers of sailing in the earlier era.

Another of the century's most popular ballads, "Riley to Ameriky," which appeared sometime before 1866, exploits these maritime perils in a tragic tale of two lovers. The problems in the voyage made the decision to leave more difficult. Riley returns from his stay abroad to bring his lover to America over the objections of her father. The couple's watery grave, the ballad adds, should be an example to others. It concludes:

> So let it be a warning to all young maidens gay,
> And never let the lad they love sail to Ameriky.[27]

The most famous ballad of a returned emigrant with a similar moral was the tragic "Noreen Bawn." This warning against emigration likely appeared just prior to the Civil War. The heroine was a widow's daughter who did return to Ireland after a prosperous American stay; but during that period various problems encountered in the strange land made her suffer emotionally. Her mother weeps at her daughter's death, concluding, "Twas the shame of immigration / Laid you low, my Noreen Bawn."[28]

For the over four million Irish immigrants who came to America in the nineteenth century, their culture and settlement patterns both persisted and changed from those they had known in the homeland. Their songs expressed mixed sentiments about the new conditions in a new land. Some were optimistic about potential opportunities, but many more were discomforting. They highlighted the general ambivalent feelings about coming, for they found, for example, on the one hand continued discrimination in getting settled and finding employment, while on the other they sensed the exhilaration of greater freedom. These latter sentiments certainly encouraged their ethnic nationalism, recruiting more arrivals to work for Irish independence. The result was the acquisition of a new Irish American identity having more awareness of other groups and finding a similarity of the liberal philosophy they shared with their host society, America.

The sense of being an exile as expressed in emigration songs persisted, having been forced out of the homeland and, while appreciating the benefits of American democracy, they still wished to see and often to return to a free Ireland. Undoubtedly the Irish became aware of their own ethnic identity while in a more pluralistic, fluid American society in which groups easily exchanged cultural influences. So while Americans were similar to the English as a predominantly hostile Anglo, non-Catholic culture, the Irish sense of being different did not depend as heavily as it had in Ireland on British oppression.

One continuing feature of Irish cultural life was the ubiquity of musical performance. In fact the occasions for song and dance probably increased in America. Not only did immigrants continue to entertain themselves at taverns and home parties (later known as *seisun*) with family weddings, christenings, wakes, and the like but also in more formal New World venues such as at club, nationalist, and labor meetings and outings as well as in cabarets, dance halls, and commercial theaters.[29]

The greatest difference for the Irish in the New World was in the location of these gatherings as well as most Irish American settlements. The latter were in large cities, settings that offered a better life than the more rural areas in Ireland. While initially isolated physically in a large American metropolis, the Irish soon became situated with other minorities on much more congested terrain. In these tightly packed Irish American quarters, with limited income from unskilled industrial work, where employment was uncertain, and living in overcrowded tenements, males naturally sought a comfortable outlet for relaxation, places where they could socialize, meet friends, and get the latest news from newly arrived countrymen. They found that desired fellowship in the neighborhood saloon. It was a place they frequented to alleviate the stress of being a discriminated minority, where they could find both social and cultural comfort, particularly in drink.

The local American ethnic pub was, of course, not unique to the Irish; other groups had similar sanctuaries. But the Irish use of music and song there was distinctive. As a recent scholar put it, the saloon and its owner provided an emotional safety valve for the frustrations of the ethnic working class. It was also a place where one could "climb into the minds" of the workers. Tavern entertainment was often especially grassroots in nature as Irish patrons often chose their songs to be sung. They indulged there in the entire ethnic repertoire of emigrant ballads.[30]

As stated, one of the major frustrations of the Irish in America was continued ethnic discrimination. The emotional distress from this abuse certainly was not new, for anti-Irish and anti-Catholic prejudice had been well known in the long history of Great Britain. But as many newcomers left agriculture to do unskilled work in the construction and other industries in American cities, the barring of

Irish laborers from certain areas of employment or simply exploiting them on the job was an open and common experience in the New World. The situation produced two of the best-known Irish American ballads, both of which deal with economic injustice. These were "No Irish Need Apply" and "Drill, Ye Tarriers, Drill."

A full history of the former song remains incomplete since sources contradict its origins. But while "No Irish Need Apply" has several versions, both with similar or even very different lyrics, they all do express the traditional feeling of dissatisfaction over critics demeaning the group's considerable physical and intellectual contributions. The versions of "No Irish Need Apply" all have related titles and hence similar sentiments, among them "The Irish Labourer," "No Irish Wanted Here," "I am Proud I'm an Irishman's Son," "The Irish Are Preferred," and "What Irish Boys Can Do."

The specific universal complaints are over the reluctance of the outside majority to accord any positive traits to the Irish workers and their culture, in particular their warm hospitality to outsiders and their attractive cultural gifts. The singers complain also about the general abuse and exploitation of ordinary group members by both the British and Americans. Both Anglo societies were blatantly hypocritical, for they were entirely willing to depend on outsiders being recruited for military service to protect all citizens from their enemies.

The Irish contributed substantially to the struggle of the British against Napoleon in Europe and to the Americans against the rebel Confederacy. Yet for all these sacrifices the Irish and Irish American recruits encountered mistreatment from their superiors. And when they later sought suitable employment, they were either rejected or exploited when on the job *or believed themselves to be.*[31]

While the two major musical texts of these versions were well known and similar, the information about their degree of popularity is conflicting. One version of "No Irish Need Apply" is by John Poole, a business manager for the famous vaudevillian Tony Pastor in New York. Poole probably was inspired to write his song by another version popular in London in 1863. It begins with an immigrant complaint:

> I'm a dacint boy, just landed from the town of Ballyfad,
> I want a situation: yes, I want it might[y] bad.
> I saw a place advertised. It's the thing for me, says I;
> But the dirty spalpeen ended with: No Irish Need Apply.
> Whoo! Says I; but that's an insult—though to get the place I'll try.
> So, I wint to see the blaggar with: No Irish need apply.

The man repeated his charge, which infuriated Paddy, the jobseeker.

Thin I felt my dandher rising, and I'd like to black his eye—
To tell an Irish Gintleman: No Irish need apply!

The immigrant physically beat him, saying that he thought America was a democratic land where an Irishman was supposed to be "just as good as any other
man." He then expresses his belief in American tolerance, though observing that
bigots are always evident. He concludes with an ultimate faith in the American
principle of equality. The Civil War showed authorities that Irish immigrants
made devoted soldiers; thus when they sought more recruits, "None but Irish
need reply."[32]

It is important to add that another version of this song, likely also popular
under the same title but different lyrics, suggests that job discrimination was also
felt by Irish working women. It was made famous by the performance of an Irish
American female singer, Kathleen O'Neil, who speaks as a domestic. It begins,
"I'm a simple Irish girl, and I'm looking for a place."[33]

Another popular labor song addresses the arduous conditions of the work of
Irish laborers. While known as a "comic" tale among Irish laborers, it still con-
centrates on the physical abuse and exploitation that a foreman could inflict upon
them on the job. Unlike "No Irish Need Apply," this ballad, called "Drill, Ye Tarriers, Drill," offers no relief in the future. It remains a satire, complaining about
the difficulties of employment. The "tarrier" is a worker who uses steam drills
and explosives to break up rocks and build roads, particularly railroads, in the
later 1800s. Throughout the century, of course, many Irish workers were involved
in such dangerous manual labor.

The origins of the piece seem to be even more obscure than "No Irish Need
Apply," although it is likely that it appeared and was performed in an earlier version in the 1860s. The best-known lyrics were popularized by an Irish worker-
entertainer in the late 1880s who sang it in New York Irish clubs and taverns. It
later appeared in vaudeville.[34]

The narrator is an Irish "tarrier" who complains about mistreatment by his
foreman, who cheated the working gang out of its fair wages. The most popular
segment of the ballad is its conclusion. After a premature explosion hurls one
man into the air, that "mean" boss docks that worker's pay for the time he spent
off the ground.[35] Other, less-popular work songs, particularly from the mines,
which employed mostly Irish, hardly offered such humorous, lighthearted scenes.
They contain more-serious protests, as in "Pat Works on the Railway" in which
a Yankee pay clerk also cheats a laborer; "The Lament for the Molly Maguires,"
which recounts how several Irish mineworkers were executed in the 1870s for
defending workers' rights; and "The Mines of Avondale," which laments 110 Irish
miners who died in an 1869 cave-in disaster. Poor working conditions were also

given in the late-nineteenth-century song themes of Butte, Montana, miners who, feeling like exiles, yearned to return to Ireland.[36]

A particularly pessimistic statement, entitled "Give an Honest Irish Lad a Chance," was that of a young immigrant looking for work in America. He dwells first on his reluctant leaving of his beloved home in County Clare, where the "mountains and hills, the lakes and rippling rills, / Are singing sweetest music all the day," but "our little farm was small, it would not support us all, / So one of us was forced away from home." He had to "bid them all good-bye with a teardrop in my eye" and "sailed for Castle Garden all alone." What he seeks in the chorus of the song is work that no one will offer. He then becomes miserable and depressed:

> When I landed in New York, I tried hard to get work,
> And I traveled through the street from day to day;
> I went from place to place, with starvation on my face,
> But every place they want no help they say.
> And still I wandered on, a-hoping to find one
> That would give a lad a chance to earn his bread;
> But then it's the same, for I know I'm not to blame,
> And oftentimes I wished that I was dead.[37]

An intriguing subject to explore, if it did exist in the songs of the Irish immigrant, was any mention of their relations with other minorities, especially African Americans. Unfortunately, the available sources offer little on the subject. How these immigrants related to other minorities is a currently significant issue, for recent and widely accepted interpretations describe the growth of a "whiteness" consciousness among American workers, particularly the Irish, who seemed especially sensitive to competition with black labor. According to this view, Irish American labor was at pains to differentiate itself from African Americans, with whom others, such as the upper classes, viewed the emigrants of the Emerald Isle as having much in common socially. To avoid, and perhaps stung by, such comparisons, the Irish treasured and stressed their racial difference, their "whiteness." Other evidence for the group's sensitivity about their racial difference is their coolness toward the antislavery forces around the Civil War era, shown in particular in the heavy Irish involvement in the antiblack draft riots in New York City in 1863.[38]

Unfortunately, research uncovered only one Irish ballad on the topic, and it does suggest a demeaning attitude toward the black minority. "Sambo's Right to Be Kilt" is apparently a popular Irish song that appeared in the *New York Herald* in 1862. It was written by an army recruiter to justify the widely controversial policy of having black soldiers participate in the conflict. The musical reference offers a degrading comment on African Americans by reminding its audience that the more "Sambos" in the ranks as gun fodder, the fewer whites will be in danger.[39]

A final genre of popular ballads that was evident not only during the Civil War but also throughout the nineteenth century was the purely political pieces. They helped construct an Irish American identity by showing that their group principles were identical to those of native Anglo-Americans. Those guiding rules were the democratic ideals underlying the Constitution. As suggested, politics was an integral part of the Irish social history and musical tradition long before many arrived in the United States in the 1800s. Their historic enemy was the British, and the Irish had often expressed their resistance against Anglo-Saxon domination through song. The struggle for freedom continued throughout the nineteenth century; again, as noted, most emigrants considered themselves exiles rather than permanent immigrants.

As the well-known ballad "Skibbereen" and others suggest, some of the Irish looked upon departure to America as a way to realize their own sovereign nation. Whether it was a sense of guilt over leaving or simple idealism that prompted them, the immigrant support for homeland struggles was constant. The major campaigns for freedom were Daniel O'Connell's drive for Catholic emancipation in the 1820s and his 1840s repeal movement, the 1848 insurrection by Young Ireland, the efforts of American Fenianism in midcentury, and the aid the Clan-na-Gael provided for Charles Parnell's Irish Land League and Home Rule in the 1880s. As justification for their efforts, immigrants frequently referred to the similarity of Irish and American political principles.[40]

As important as is the content of the familiar political songs in revealing the immigrant mentality, it strengthens the idea of Irish nationalism among Irish Americans. These songs were sung in the informal surroundings of cafes and taverns. But the most conspicuous occasions for voicing the Irish bond with America were the annual observances of St. Patrick's Day.

These commemorations began very early, in the first years of the 1700s, and dwelled on the common Irish and American principles. They consisted of banquet dinners with speeches, toasts to heroes of both cultures, and music and song. Later the celebrations became more elaborate and included parades. Especially by adding marches, the observances widened popular participation and heightened the emotional and psychic involvement of immigrants.[41]

It is true that in the early years of the 1800s, these festive affairs were largely run by the Irish elite. But they became less upper-class affairs when the emphasis became more pointedly nationalistic. For example, the large Irish American fraternal organization, the Ancient Order of Hibernians, dominated the celebrations in the post-famine years.[42]

Throughout the era, the subjects of the songs sung at these banquets did not change, stressing the similarities of Irish and American democratic goals and the haven America provided for these European "exiles." Especially effective in reviewing the commonality of both peoples in the early years was the joint reference to their common oppressor, England, with its monarchy, its court, and its highly stratified social classes.

For example, at a typical St. Patrick's Day celebration, Irish immigrants would sing American patriotic songs like "Yankee Doodle," "Hail, Columbia," and the "Star Spangled Banner" just prior to their native strains, the "Wearing of the Green," "God Save Ireland," and others.[43] Another representative tune was "Saint Patrick's Day in New York," which concludes:

> Cheer up, ancient Hibernia boys, the time it is not far,
> When that dear isle on us will smile, protected by the [American] stars.
> And when the stars and stripes, my lads, and eagle of liberty,
> When the whole day long will be our song, old Ireland she is free![44]

As a huge contingent of Irish immigrants fought for the North in the Union army, the Civil War gave tunesmiths an ideal opportunity to reaffirm the similar Irish and American identities. The group made up perhaps as many as one-half of all Northern soldiers. Their coolness toward African Americans did not mean a reluctant support for the North, particularly when the British government and upper classes favored the Confederacy.

Particularly famous in fighting for the Union cause was the heroism of the Irish 69th New York Regiment. A familiar song speaking about the exploits of that military unit is representative of others, for it pulls together nearly conflicting emigrant opinions about the war. These were the dissatisfaction over the inadequate recognition of the Irish military contribution along with heralding the identity of Irish and American liberal goals.

"Pat Murphy of the Irish Brigade" tells the story of an Irish Union volunteer who like so many of his people gives the ultimate sacrifice in battle. America should never forget his contribution, the song advises, so that when Ireland needs help in its drive for independence, the American flag should be there accompanying the Irish banner.[45]

Thus these Irish American political ballads, unlike the labor and departure songs that tell of the agony and discomfort of emigrants, were more positive about their stay in America. The immigrants' arrival and settlement would lead to Irish freedom eventually. But that hopeful prospect was still a mixed one, for it required more Irish sacrifice, like the death of Pat Murphy, to prove their sincerity.

The conclusion of the song returns to the traditional lament, "He died far away from friends that he loved, and far from the land of shillelagh."[46]

Overall, then, whether communicating about leaving Ireland, family, and friends; crossing the ocean; meeting a new society; finding a job and keeping it; or defending the similar American and Irish objectives of liberty and democracy, the repertoire reveals an ambivalent Irish mentality. The dominant theme of the songs, and hence the mentality of the group, while reveling in American freedom, still is one of great sacrifice and economic, psychic, and physical hardship. A leading Irish nationalist historian has referred to the emigrant sentiment as filled with "humiliation, resentment, and bitterness," feelings that their songs certainly express as well.[47] With some distinctive exceptions, the corpus of German emigrant songs offer a similar complexity of hope, resignation, and reservation about a new life in the United States.

The Germans

"Kultur" and Complexity

In their attempt to find generalizations that would apply to all immigrants, some students, such as the earlier migration historians, might consider that the nineteenth-century exodus of Europeans to North America was a movement of peoples who had similar migration experiences, adjustments, and attitudes. Certainly some of the major causes for those diasporas were indeed the result of encompassing international changes. These were such dynamic forces as industrialization and urbanization, with the concomitant decline of traditional agrarian life, resulting in vast changes in land ownership and distribution, extensive agricultural distress, and the rise of free trade. These developments were widespread in the world, hence it is true that they affected European peoples regardless of national borders. Still, it is also important to recognize how their migration experiences differed.

German immigrants shared some of the practical features of movement and settlement with the Irish, one of which was the emotional discomfort accompanying the migratory experience. The most popular songs of these migrating central Europeans also suggest the psychic burdens they too bore with them as they left home and family. But while similar, differences were evident too in the move of the Germans. They were at a somewhat better economic level, hence they encountered lesser discomfort in their coming and brought with them a greater self-confidence in the durability and superiority of their culture.

The similarities of experience are obvious. Both groups left Europe over generally the same period of time, fewer in the pre-Revolutionary era, and many more after 1815. Both also came in large numbers. The German influx amounted to about 5,500,000 over the next century; the Irish figure was only slightly less. In

addition, some motivating forces for movement were the same. The economic dis-
location of the Industrial Revolution, religious persecution, other legal restrictions, and general mistreatment by authoritarian governments were all common
reasons for both peoples' departure. In addition, their obstacles in leaving were
similar: the reluctance to leave loved ones, the fear and hardships about transportation, and the difficulty, lesser in the Irish case, of reconstructing lives in an
unfamiliar and even hostile Anglo-American society.

Nevertheless, the *mentalité* of these central Europeans as expressed in song was
not as distressing and less upsetting and disruptive in many respects than that of
the Irish and even many other groups. This may have been due to the more rapid
social mobility of German immigrants. In addition, unlike the nearly common
goal of the Irish for an independent homeland, the Germans did not consider
themselves as simply "exiles." Unlike their English-speaking neighbors to the west,
they generally did not expect to return at some time to a free motherland. The goal
for most of them was to settle permanently in America.

Perhaps the most notable difference, however, was psychological. Unlike the
Irish, who anxiously sought the respect of their Anglo-American hosts, the Germans did not suffer from any inferiority complex toward their hosts. In fact,
their sense of "Kultur" represented a strong feeling of cultural pride and provided
them with a substantial group confidence, even superiority, especially when comparing their cultural heritage to that of Anglo-Americans. The character of their
song repertoire in America proves that.[1]

Overall then, while Germans certainly did encounter majority hostility and
discriminatory barriers to individual success, they still retained a considerable
affection for the United States. To them as to many others, this new land offered
greater freedoms than Europe and thus more opportunities. Yet they still tempered that positive outlook with some hesitation, an ambivalence about their
transfer, and dissatisfaction over what were generally regarded as inferior Anglo-
American traits.

One explanation for German immigrants' dominant optimism about their future was their possession of considerable economic and social resources compared
to others. Characterized by a wide social diversity, these non-English arrivals certainly came with more substantial material and educational endowments than
those of the generally unskilled and poorer immigrants from the Emerald Isle. The
situation enabled the Germans to adjust to the new culture more easily than the
Irish. Despite the extraordinary diverse social makeup of German arrivals, one
can still cite certain generalizations applicable to that entire contingent. To understand that complexity requires a brief historical review of the socio-political situation of their homeland.

For centuries until 1871, "Germany" was a concept, not a homogeneous, unified nation. For a number of centuries before and through most of the 1800s, ethnic Germans inhabited many different and distinct regional and political units. Emigrants, therefore, left home with a wide variety of local identities originating from a large array of duchies, kingdoms, and city-states. That geographic complexity extended into the social realm, and Germans also represented many faiths and religious denominations, even philosophies. Besides consisting of a host of different Protestant sects, immigrants included many Catholics and Jews. Further, Germans were splintered along philosophical lines, spanning another wide spectrum of beliefs, as secular freethinkers, monarchists, nationalists, liberals, and of course socialists. Alternatively, still another element of internal difference was the rather varied occupational composition of the German immigrating masses, more fragmented than other Europeans. Many were peasants and unskilled workers, but a significant percentage too were artisans, intellectuals, and shopkeepers.

Overall, that considerable social and intellectual fragmentation and diversity enabled this group to fulfill the numerous occupational opportunities that America, a rapidly growing young nation in the nineteenth century, offered. In the early years to about 1870, most Germans, having been peasants, were attracted to the thinly settled and low-priced lands of the West. That vast, undeveloped inland region was appealing since it allowed some to carry on their traditional life as farmers, while the growing American urbanization during the century provided a high demand for those in other occupations, such as German tradesmen.[2] The many artisans and skilled workers responded to the great additional need in America where, unlike in Germany, those abilities permitted them to continue their occupation and hence their culture.

It was only the third element of Germans, the unskilled workers originating from east of the Elbe River, who like most of the Irish had the greatest difficulty in the transfer. They arrived mostly toward the end of the 1800s and at least initially encountered significant obstacles in securing steady employment in the then-booming American heavy industry. In that capitalist society, their efforts at economic advancement and security were much more problematic. Understandably, these later immigrants were occasionally more hostile to the American economic system and its treatment of workers. They expressed both the attraction of and their dissatisfaction with America in song.

Fortunately for a cultural study of this sort, whatever the scope of all their internal diversity, Germans as a whole in both the Old and New Worlds traditionally regarded music and song as a central feature of their daily lives. Perhaps the leading and thus distinctive feature of their singing in America was a decided adherence to retaining and disseminating the traditional ballads along with adding a few others about their migration. Their repertoire thus consisted of a paucity of tunes that referred to their everyday experience in America. Their high regard for the transcendent quality of the old songs sung in the homeland was part of that secure sense of Kultur, their feeling of cultural superiority.[3]

It is also important to note that even for those songs that originated in one region of Germany and were brought from the old country, some became popular among the entire ethnic group in America. Thus one can conclude that such tunes certainly contributed to a new consciousness among the German immigrants. Not only did songs fulfill new emotional needs of performers and listeners but also the group's rich musical traditions were again considered to be a basis of ethnic pride and superiority. As one German musical scholar put it, the songs the emigrants sang as they left and were carried on the way to the new land were the "voice of the people . . . , first hand accounts from the emigrants' point of view." Certainly, the emigration ballads reveal the diverse and mixed motives about leaving.[4]

German music and song not only helped unify these fragmented immigrants into an American ethnic community but also represented an extraordinary ethnic self-confidence. The Germans believed that their long-held musical traditions and songs were of such high quality that they could even affect outsiders. Their musical talents would act as prods to raise the aesthetic standards of their more backward and less civilized Anglo-American hosts. Additional evidence of music's universality and high status among German Americans in particular is the large number of publishers who throughout the century disseminated broadsides and sheet music widely among their literate clientele.[5]

While much of the content of those German emigrant songs concerning migration itself is similar to that of the Irish, there are significant differences. Both groups did sing about, dwell on, and contrast the iniquity of their oppression in Europe with the freedom they found in America. The German songs, however, followed a more discernible trend over time. In the early years of emigration, their ballads more emphatically trumpeted the attractive liberal principles of American liberty and equality. Later in the century, when the emigrants were poorer and less skilled, their song lyrics became more pessimistic about life in the new land. They began to complain more often about the social problems of the burgeoning industrial society, especially the increasingly difficult requirements for success and the excessive materialism of their hosts. In other words, one could conclude that over the course of their coming during the nineteenth century, the German emigrant song reflects a shift in the mentality of the immigrants from enthusiasm to ambivalence. While the precise dating of any folk song is always problematic, in the case of German emigrant ballads in the century after 1815, that same trend of an initial glorification of America was followed by greater fears about traveling there.[6] Lyrics clearly reflect that attitudinal change.

Before discussing the specific content of the most popular emigrant songs and their performance venues, one must review briefly the scope and main features of the German movement to America. Particularly notable was the early establishment of their New World communities. Those colonial settlements of German-speakers offered clear evidence of a rich and vibrant musical culture in America even before their mass movement here in the nineteenth century.

William Penn first recruited some German pietistic sects for his new Pennsylvania colony just before 1700, and over the next century about 100,000 concentrated there and in the inland fertile valleys of Maryland, Virginia, and the Carolinas. These arrivals were mostly farmers and artisans. Their settlement clusters constituted definite ethnic communities by the time of the first U.S. census in 1790. By that early date, surprisingly, almost one-tenth of the white American population was of German descent. As most had been religious dissidents in Germany, they brought their various faiths with them and carried on religious practices that included traditional church hymns with distinctive instrumentation. Benjamin Franklin, for example, was printing hymnals for Pennsylvania Germans as early as the 1730s.[7] Secular vocal music about emigration, though, was virtually nonexistent.[8]

The larger numbers of Germans who began to leave later in the early nineteenth century were chiefly peasants from the western territories. These travelers were forced out by the disastrous harvests of 1816–1817 and other economic dislocations resulting from the Napoleonic Wars. This emigration generally increased in later decades, reaching a high point in the early 1850s as a result of a number of other causes, such as the deleterious effects of the continent's growing free-trade philosophy and the Industrial Revolution on its farmers and artisans, Old World religious persecution, the failure of the 1848 revolution, the desire to avoid military conscription, the gold rush in America, the high demand in the New World for labor and settlers, and especially the magnet of liberal American land policy.

The height of the German exodus came in the 1880s, when almost 1,500,000 went to the United States chiefly from the eastern lands. The character of the post-1860 community then had changed. By around 1890 almost half of the German Americans had gone to cities as laborers; the unskilled became so numerous that by that time they made up about half of all arrivals. By then too they had spread westward around the country, with the heaviest concentrations in the north-central states from western New York and Pennsylvania to the upper Mississippi Valley and into Missouri and Texas.

With this placement and portrait of the emerging German America, we can now concentrate on the most popular songs that the group sang in the era. One other important encouragement to German singing was the coincidental influence of the liberal ideas of the late-eighteenth-century Enlightenment, which contributed to the naturalness of vocalizing one's emotional feelings. The philosophical ideals of the era promoted the individualism and the need and desire for ordinary people to express their most personal and intimate ideas. The secular ballad, particularly in the German case, then became an ideal way for a person to shape and reveal one's own destiny, thus offering some opposition to established authority.[9] Indeed, the very act of singing about one's cares became a recognized and common safety valve for dissatisfaction. Hence song covered a host of grievances, including concerns about emigration.

Fortunately, writers have cited the earliest song that was popular among many German arrivals in America. Appearing in the late 1700s, it has value in helping reveal the early emigrants' mental state. The piece was to prove a model for many later ballads throughout the entire era of mass immigration. One sentiment similar to Irish ballads concerns the circumstances of departure. It expresses an ambivalence about leaving friends and family for an unknown land. Surprisingly the work is not a folk piece or broadside but a published composition called "Kaplied" ("Cape Song"). It appeared in 1787 and was continually sung often among these westward-bound central Europeans until about 1840. While its original version was as a military piece that referred generally to a German soldier going off to do (likely mercenary) service in Africa, those destined for America in those early years also adopted it.

> Away, away, brothers, and be strong,
> The day of departure has come!
> It weighs heavily on the soul, heavy!
> We shall go over land, across the sea
> to America. [substituted for Africa.][10]

Other ballads widely known on both sides of the Atlantic in those early antebellum years illustrate the universal emotion of inner frustration and hesitation over leaving loved ones. One of the most famous of this type originated in Swabia in southwestern Germany probably in the 1700s. At that time the region was very poor and thus for sometime afterward was a major producer of German emigrants to other parts of Europe, out along the Danube River, and later to America. While originally known and sung only locally, the song soon became an anthem for all those going anywhere. It is far more than a simple tune sung by departing emigrants, for it is still performed in many areas of the world even outside America, wherever Germans have concentrated.

"Muss I denn zum Städtele N'Aus?" ("Must I Go Away from the Town?") is a statement by an emigrant who promises that his going will not change his feeling for his lover. The lines run, "Thou dost weep, thou dost weep that I'm wandering forth," and in summary assert that he doesn't think he will forget his love because he will return in a year. He concludes, "Then shall the wedding be"; the emigrant was leaving with a heavy heart.[11]

Another popular song that added to that personal burden was a more cosmic one on the minds of many peasants. It contrasted conspicuously the "push" of the economic devastation of the Napoleonic Wars with the "pull" of the promise of America. Entitled "The Decision to Go to America; or, the Farewell Song of the Brothers," it too exemplifies the emigrants' awful dilemma. A reviewer has referred to this piece as *the* "typical [expression] of the mentality prevailing among emigrants" in the early years of the century.[12]

It conveys like most others the emotional distress of emigrants. One sibling asks God to help him convince his brother to leave and for them both to offer some rationale to their dear parents to ease their sad parting. The anguish of the two youths is obvious. They finally offer two justifications that most actual emigrants felt. One is, as in "Muss I Denn," the greater income potential, or "gold," in America, while the other is the intolerable slavery at home. Likely the greater influence is to leave their unalterably low social status and enforced dependency that Old World serfdom had created.[13] In any event, clearly their departure, while necessary, is fraught with bitterness and pain.

Two of the most popular German emigrant songs from the 1840s through the early 1900s include the conflicting mental pressures that earlier lyrics articulate with a greater stress on the attractions for agrarians of new land. One is a published work authored by Friedrich Sauter. Its appeal must have been enormous, for it had at least one hundred variants and differing titles. "Farewell Song for German Emigrants Going to America" was written in 1830 and likely sung at that time, but it gained its widespread appeal after appearing in print around 1845. In it a male speaker says goodbye to loved ones as he goes off with his wife and child. He ends his song with a visit to the group's well-known American social center, the saloon, with a kind of nostalgic toast to the homeland:

> The time has come for me to go,
> I'm leaving for America.
> The wagon's waiting at the door.
> And I shall see you never more.
>
> The wagon's waiting at the door,
> With wife and child I climb aboard. . . .
>
> And when the ship is on the sea,
> Then we shall sing a melody.

I'll keep the tears down with a smile,
Thanking God then all the while

Now we land in Baltimore
And extend our hands before us. . . .
And cry out, "Victoria."

It's to the tavern straightaway
To put a bottle of wine away,
To put a bottle of wine away,
And let Germany stay where it will stay.[14]

One variant stresses the agrarian and material delights awaiting in the New World:

In America things are great,
The wine flows there right through the gate,
The clover there grows three feet tall,
There's butter and meat enough for all

It concludes:

Chocolate grows there, take your pick,
As sugar candy on a stick
I know it's real hard to believe,
But cotton grows on every tree.[15]

The other leading ballad popular throughout the nineteenth century was "Heil
dir, Columbus, sei Gepriesen!" ("Hail to Thee, Columbus, Be Praised!" 1833). It
also promotes going to America, though particularly for political reasons and to
reap the other benefits of the new democracy. The Great Discoverer is cited symp-
tomatically in many group repertoires in contradictory ways: as both a hero for
opening the new land and as a villain for luring poor immigrants to their ruin. In
this case the lyrics are largely positive, for they certainly express the yearnings of
both ordinary people and liberal refugees, like the Forty-Eighters. Both were fed
up with officious government bureaucrats and martinets who rigidly and mind-
lessly enforced onerous restrictions, military conscription, in particular. These
officials are referred to as *Gauners*, tricksters, and rogues, known for exploiting
and harassing people in their daily lives.[16]

This long "Columbus" ballad, contrasting Old World restraints with New
World freedoms, does not openly describe the emigrants' distress, but it does say

that "leaving home" requires considerable courage, suggesting self-sacrifice. The second stanza has a decidedly modern ring, with its attack on taxation. When it says that such Old World laws steal hard-earned income, it expresses the traditional American suspicion of a strong, central governmental power, hence suggesting an early Americanization. These are some representative passages:

Hail to thee, Columbus, praise!
Be honored for all eternity!
For you have shown me the way
And led me from servility.
Away, *if one will dare*
To leave his home for over there.

[No restriction] holds a person [in America]
What you earn is yours to keep. . . .
For honest work you'll get your bread
Will not suffer from lack or dread. . . .

Here in America's spaces free
We have no nobility.
Here the man from every class
As a man is judged to pass.
Here the earl and the baron
Count no more than the farmer's son. . . .

Now I wish to close this song,
Wish to bid Deutschland a warm good night
And should someone smarter come along,
Then let him do what's in his might
I for my part, though, I'd say it's right
To bid this Deutschland a last good night!

This particular piece was widely sung first in Westphalia, Hanover, and Prussia and later elsewhere. Its meteoric popularity so alarmed German authorities that they considered it having the virulent and ominous potential for causing widespread protest. It was clearly an "agent for social and political unrest."[17]

This ballad indicates that the bureaucracy itself was a common source of emigrant dissatisfaction. Another early and well-known vocal piece that complains about the treatment of officials and the red tape that German emigrants had to face, not only in their country particularly but also anywhere when they found it necessary to leave, is "Ich Verkauf Mein Gut" ("I Sold My [Worldly] Goods"). It is the story of a German couple who try to sell their property but are hindered, in this case, by French officials. They finally arrive at Le Havre and state that they will write back when they make their fortune.[18]

There were, of course, some songs around midcentury that did not reflect any ambivalence and were unequivocal about emigration. These came from the small group of liberal Forty-Eighter refugees who proclaimed their clear political reasons for leaving home. For example, one refers to King Frederick Wilhelm of Prussia, who, it says, masqueraded in democratic attire but really was a tyrant (*Wüterich*). In fact, "freedom is lost throughout all Europe, so Brother let's go off on our trip to America."[19]

While this musical contrast between an impoverished homeland rife with its political and social evils and an American paradise predominated throughout the era, the Germans, like the Irish, also had a repertoire of anti-emigrant songs. These songs that dwell on the beauties of the homeland and criticize the intentions of emigrants and their destination appeared later in the period, largely after 1870. Two matters are important to emphasize here. First, this negative repertoire did not replace the earlier, positive songs but coexisted with them, thus suggesting conflicting pressures on the emigrant. Second, many of these latter, critical pieces were sung in America as well as in the homeland; the repertoire then was not simply one adopted by officials or those who stayed behind in central Europe.

These new, more pessimistic songs in the German case differ from the Irish example, whose sense of exile, loss, and dissatisfaction was constant throughout the century. For the Germans, the growing criticism of going to America came paradoxically at a time of improved, cheaper overseas transportation, with much faster ships and hence a quicker crossing and much better onboard conditions for passengers.

Overseas travel always was an experience many Germans were reluctant to take even before 1870, for the prospect of the voyage appears in the songs to highlight the expression of a nostalgic "homesickness." This genre of ballads is known as *Heimat* songs. A good representative example of this type is "Heimathlied," published from the repertoire of the German American musical theater in 1903.

> When far away from childhood's home,
> Our thoughts to it will never roam,
> Where youth was passed, there is the place
> Where naught from mem'ry can efface. . . .
>
> But fate drives us on now here, now gone,
> For hither and thither our lot's to roam,

A singing (German) emigrant in the lower deck of a sailing ship, 1840. (Courtesy Deutsches Shiffartsmuseum, Bremerhaven, Germany.)

But though many sorrows may come our way,
We can never forget our old home.[20]

Such music was likely sung widely and informally, both when emigrants left *and at their destination abroad;* the Germans did not have anything like the elaborate American wake ritual of the Irish. Certainly, these *Heimat* pieces were played when emigrant ships debarked from German ports. One writer refers to what was apparently a familiar sight in the late nineteenth century at Bremen harbor when brass bands played the popular "Muss I Denn" for emigrants. Other musical groups similarly greeted the voyagers upon their arrival in America.[21]

Another example of musical nostalgia at departure is another scene described by the famous Serbian immigrant engineer Michael Pupin. He recalled as a passenger leaving Hamburg in 1874 on a ship and hearing German emigrant passengers sing an untitled but "famous . . . emigrant song." The lyrics express great anticipation, not at going west but rather looking forward to the time the migrants could return home:

Oh, how hard it would be to leave the homeland shores
If the hope did not live that soon we shall see them again,
Farewell, farewell until we see you again.[22]

In referring to "German" emigrant songs, another writer insists that as they possess their own distinctive repertoire, so the ballads of German-speaking Swiss must be considered separately. But the representative selections he lists turns out to be essentially the same as those of the people to the north. The Swiss emigrant *mentalité* as expressed in song is almost a copy of that in Germany.[23] The only possible difference may have been the more intense homesickness toward their native land based on that nation's more dramatic Alpine setting. Reference to this rugged natural endowment of the homeland is replicated in the songs of other groups, especially the Norwegians.

This Swiss romantic nostalgia in song was expressed early, about midcentury. An example is "Farewell to the Sons of Scham," which glorifies Switzerland's dramatic natural beauty and expresses wonder at why one would leave it. Another, written in America in 1835 and entitled "The Song of an Emigrant to America," lists the dangers of leaving: the horror of the crossing, American materialism, and the difficulty of establishing farm life in a country with hostile animals and snakes. This Swiss *Heimat* and *Amerika Lieder* also convey other themes, such as the pain of leaving family, the male emigrant as a prodigal son, and the lure of gold as a phantom.[24]

Other German songs raise the specter of ship disasters that awaited emigrants. Probably the best-known ballad of this type tells of the tragic collision and shipwreck of an Austrian and English steamer in 1883 that resulted in the drowning of one hundred passengers.[25]

Still other threatening advisories came from ballads known as *Bänkellieder*. They in part castigate emigrants for neglecting their family obligations and community responsibilities as the Swiss songs do for the sake of greedily seeking income abroad. They too condemn the departing travelers for being too materialistic and for trying to achieve unrealistic goals. America was not the place for Germans, this genre of song points out, since except in rare cases, adjusting to the new society was impossible. The new land was simply too raw, uncivilized, and anarchic.[26]

The originators, social circumstances, and aims of this repertoire of negative songs on emigration and even the degree of their popularity are not entirely clear. Some critics have stated that the ballads were promoted by homeland officials who sought to staunch the outward flow of the emigrants; likewise, they wanted to support those who did not leave and provide them with some solace and rationale for staying at home. Also, it is known that conservative institutions such as the churches supported and may have even composed some selections. Certainly, these songs were not spontaneous, popular expressions and thus were likely less representative of widespread feeling than those urging emigration.[27] But whatever the proportion of sincere positive or negative statements about leaving, representative German song lyrics still offer mixed messages about the decision, a situation that must have added to the emigrants' uncertainty and doubt.[28]

To this point the songs referred to are chiefly European or ballads that originated in the Old World, though in many cases familiar in America. Research suggests that only a very few were composed on this side of the Atlantic. Certainly,
crossing the ocean to an alien land did not force travelers to abandon their traditional love of folk and popular music. In fact, nearly every German community
in America had its own singing society, some extending back to the pioneer era of
the 1830s; and larger settlements had several. They not only promoted singing but
also held formal songfests, or saengerfests (German, *Sängerfest*). These were competitions, some of which were huge gatherings, of many group societies organized
into regional confederations, or saengerbunds.

Informal and more-spontaneous singing was common in both rural settlements and urban "Little Deutschlands." Groups would sing not only for pleasant
diversion and entertainment but also to maintain their group identity. Newcomers commonly and spontaneously would break out into song in many private and
semipublic venues, their homes, neighborhood house parties, local taverns, parks,
beer gardens, or any place to celebrate that distinctive quality of German American ethnic life, *gemütlichkeit*, or festivity.[29]

The most popular setting for both spontaneous and organized German American singing was the local saloon. One must remember that the term "saloon" does
not refer to a particular generic institution; at that time it really referred to a variety of places of recreation and entertainment that served alcohol to its patrons.
Saloons included establishments ranging from the simple watering holes to the
most elaborate beer palaces. Some were termed "concert saloons," and others,
called outdoor "gardens," offered music and professional entertainment. Patrons
included all social classes, from the lowest to the most wealthy.[30]

The great need for a place in a city where workers of any background could go
to relax, socialize, and get relief from the congested living and arduous working
conditions made the saloon immensely popular among both immigrants and the
native born. But this German American institution differed from the rest, first because it was also a place for the group's distinctive form of entertainment, singing
and music, and second because it was far more than the typical "workingman's
club" that was common to other ethnic communities, such as the Irish or the Slavs.

The German tavern was generally a much more elaborate, clean, well lit, and
comfortable place than those of other groups. One appealing feature of such a
saloon that patrons especially loved was the pervasive greenery conspicuous
both inside the structure and outside. The typical tavern often had open-air
gardens in parklike, well-landscaped settings. Thus the ambience was distinctive
and the venue offered pleasant places to which workers could and did bring families. It was common, for example, for German American women and children to
accompany their menfolk there after church on a Sunday afternoon to listen to

music and sing familiar songs. It was common too for the entertainment to be of a better musical quality than the amateur audience participation at other ethnic saloons. German beer gardens, then, would more often serve as theaters, with vaudeville skits and instrumental concerts.[31]

That German Americans loved to hear, play, and sing music is quite obvious. That passion for such entertainment was also particularly significant in another way. Both the spontaneous and organized ritual festivities helped weld together the widely divergent elements of the group to create some sense of a unified German America. As one observer of an Evansville, Indiana, singing society put it, the *gemütlichkeit,* which its members' love of song and festivity produced, "is a rich index of identity which affirms their local community while simultaneously connecting them to a larger German and German American culture."[32]

The critical issue here, though, is to analyze the content of the song repertoire in order to understand what those songs reveal about the German immigrant experience. Ironically, despite the universality of and the reverence for vocal and instrumental music sung and played, with one notable exception German American ballads treating the group's daily existence and living and working conditions in America appear to be rare.

For example popular works sung in private venues were mostly of the *Heimat* theme—that is, songs about the Old World home. Almost none were, like many other groups, concerned with the experience of finding shelter, getting employment, or encountering Anglo-American hostility.[33]

An exception to the dearth of German songs about their American life can be found in the group's immigrant theater. This institution also provided an outlet for a number of other ethnic groups to express themselves about life in the New World. The formal German American theater was an enduring and significant institution that produced well-known stage plays, many of which were brought over from the homeland. Generally, however, these productions consisted of serious, high-level, classical drama.[34]

Still, even though exceptional for this group, a few stage productions were light, musical comedies that dealt with the real-life social problems of ordinary immigrants. And these particular productions were plays that many German immigrants, as well as Germans abroad, loved. Thus reviewing the content of those musical works offers further insight as to their influence on and representative character of the audience. For example, a common theme that playgoers enjoyed was the comic depiction of the naïve newcomer, that is, the "greenhorn" just off the boat.[35]

The aim here is to determine whether these musicals could have eased the New World transition for its audience or made it more uncomfortable. The comedies may have benefited the more assimilated German Americans at the end of the

century by showing how far they had progressed in sophistication. This satisfaction, however, came from the parodying of their newly arriving countrymen at
the American port. This stage treatment could only have made the adjustment
that much more difficult psychically for the most recent arrivals.

It is difficult to obtain much information on the German comedy theater, probably because ethnic group drama critics were so hostile to them. An exception to
that obscurity was the work of the unusual immigrant playwright Adolph Philipp
of New York. Despite elite reviewers' condemnation of his work as trash, Philipp's
German American musicals were enormously popular in the community when
they first appeared in the 1890s. German Americans attended his plays en masse
throughout the decade.[36] His two greatest hits were "Der Corner Grocer of Avenue
A" (1893), which ran to 750 performances, and "Der New Yorker Brauer und seine
Familie" (1894).[37]

Unfortunately, the scripts of these very popular shows and the other eighteen
productions Philipp staged have not survived, so the full plots are unknown. But
one can obtain their themes by other means. As suggested, they indulged heavily
in ethnic self-parody, satirizing in particular the backward manners of German
greenhorns. Particularly caricatured was the newcomers' abuse of the English language. Philipp's obvious theoretical purpose in his works, besides offering good
comedy, was to stress the need for raw immigrants to assimilate. He wanted the
most recent arrivals to Americanize quickly, abandon their traditional or marginal
condition, and climb the socioeconomic ladder to success.

Philipp was likely basing that universal plotline on his own life, which was a
Horatio Alger story of achievement. His rapid advance as a playwright beyond the
confines of his German community to creating and producing English-language
dramas brought him considerable success and wealth. Thus his earlier musical
plays, "Der New Yorker" in particular, and the songs from them all present the
early years of immigrant life as a state of degradation. Newcomers, Philipp advised, came in a condition that Germans ought to quickly put behind them. They
were to start immediately on the assimilation process.[38] Their awkward speech
was real and a common target of humor and satire in German America. The newly
arrived immigrants, struggling to find employment and economic security, were
therefore the butt of derision by their own people.[39]

Oddly, Philipp was ambivalent about total and rapid assimilation, whether one
should shed the traditional culture entirely or retain aspects of it. He did recognize the widespread immigrant need to reflect fondly on the Old World home.
So his plays did dwell approvingly on the inevitable warm nostalgia for family
and lands left behind. One of the few hit songs from "Der Grocer," entitled "Heimathlied," romanticizes the circumstances of life in the homeland. It concludes by
expressing the pain of being abroad:

But fate drives us on now here, now gone.
For hither and thither our lot's to roam.
But though many sorrows may come in our way,
We can never forget our old home.[40]

While it is axiomatic that music and song were a significant part of German
American life, trying to find and identify those tunes sung informally beyond the
theater in private venues is rather difficult. Listing the repertoire of the most familiar pieces performed at home during weddings or other family lifecycle events
remains problematic. Yet, while little of the entertainment at those intimate occasions is known or accessible, events where one can identify the most popular
songs are public occasions, where the ubiquitous German singing societies enter-
tained. These *saengervereine* regularly performed for their communities in well-
publicized competitions (saengerfests), at German meeting places like saloons,
or more conspicuously on formal occasions for the general public. They were a
common sight at celebratory town and civic occasions in the late nineteenth and
early twentieth centuries.

As an integral part of German and German American culture, these singing
associations were established in almost every group community in the nation. But
generalizations about them remain difficult, for despite the fact that they were
so numerous and varied around the country, they have attracted only limited
scholarship.

Still, a preliminary and selected review of their published musical programs
indicates a song repertoire that consisted mostly of enduring traditional works.
Their performances were normally made up of selections either that German
immigrants had known *in Europe* or, if composed in America, were traditionally
styled songs. The vocal offerings were similar to the dramatic selections of the
German American theater. They were typically an eclectic mix of choral works of
the masters, classical selections such as symphonic pieces, chorales, oratorios, and
arias. They did include stirring nationalist, folk, and popular tunes, such as student and drinking songs from the various regions—again, really works of the Old
World, not the New.

These *saengervereine* then were hardly involved with works concerned with the
everyday lives of ordinary immigrants.[41] Part of that avoidance likely stemmed
from the origins and traditions of singing societies, whose song competitions had
been established long ago. Their offerings dated from medieval times, when
courtly singers encouraged competitive musical presentations.[42] Later performances of these musical societies retained *European* art and folksongs as a continuing tradition. When these groups were established or reestablished in the New
World, they retained much of that old repertoire. Their list of musical selections

in America was a solid affirmation of the high quality of their cultural traditions. The old songs performed were to be a model to instruct Yankee America on how to attain a higher level of culture.

Thus, just as soon after large-scale German immigration commenced in the 1820s, *saengervereine* sprang up. The first appeared in the mid-1830s in the larger pioneer German centers, such as Philadelphia (1835) and Baltimore (1836), and thereafter spread westward over the next two decades to the Midwest, South, and Far West. Their performances regularly contained works of the masters, German composers like Schubert, Beethoven, and Mendelssohn. The compositions of these figures were widely popular since Americans *generally* had known of and had esteemed their music even before the German influx; thus a large American audience already existed for those choral works. The rationale for societies performing these classics was not just entertainment but also ethnic pride—to show up the deficient Yankee culture. Another basis of German self-assurance was the belief that their folksongs in particular would be beneficial to Americans, for the singing of these pieces too, being festive, would alleviate the excessive materialism of the majority culture.[43] In any event, with that purpose again, whatever songs the *saengervereine* performed, none need deal with the German immigrant experience.[44]

There were, however, two other types of music that were common in the German immigrant community that do offer at least a hint of the group mentality about its adopted country. One is the frequent inclusion of patriotic American music in singing society programs during the post–Civil War era. Often mixed in with the works of Beethoven, Mendelssohn, and traditionally styled German American composers like Franz Abt would be selections like "Hail, Columbia" and "The Star Spangled Banner."

Also, it was not unusual for the *vereine* to participate in general civic celebrations commemorating the founding of civil communities. The regular inclusion of these American works with the classics suggests widespread German American appreciation for life in the United States, or at least gratitude for the political freedom immigrants had in their adopted country.

One might understand this acquired loyalty better by concentrating on a specific, possibly representative, case of particular singing societies that appeared to bridge ethnic and majority cultures in one large German American community, Baltimore. There a new country loyalty of the group was evident as early as 1858, when the Germania Club singers participated in a festival for, most appropriately, General von Steuben, the German hero in the American Revolution. In another situation, in 1863 one of the oldest *saengervereine* in Baltimore, the Arion Club, helped memorialize all the city's Civil War dead by providing musical accompaniment for Lincoln's famous Gettysburg Address.[45] Most notable of all

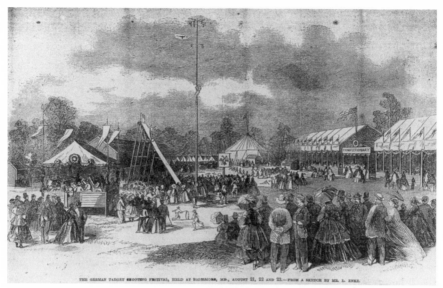

A German American shooting and music festival in Baltimore, August 1869. From *Frank Leslie's Illustrated News*, Sept. 16, 1869. (Courtesy Enoch Pratt Free Library, Baltimore, Md.)

these German American bonds with their adopted country was the deep involvement of the city's many German singers and singing societies in the ceremonies memorializing the city's 150th anniversary in 1880. The venue was notable since it tied German immigration to America in the city's general observance, for the ceremonies took place in the group's major recreational center, Schuetzen Park. There, in an elaborate program that included the mayor's address, two hundred voices from the several *saengervereine* combined their singing of German folk songs and a familiar piece by the popular German composer Franz Abt with the state's anthem, "Maryland, My Maryland."[46]

The high point of the occasion was an afternoon speech by one of the city's non-German leaders, a General Phelps. In a succinct and pointed address, he recognized and even glorified the considerable contributions of the city's Germans, who then made up a quarter of the population. As he put it, "We owe them music, we owe them lager beer, and to be perfectly candid, it must be added, we owe to them the Sesqui-Centennial [itself]." His oration was followed appropriately by the singing of "The Star Spangled Banner."[47]

Later in the century, a 1903 national gathering of *saengervereine* in the city reminded participants of the close ideological bond of German culture with American political principles. The program for that twentieth national assembly of the Northeastern Saengerbund offered works by Wagner, Mendelssohn, and the folk piece "Muss I Denn" along with "Amerika," "The Star Spangled Banner," and "Hail Columbia." Again, such a program was typical around the country in the late nineteenth and early twentieth centuries.[48]

In another major nineteenth-century German American center, that association of traditional and adopted cultural characteristics in the music and performances of singing societies showed not harmony but the tension involved. In Milwaukee, where two-thirds of the population was German speaking in the late 1880s and early 1890s, the longtime leader of the Milwaukee Musical Society was involved in a controversy that revealed the mental conflict that existed in his mind and those of his musicians. Eugen Luening became embroiled in a serious controversy when, at his group's 1890 banquet, he felt impelled to compare in his speech "Yankee superficiality" with German cultural superiority. As a writer concluded about his significance, "Clearly Luening was an important part of Milwaukee's cultural life during this period, not only because of his long tenure as [leader] of the Musical Society, but also because his attitudes were quite typical." That was "his pride in his German heritage, his appreciation for American democracy and opportunity, and his occasional inability to keep these sentiments in balance." Again, that sense was not an individual one: "they reflect[ed] well those of many German American musicians and musical societies in nineteenth century Milwaukee."[49]

Thus, while singing societies in nearly every sizable German settlement often did refer positively to the identity of ethnic and American *political* values, this did not extend to culture. In addition, in more practical terms, there was no satisfaction among the group about the day-to-day living and working conditions in America. This later expression of unhappiness has much to do with the changing class composition over time of German America in general and the singing societies in particular.

Again, determining precisely the social makeup from a picture of all American *saengervereine* is difficult because sweeping generalizations have been lacking. It is certain, however, that in the early years of the nineteenth century, most of these musical bodies probably consisted of a mixture of both upper-class and working-class members. While skilled artisans joined middle-class countrymen in many groups, it was clear that the upper classes dominated these musical ensembles, notably, for example, in the *saengervereine* of Missouri, Maryland, Texas, and San Francisco.[50] This social character, however, changed as the century wore on.

It is clear that in the later 1800s the social effects of the Industrial Revolution, the rising popularity of Marxist and socialist theory, the liberal 1848 revolution, the 1871 Paris Commune, and the emergence of the German Social Democratic movement all caused greater working-class solidarity and identity, and hence social division, in Germany. And a new genre of music and song reflected that. It became extremely important in conveying the innermost sentiments of that rising working-class consciousness.

As one historian put it, the hundreds of working-class songbooks that were published between 1870 and 1914 offer "what ideas were heard repeatedly and . . . were likely to be imbedded in the consciousness of Germany's organized workers." The anthem of the rising German social democracy was the famous French Revolutionary piece, "Marseillaise." It provided the music for the lyrics of the German variant, known as the "Arbeiter Marseillaise" ("Workers' Marseillaise"), which was introduced in 1864 and sung at all party meetings.[51] Since immigrant German Americans composed few of their own songs about their living or working conditions, the radical German American periodical *Fackel* in Chicago reproduced those Old World songs and apparently became the source of the most popular works sung on this side of the Atlantic.[52] This presumably included the popularity of "Marseillaise."

This growing class conflict in both Europe and America was reflected in both places in the fragmentation and transformation of the membership of singing societies. The older singing groups lost much of their working-class character as new, more purely working-class ensembles appeared. This change in the social makeup of choral groups occurred as early as the 1860s in Germany and a little later in America.[53] While some singing societies, particularly the male ensembles called "Männerchor," had always been of a working-class character in Europe, the splintering in New York, for example, based on class took place at the close of the Civil War.[54]

The rising class-consciousness and animosity was particularly evident in the German community in Chicago. There, by the 1870s, workers developed an active singing tradition among their own network of groups. While the working-class *vereine* agreed with its upper-class counterparts in heralding American republican and democratic principles, their song repertoire certainly and rather decidedly adhered to the liberal spirit of the French Revolution and its egalitarian goals. But German American workers began to realize that upper-class influence also blocked lofty American ideals.

The high point of worker dissatisfaction with local authorities came in the period between the depression of the 1870s and the Haymarket Square Riot of 1886. A Chicago composer, Gustav Lyser, wrote popular songs that expressed the need for German workers to take up arms against political corruption and oppose the anti-labor sentiment of the middle class and its militia.[55]

One observer cites two German American songs as representative of the growing class conflict felt by Chicago workers in the 1880s. One is the powerful, emotional "Die Klöpplerinnen" ("The Bobbin Lace Workers"; 1883), which protests the exploitation of female and child workers. It offers a "biting sarcasm and sharp contempt for the upper class."[56] The other is a labor hymn for the major socialist organization in the city, the Chicago Education and Defense Association. It concludes:

> Sing joyously toward the day of victory,
> Which will break the old chains,
> And will grant the people of the world,
> Blessing, freedom, joy and wealth!
> Victoriously above all the misery
> Beams freedom's dawn![57]

Thus while the working class did esteem American constitutional principles, the Chicago Männerchor certainly identified and protested the evident hypocrisy of theory with practice.[58]

It is admittedly true that labor dissatisfaction ebbed as the turn of the century approached and radical groups found German labor less angry and more assimilated. Thus radicalism in general declined in the group around the end of the century. But this shift has been ascribed, not to a change among immigrants, but rather to a decline in arriving newcomers after 1900, along with the social mobility of the second generation.[59]

An important work that aims at uncovering in a general way the ordinary mentality of the people over the entire era of the mass movement of Germans is a recent collection of immigrant letters. While these are valuable social documents in revealing grassroots sentiment (though perhaps not representative of all German immigrants), they do on the whole give some further insight into the mind of at least some ordinary newcomers. Furthermore, they generally reflect the content of the songs covered here.

Above all they show obvious sentiments, such as the emotional difficulty of leaving and the enormous concern and obligation that immigrants had for relatives at home. Conveyed too is the general attraction of America as a better place to live because of its egalitarian principles and the great potential wealth immigrants could obtain. Yet political freedom and economic security still would exact a price in a list of the obstacles and pitfalls to success. One drawback already referred to was the unrealistic expectations many immigrants had of acquiring wealth quickly and with little effort; that would result in some disillusionment. Another difficulty was the period in which the letters were written, the 1850s and the 1880s, which were eras of considerable economic distress and anti-immigrant nativism.

The correspondence of one worker seems to be representative of a larger body of letters. An older immigrant in his fifties, he lists his observations in correspondence just after his arrival in 1881 about the difficult course of adjustment that most others also encountered. The worst part of his experience was, despite the existence of German American mediating institutions, the early greenhorn months. It is then that with no knowledge of the language most immigrants suffered the greatest from mistreatment and exploitation. Other problems were the extraordinary hard work necessary to succeed, the lack of stable and steady employment and other baleful effects of a capitalist and individualist society, the anti-German character of Sabbatarianism, and the constant discomfort of being an outsider. All in all though, with all of this mental and physical hardship, if one did persist, he concluded, America would provide immigrants with a better life than they could have in Germany.[60]

On the whole, then, this survey of German immigrant song reveals a predominant sentiment similar to the Irish in its general complexity, although clearly these emigrants from central Europe were more optimistic about their transit to and life in America. This was particularly evident in the early years, when the German American community consisted of a close alliance of middle-class professionals and skilled artisans. For them, as for those leaving Ireland, the departure was always a trial, chiefly with the mental reservation and difficulty of forsaking family, friends, and the beautiful natural environment with which they were familiar.

As German migration transformed in the late 1800s to a more proletarian, working-class character, people generally with fewer economic and cultural endowments, the songs they sang tended to be more bitter about their new surroundings. True, to a greater or lesser extent, all immigrants, both early and late, certainly prized the new and greater freedom they found in the United States throughout the nineteenth century, but as the early 1900s approached, the social misery caused by the Industrial Revolution and middle-class exploitation in both Europe and America made the newly arriving working class (and especially the greenhorns least familiar with Anglo-American society) much more dissatisfied with their life in the new land.

The Scandinavians and Finns

Natural Longings

Certainly, when anyone thinks of northern Europe and the Scandinavian peoples who live there, the obvious and enduring image of the area is the region's natural phenomena, its rugged mountains, deep fjords, and its many small communities. So particularly indelible to both visitors and residents are the setting and the climate, the dramatic scenery as well as the great seasonal changes. Anyone can understand that the fjords of Norway, its high mountains and deep valleys, and the notable shift in weather from cold winters to bright summers all leave a profound and memorable impression on the people who live there. Thus when some northerners had to leave for new homes overseas, that familiar environmental setting became in their minds a powerful force that helped them define their "home." And as one might imagine it was a picture that the people expressed often in song. Indeed, whatever the conditions of departure, this musical recollection helped develop a warm nostalgia among Scandinavians in America of their homeland, one that led to a greater appreciation of the land they had left behind.

Before a consideration of that transformation, it is necessary first to more clearly define and identify the several northern European nationalities of interest. Among these are, of course, the Norwegians, Swedes, and Danes, traditionally known as Scandinavians. To them are added the Finns. Except for them, these groups have similar ethnic roots and thus possess cultures and histories that traditionally have been closely interrelated.[1] Certainly in America too, the Norwegian, Swedish, and Danish communities have shared elements and songs and ballads in their immigrant experience that justify a unified treatment.

While the anthropological and cultural origins of the Finns were totally separate from their Scandinavian neighbors, they did have a political connection with

41

the Swedes and lived under them as a minority for a time. Some, in fact, were called "Swedish-Finns," while others living in Finland were "Finnish-Swedes." So while there may be few cultural features that justify including them here with the others, there is certainly a thematic one. A minor but still significant example is that on occasion, a song that was popular among the three western northerners like "Farväl moder Svea/Norge/Danmark" also existed as "Farväl du moder Suomi."[2] The Finns' immigrant experience was not totally distinctive, and even to the extent that it was similar or different, it still substantiates the general thesis that songs generally depicted the psychic discomfort of all these newcomers.

The emigrant songs of the Norwegians, Swedes, and Danes suggest two predominant themes in their departure. These sentiments were, of course, not unique to these groups alone; they were certainly evident for the Irish and Germans. Still, they were more pervasive among the northern Europeans. One was that songs reflected and were a part of the bitter controversy in the homeland in the mid-1800s over the desirability of emigration.[3] While one theme urged people to leave, another warned of the evil consequences in doing so. Even though it was homeland authorities and those who did not leave who criticized emigration in essay and song, it is still plausible to believe that their negative stance did have some effect on those who left (see below).

The other common sentiment was a widespread and complex homesickness, heavily based on the attractive natural and physical features of the old country. While other immigrants also referred to their homeland's appealing geography and topography, the sentiment was particularly strong among those from Norway, Sweden, and Denmark.

The history of the arrival in America of Scandinavian immigrants in the nineteenth century clearly suggests two distinctive features. One is the huge percentage of those leaving compared to the total population—it was a massive hemorrhaging of inhabitants. The first of the three groups to create a permanent community presence in the United States were the Norwegians in 1825, with arrival of a boatload in New York City. Over the next century their exodus numbered 850,000 people. For the Swedes, it was 1,200,000 who emigrated mostly after the 1840s; and 300,000 Danes arrived, chiefly after midcentury. These statistics reflect a percentage of national populations going to America second only to the Irish. While historians have listed the motives for their leaving as typical of that for other groups, economic distress, along with social and religious causes, one can characterize this northern European phenomenon as unusually frenetic, as an "America fever."[4]

This rush overseas and rapid depopulation in the 1800s helped cause the other characteristic feature of Scandinavian emigration, a bitter debate in these three countries over the deleterious consequences of the mass exodus on national health. While the argument took place at the upper levels of public discourse in Norway and Sweden in the 1830s and 1840s, the fact that popular songs mirrored the issue suggests that the conflict was also on the minds of those at lower social levels, those who left. As the major translator of these works has observed, despite the liberal 1814 Constitution, the songs give "the sense on the part of so many of social and political inferiorities . . . [that] the little folk lost hope." Clearly "the [song] translations . . . give the sense" of emigrant feeling.[5]

The Norwegians and early departing Swedes were largely agrarians who were simply unable to feed their families from the meagerness of the soil and smallness of their fields. Thus the cheap, vast land in America was their magnet, but they continued to harbor a warm attachment for their ancestral origin.[6] One can conclude, then, that the extensive national opposition to their travel, along with their love of home and its setting, produced a musical repertoire of ambivalence.

One song fragment put the dilemma of conflicting pressures of practical need and national loyalty succinctly:

> Farewell, Norway, and God bless thee.
> Stern and severe wert thou always, but
> As a mother I honor thee, though thou
> Skimped on my bread.[7]

Another, longer version of the same song is entitled "Farväl Du Moder Norge" ("Farewell, Mother Norway"), probably from 1847:

> Farewell, mother Norway, I am going away;
> But I bring you thanks for
> Having nursed me and reared me thus far
> You skimped a bit on the board you gave us. . . .

It includes a fond reminiscence about the country's natural attractions.

> Still I love you dearly, with your mountains and lakes,
> And exchange them unwillingly
> For the prairies of the [American] West.
> But when it is a matter of our daily bread,
> Our hesitation is gone.
> Then, like the birds of the forest,
> We must leave our nests.

It concludes with the possibility of return.

And if I should ever get back in my lifetime,
I will hurry there first of all;
For there my spirit is at home,
There I first saw the light of the sun;
Nor will the longing in my heart
Ever suffer me to forget.[8]

Just as popular was the Swedish echoing of those thoughts in a song with a similar title, "Farväl, O moder Svea."

Farewell, O Mother Sweden, now I am leaving you,
And I thank you from my heart for having fostered me.
The bread you gave so little [of that] it hardly sufficed,
Though to many others you have given more than enough of that.

Still I love you, Sweden, my dear fatherland,
And would rather not trade you for the prairie sand of the west,
But when it comes to bread, [my] hesitation is gone,
We must like in the forest leave our [beloved] nest.[9]

One of the more forceful references to Norway's environmental wonders in an
emigrant song was written by the group's famous pioneer emigrant Ole Rynning
during an 1837 Atlantic crossing. Rynning was the founder of one of the early Norwegian American settlements in Illinois but was better known as the author of the
group's most popular guide to America. As the song text indicates, he too was rap-
turous over his homeland's natural endowments:

The cliffs of Norway lie hidden now behind the waters,
But our longings go out to those shores,
With their dim and ancient oak-forests,
Where the soughing of the pines and the thunder of the glaciers
Are music to Norway's son . . . [who] will cherish always
The mountains of old Mother Norway,
And yearn with pious longing
To see his beloved home once more.[10]

Similarly, the birds, lakes, and especially the beech forests of Denmark bulk large
in that country's emigrant song literature.[11] A common Danish ballad of 1856 includes a wish for social justice, blaming the aristocracy for forcing out ordinary

people. It laments having had to leave the "beautiful land of Denmark" because the "lords and counts . . . have added land to land and forced us away in wrath."[12]

As stated above, the emigrant song was an integral contributor to the debate over whether people should leave their home and family. As news of America's advantages came back in letters and other sources to peasants struggling to feed their families in midcentury, conservative humorists used musical satire to counteract the hyperbole of the new land's material advantages. This criticism was undoubtedly very popular among all Scandinavian peoples and familiar to both those who left and those who stayed.

The best-known example was the critical reaction to the colonization experiment of Norway's most popular violinist, Ole Bull. He went off to America in an attempt to establish a utopian settlement, New Norway, with its capital, Oleana, on 120,000 acres he purchased in Pennsylvania in 1852. But the colony failed, and its great promise was dashed due to fraud by the sellers of the land and other factors. A homeland critic, Ditmar Meidell, composed "the most famous of all 'America songs'" the following year, which satirized the effort for its unrealistic objectives.[13] Selected passages of the lyrics suffice to show the satire, making fun also of the colony as a panacea for homeland ills. It opens with a typical justification for joining the enterprise.

> In Oleana, that's where I'd like to be,
> and not drag the chains of slavery in Norway
> Ole-Ole-Ole-oh! Oleana!
>
> In Oleana they give you land for nothing,
> And the grain just pops out of the ground. Golly that's easy.
> Ole, etc.
>
> And the salmon, they leap like mad in the rivers,
> And hop into the kettles, and cry out for a cover.
> Ole, etc.
>
> You bet, they give you two dollars a day for carousing;
> And if you are good and lazy, they'll probably give you four.
> Ole, etc.
>
> Oh, I'd much rather live in Oleana
> Than drag the chains of slavery over there in Norway.
> Ole, etc.[14]

Similarly, a Norwegian newspaper published representative positions on the emigration debate as expressed in an exchange of songs in 1846. The text later appeared in a leading immigrant paper in America. The first offers one emigrant's typical reason for leaving, complaining that since "Norway is a poor and wretched land" where "I have to slave and suffer want," he was going to America, where "everyone can make a living." The reply, also in song, reminds the complainant what he would lose. "Poor fellow! You'll soon regret you've left friends . . . kin and home behind you. . . . Even should you find there gold abundant as the sand of the sea, one thing you will never find—a fatherland."[15]

A significant example of the sincere psychic ambivalence of the ordinary Norwegian in leaving home may be a folk ballad in the *stevleik* tradition that appeared in a song collection published in Chicago in 1894 and uncovered by a leading Norwegian literary scholar, Einar Haugen, in an article in 1938. The piece is in the form of a debate between an assimilated Norwegian American, who has been here for some years, and a greenhorn who still is unsure of his decision to leave Norway. To the justification of the earlier arrival that he had won a more "decent living" in the new land, the ambivalent newcomer replies, "You are welcome to enjoy your pretty little dolls! . . . the thing that I have learned for sure is that in Norway I had greater happiness."[16] Norwegians thus had to balance material success with more-spiritual concerns.

The two most popular Swedish American ballads also referred to the difficult ordeal of departure, passage, and settlement. One was the leading ballad "Petter Jönsson Amerika Resa" ("Peter Johnson's Trip to America"), composed in 1872 by a journalist, Magnus Elmblad, and soon after printed in broadsides for a wider audience.[17] While more lighthearted than the more caustic satire of Oleana, this song is still important, for it cautioned listeners not to overestimate New World advantages because of the dangers of getting there. It describes the migration of a fearful immigrant who, despite his looking forward to the material benefits of America, is convinced by the arduous transit to return and remain home.

> And Peter Johnson he read in "The Fatherland"
> That bureaucrats had ruined the northern land.
> He got disgusted and thought: "The devil take it!
> I guess I'll hurry away and that immediately." . . .
> From the left eye he wiped a tear with his mitten
> With God in mind he set forth upon the Atlantic.
>
> He would away to the great land in the west,
> Where there is no king and no difficult priests:
> Where one may sleep and eat pork and potatoes,

And then with the grease smear one's boots gratis. . . .
Where no sheriff dares knock a farmhand on the head,
And distilled whiskey may be had for six pence a quart.
Where more money is found than [fleas] in Trosa [a backward Swedish
    hamlet]
Thither Peter would go, and thither steered his course.
On the ship he stood and kind of held his belly,
Because his soul was with great anguish beset . . . [because of his fear of
    the ship][18]

The other leading ballad was "Vi sålde våra hemman" ("We Sold Our Homesteads"), which originated in 1854 in Värmland, later one of the leading emigrant-
producing provinces in Sweden. The tale is a sad one told by a lay preacher whose
emigrant party is dogged by homesickness, misfortune, sickness, and even death
on their way to America.

We sold our farms and then went away . . .
But we will ne'er see again our dear fatherland

We departed from Sweden feeling somewhat daring
We knew not the fate that awaited us yonder

Nostalgia hits them hard early at Liverpool, England.

The tears of deep regret began to flow freely.
Heartache and longing grew in every breast.
Now all spoke only of Sweden and of our former home.

They are swindled out of their money in Liverpool. Later, on the next leg of their
trip across the Atlantic, the misery continues. The ship's captain is a devil, passengers are often cold and hungry, and some die from the ordeal. The emigrants
finally land at Quebec only to encounter a cholera epidemic in which many perish.
One laments:

O Lord God, protect every one on earth
From exposing oneself to danger, and believing a preacher's word.
My song is a curative, for those to take in
Who intend to emigrate and have a flighty mind.

Emigrants, he concludes, are thus like uprooted weeds in Sweden, "sent to distant
foreign countries where pride is rooted out."[19]

Even the most optimistic of the more popular Swedish songs about America is in its very title apprehensive. "Bröder vi har långt att gå" ("Brothers, We Have Far to Go") is also known as "Skada att Amerika" ("Pity That America Should Lie So Far Away"). This piece is actually of Danish origin, from an opera of 1836, and dwells on the delights of the New World, where "Trees . . . are as sweet as sugar . . . , the land [where] girls [are like] comely dolls," and "Chicken . . . rain down cooked well [onto] the table with knife and fork in their thigh." But to get all that, again, "we have far to go."[20]

Clearly then, as a whole, all these songs sung so often by immigrants through the century suggest a mental retrospective of considerable discomfort. Certain other evidence of the most popular songs composed *in America* and sung by immigrants and their descendants, not just those that emigrants sang, suggests that that homesickness was based largely on and characterized by the physical features of the homeland.

An authority on Scandinavian American literature has emphasized the Norwegian mountains, Swedish lakes, and Danish beech forests as pervasive, focal-point settings in the immigrant memory of home, especially later in their American experience.[21] The best articulate expression of that feeling is the work of a lyric Swedish American poet, Arthur Landfors (or Landors) (1888–73). A socialist, he was one of the rare Scandinavian writers who dealt with the sensitive innermost feelings of his alien New World countrymen about their daily lives and problems. While not a composer of songs, this writer did articulate in verse a homesickness that described the immigrants as forever strangers in America. His poem "Fosterlandet" ("My Homeland") certainly conveys the immigrants' review of their European origins and once again its physical appeal.

> [My homeland] is a coast with bare cliffs,
> Where the sea rushes in.
> It is a smiling archipelago,
> When shadows play among the islands . . .
> It is the valley walk,
> Where the river runs and the mountains the sun goes down behind . . .
> This is my homeland.

With those thoughts on the mind, the immigrant became an eternal, emotional pariah.

> We never become at home here,
> Never feel ourselves truly at home.
> We become citizens,

We cast our votes . . . but . . .
We always remain strangers.[22]

A common theme of songs tugging at Swedish immigrants and romanticizing their past concerned females. As we have seen already in the case of the Germans (and will note especially for the Jews and Chinese), songs about women especially idealized the old country. While the popularity of each work is unclear, at least two may have been representative of others in rooting homesickness in their reference to women. One pre–World War I piece, "Till Svenska sångmön I Amerika" ("The [Female] Swedish Singing Muse in America") indicated that women too would not find emotional comfort until they returned to a familiar physical setting.

How richly nature paints for us [at home]
How the meadow smiles, and flowers smile to us
And stars, they send their bright rays
Down to us from a heaven high and wonderful.

The Swedish muse would rather turn to her home
As the arc's dove, she will not find any peace,
Until she will return over the troubled sea
To the childhood home, where the near and dear live.[23]

Another writer refers to two other ballads in which Norwegian and Swedish women are reluctant to emigrate. One, "The Swedish Girl or Nils Who Will Travel to America," recounts a lover who wants to leave and become rich, and he promises to send for her. After she refuses his plan, she finally convinces him to stay, for he concludes, "I will die with you."[24]

In any discussion of homesickness in the songs of northern European Americans, one would have to include three of the most popular examples. Significantly, this trio of vocal compositions appeared late in the coming of these peoples, just prior to and after World War I. While none actually refers to life in America per se, it seems clear that they still were an emotional response to their twentieth-century situation. In short, these ballads perpetuated that sense of homesickness, with their idealized natural setting. But one, "Nikolina," which expresses a warm nostalgia for the simple, rural life that immigrants had lost, added a new dimension. It is necessary to review all three compositions, for they certainly represent the immigrants' heartfelt sentiments. Indeed, they could be termed Scandinavian American "anthems."[25]

These "beloved" tunes were "Där som Sädesfalten boja sig for vinden / Barndomshemmet" ("Where the Fields of Grain Are Rippling in the Wind / My

Childhood Home"); "Hälsa dem därhemma" ("Greet the Folks Back Home"); and "Nikolina."[26] Once again, all appropriately glorify the homeland's natural settings.

Oddly, the music for "Barndomshemmet" was originally that of the American tune "On the Banks of the Wabash," popular around the turn of the century. It acquired its Swedish text in 1914. "Barndomshemmet" later came back across the Atlantic about 1922 and certainly echoes Landfors's theme, a homesickness for the old country.

> There where the cornfield sways before the wind
> And where the dark green spruce wood shines behind it
> Stands the little red cottage near the gate,
> Which in earlier days was my childhood home . . . [but alas]
> No more I sing then of the homeland's valleys
> And about my dear ones in my childhood home.[27]

"Hälsa dem därhemma" was written in 1922 by a Danish railroad worker for the Copenhagen musical theater.[28] Its lyrics express the longings of a lonely sailor who, upon seeing a swallow flying north, tells it to send his greetings to his family and "the meadows green at home." Its sentimental hold on group members endured at least to the 1970s, as a revival of Scandinavian music at the Minneapolis Snoose Boulevard Festival showed.[29]

Probably the most important of the "anthems" that dwells on the love of the native land and reveals the immigrant mentality best is the song "Nikolina." This piece was made famous in America by the Swedish American rural comic Hjalmar Peterson, better known as "Olle I Skratthult," and his vaudeville troupe. To understand the extraordinary appeal of this song and the yearning of New World Scandinavians for peasant life, which was central to Peterson's musical entertainment, one must remember that a drastic change occurred in the composition of the Swedish immigrant community over the course of their nineteenth-century settlement in America. While most of the early arrivals left the countryside as farmers and rural labor, toward the end of the 1880s the origins and destinations of the emigrants became much more urbanized, settling in the larger American cities of the Midwest. For example, while only one-third lived in urban areas by 1890, that number had increased to two-thirds by 1910, especially in Chicago and Minneapolis.

But despite, or perhaps even because of, its more citified environment, the Scandinavian American community developed a profound nostalgia for the rural life. These people had a long tradition of humor that originated in their agrarian society. It was no surprise then that the folk comedy known as *Värmlänningarna* (*People of Värmland*) won the hearts of Swedish peasants decades after it was

Publicity poster for the popular Scandinavian musical play, *Värmlänningarna,* from the late 1920s. From the Emigrant Institute, Växjo, Sweden, as published in liner notes, *From Sweden to America: Emigrant-och immigrantvisor / Emigrant and Immigrant Songs* CAP 2011 (Växjo, Sweden: n.d.)

first performed in 1846. Its American premier was in Chicago in 1884, and since Värmland was the home of many immigrants, it warmly reminded them of their origins. When the presentation added costumes and song, its wide appeal broadened, and the show soon became far more popular with the urbanized Scandinavians of the United States than it ever had been in Europe.[30]

Besides the gaiety of the color and the music, another reason for its appeal was the addition of the traditional comic figure in Scandinavian theater known as the *bondkomik.* He was a rural yokel, a big, clumsy, slow-witted clod with yellowed, unruly hair and ill-fitting clothing. The immigrant Hjalmar Peterson, who was born in Värmland in 1886 and had gone to America in 1906, returned to his birthplace three years later and quickly adopted that rural character in his performances. He formed his own comedy troupe, "Olle I Skratthult" ("Olle from Laughtersville"), and brought it back to America to wildly appreciative Swedish and Scandinavian audiences.[31] From Minnesota it occasionally toured the region, and from its stage presentations and recordings remained popular for the next twenty-five years.[32]

Part of Peterson's appeal was his characterization of Olle, whom the audience saw as not just a country hick but also someone they plausibly could have viewed as a naïve greenhorn immigrant. The fact is that the American theater had already established that simpleton to represent Scandinavians stereotypically by the early

1900s. It is unclear just how much Peterson drew his character from his stay in Sweden and how much from the parody by Americans. The important fact is that he knew his immigrant audience would enthusiastically accept his characterization of Olle as a dimwitted but lovable peasant. His *bondkomik* attire added to his appeal. "Nikolina" then became his signature vocal tune, with its emphasis on rural innocence.[33] The lyrics are themselves simple, the story of a young peasant couple in love. They tell of the two having to wait until the father of the maiden, who had refused the match, dies to consummate their love.

One authority has analyzed the significance of what she calls this simple "Yon Yonson" figure along with his female companion figure "Hilda," with her gingham dress and blond braids. They represent several important elements of the Scandinavian immigrant mentality. Anne-Charlotte Harvey sees in these two figures and Peterson's popular depiction of the old country hick the fulfillment of a number of needs of the immigrant.[34] First, it was nostalgic and comforting for the city-dwelling Scandinavians to empathize with the couple and remember their old life in a less complicated, non-urban-industrial milieu. Second, in comparing themselves to these less sophisticated types, including peasant rustics and newcomers just off the boat, they felt more secure in what they had accomplished and understood how much better adjusted they were to the adopted American culture than their old-country cousins. Third, this greater emotional security gave them a sense of community with other ethnic members in America. Finally, while the Scandinavian American may have laughed at Olle, Yonnie, Hilda, and greenhorns for their naïveté and simplemindedness, they still felt sympathetic toward them.[35] But despite the therapy that Peterson's "Nikolina" may have provided, the major point here is that immigrants remained under some continual emotional tension to show how well they fit into the host society.[36]

While these last three nostalgic songs are really "Scandinavian" rather than connected to any one group, one must remember that the three constituent nationalities also had subtle differences in the types of vocal music that were popular among them in both the homeland and America. Nature did play a paramount role in their memories, but the repertoires were not all the same, depending on historical circumstances.

The Danes, for example, from their history and hence their songs, appear to have conveyed the *least uncomfortable life* in America of Scandinavians and perhaps of all non-English-speaking immigrants. While comprising a smaller northern European contingent, they did send a goodly number of countrymen across the Atlantic, almost 750,000 in the 1870–1914 era. But a number of factors indicate a distinctive ease of adjustment, including their wide dispersion, their substantial exogamy, their rapid acquisition of English and high literacy, and their Protestant faith, all resulting in a generally warm acceptance by their nongroup neighbors.[37]

The Danish repertoire in the homeland, as stated, is similar to that of the Norwegians and Swedes, with a debate (albeit muted) in songs about emigration as an issue, in satirical comment on the hyperbole of the American paradise, in criticism of the arriviste returnee, and the inevitable homesickness. One must keep in mind that street singing of ballads was as common a form of entertainment among the Danes, dating back to the Middle Ages, as it was for most European peoples.

Far and away the most popular emigration song in the old country was the composition authored by the most successful Danish music publisher, Julius Strandberg of Copenhagen, in the early 1880s. The lyrics once again raise one of the inherent problems of emigration, in this case the loss of romantic ties between separated lovers, although the tragedy of the song is largely resolved by the woman aggrieved. Called "I Jylland de leved en Pige saa ung" ("In Jutland There Lived a Girl So Young"), it sold fifty thousand copies the first year. It remained popular down to the mid–twentieth century.[38]

The song is about an emigrant who had left his lover, then called for her later to meet him in America, where he told of a bright future for them. But he rejects her when she arrives. He then sells her to a kindly black man, who pays the immigrant money for his marriage to her. Surprisingly, the song continues, she grows to love her African American husband, they have a child, and they live happily together until he dies. She finally returns to Denmark, where she wins a lawsuit to recover her husband's initial payment, giving it to charity.[39] Again, the woman's tragedy is largely a problem of absence and distance rather than any adjustment to the new society. In fact, she finds happiness in marrying far outside her group.

While the song repertoire of Danish Americans largely differed from the tunes sung in Denmark, the works played and sung in the United States generally followed the same theme of a relatively easy adjustment to American life. No hit vocal like the one about the Jutland lover dominated immigrant society, but it is clear from the most popular songbook used that the tunes stressed the compatibility of the traditional and adopted cultures. First published in 1889 by Frederick Grundtvig of Clinton, Iowa, the *Sangbok for det danske Folk i Amerika* (*Songbook for the Danish People in America*) went through many editions. The listed works emphasize the double allegiance the group could have to the two cultures, and in general the tunes all have a positive character. A particularly representative example is "Du Land med graenselose Sletter" ("Oh, Land with Plains That Have No End"), which dwells on the attractiveness of American nature, the freedom here, and the culture's promotion of industry.[40]

While the Danes seemed to be able to adjust most easily of the northern Europeans to their new society, clearly the group that appeared to have the greatest difficulty was the Finns. They differed because they came later, were more proletarian working at unskilled jobs and with fewer resources, and they tended to assimilate more slowly than the other Scandinavians.

In numbers, the immigrating Finns were about the same size as the Danes, just over 300,000 between the 1870s and World War I, most coming after 1893. But while some farmers prospered, overall their material advancement in America was less successful than the other northern Europeans. Most importantly, their songs reflect more dissatisfaction with their condition. To be sure, that expressed unhappiness really started in Europe. Most emigrant Finns left the agriculturally depressed western provinces of Vasa and Oulu and settled chiefly in the Upper Midwest, especially in Michigan, Minnesota, and Wisconsin. While some took up farming early there, the major attraction was the heavy demand for unskilled industrial labor, especially as mineworkers, lumbermen, and for the few women at that time, domestics. Other indications of their hardship were a frequent turnover in employment and a below-average value of their agricultural holdings. The typical Finnish American farm in 1920, for example, was worth less than half of the national average.[41]

As with the Scandinavians, the Finns had a rich tradition of music and song; their national folk epic, for example, the "Kalevala," was always accompanied by a stringed instrument called the Kantele. And singing, even spontaneous composition, was common among the village masses in the early 1800s. As one observer describes a common theme, "songs were an accepted way of telling . . . one's feelings[,] . . . [a] tradition continued in the USA."[42]

The most distinctive feature of the group, as suggested above, was the more heightened sense of oppression felt by the masses, particularly the youth, toward those in power, resulting in a hostility toward all authority. Dominated first by the Swedes in the early 1800s and later suffering under the tyranny of the Russian czar, the Finns chafed under both upper-class and foreign control. A sense of class consciousness was hence built into their musical repertoire, directed against not only outsiders but also the wealthy and societal controls in general. This yearning for freedom emanated especially among Finnish youth, who in the nineteenth century heralded in both their thoughts and songs the class hero and the carefree wanderer. The most popular ballad sung by Finns both at home and abroad (even to the present) is "Isontalon Antti ja Rannanjärvi" ("The Big House Andy and the Lake Shore").[43] It deals with the retaliation of two heroes who react to the mistreatment of an oppressive local sheriff by wrecking his home and threatening his life.

To be sure, the dissatisfaction over such abuse and exploitation of the masses was a general impetus for many Scandinavians to leave home. It was the democratic nature of American society that pulled out of a stratified class structure many of these westward emigrants. One popular Norwegian song of 1850 refers to

A late-nineteenth-century camp of loggers in northern Wisconsin, most of whom are presumably northern European. Note the accordian. (Author's collection.)

the handsome life of the "great folk" who have a monopoly on the work of that group. A Wisconsin poem of 1847 entitled "Farewell, Norway" speaks of the homeland as one of "lords and slaves."[44] But the sense of outrage appears to be especially intense among the Finns, who established a strong socialist tradition in America.

As to the emigrant songs per se, some are similar to those of other northern Europeans, even to other groups' musical literature in the hyperbolic appeal of the American paradise. But a difference again is that, in many of the Finnish songs, the motive to move was based heavily on the eagerness of young people to reject controls. According to one typical piece, they left to free themselves of not only foreign but also parental restrictions, seeking a strange land where the "hills are sugar-cakes, and the heather is honey."[45] Additional evidence of emigration as a part of wanderlust with class concerns are those songs romanticizing the vagabond in America like they had in the homeland. It is obvious that more than any other Scandinavian group, numerous Finnish immigrants supported a strong socialist movement. They founded their own ethnic Socialist Federation in 1906, and their publication, *Tyomies,* established earlier in 1903, became the group's largest circulating newspaper.[46] Thus they accumulated a rich repertoire of labor songs as an outlet for miners, loggers, and even domestics to express their dissatisfactions. Some workers and songwriters even had ties with the radical Industrial Workers of the World.[47]

A representative song with overtones of wanderlust and class struggle is "The Wandering Boy," an old-country piece that has a more bitter American version.

One section warns, "While poor, enslaved now, [as] one class, we will be our own masters, wealthy and powerful."[48] And from two other hobo lyrics, one concludes, "Although the skinflints oppress us, . . . one day we, too, shall sit in the saddle of power." The other, a poem published just around World War I, looks forward to the day of judgment, when wanderers will be king.

> Although as hoboes on a boxcar roof
> We sing our many songs
> One day in a Pullman we shall ride
> Drawing great puffs of smoke.[49]

Work songs also expressed the burdens of toil and directly or indirectly blamed capitalism for workers' "woes." In one, a Finnish immigrant-miner rues his underground place of work: "Oh so dark, oh so dark is the everlasting night . . . [where my] comrades are sitting with sweat on their foreheads" and where "capital has bought me as to be their slave, my arms and blood included."[50] A 1914 loggers' song expresses a certain pride in what those workers do but still protests under the thumb of employers: "We, the logger knights . . . working all the time as the worms . . . while they will gather the billions of which we cannot enjoy."[51]

A similar, familiar tune (about 1926) from the well-known troubadour Arthur Kylander refers to the lumberjack in America as a worker whose tasks are really little known and who has a rather difficult life. People mistake his job as romantic, but he is forced to live an isolated life like a monk, is fed beans as "sweet meats," and is visited by "big shots" and "diplomats . . . who are hiding a cruel heart."[52] Finally, another leading Finnish American entertainer of the decade after World War I, Hiski Salomaa, popularized the typically arduous case of girls as servants. In "Tiskarin Polkka" ("Servant Girl's Polka"), the mistress demands her housekeeper do all of her many chores at once, and even on her day or half-day off, she gets no respite or sleep since she must awake quite early.[53] A related folk song, with many variations that were popular on both sides of the Atlantic around the turn of the century, is "Mustalais tlytu laulu" ("The Gypsy Girl's Song"). While not charging employers explicitly for her pain, a servant woman describes herself as a "despised wanderer" and an "oppressed walker," isolated and homeless.[54]

This survey of Finnish emigrant songs, even those that concern immigrant lives, cannot be comprehensive. The entire repertoire covered other topics of immigrant life, and all of the songs did not tell of an unrelieved hardship. The numbers taking some satisfaction in their American lives appear largely in the later years of the immigrant generation, when many began to prosper in the 1920s. This later era reveals the fame of the two group's most popular entertainers, Kylander and Salomaa. They often injected humor into their repertoire and even suggested the material advantages won in America. Touring the Finnish American circuit, they attracted large audiences, especially with their bittersweet reflections on the greenhorn experience. Kylander's signature offering was his "Siirtolaisen Ensi Vatuksia" ("The Immigrant's First Difficulties").

This comic tune, however, was not like Peterson's generalized Olle i Skratthult bumpkin. "Siirtolaisen Ensi Vatuksia" refers specifically to the naïve clod just off the boat and is more ambivalent in its treatment of the newcomer. It both laughs at and empathizes with the greenhorn because of his ignorance of English. The poor newcomer's ability to respond to all questions by unwittingly saying "no, sir" gets him into humorous troubles with both his employer and his girl.[55] But even the humor of Kylander and Salomaa had its overriding class-conscious edge. Although mild in degree, their songs referring to social difference are still more characteristic of the Finns than any of the Scandinavian immigrants.

One Finnish American authority, William Hoglund, generalizes the point. Thematically, he concludes that the group's writers and composers criticized the upper class in both the homeland and the United States as they celebrated the heroic "untutored countrymen," depicted as having the ability to outwit their "arrogant" betters. The elite were not only the Finnish gentry but also the bullying boss in the lumber camp both in America and abroad.[56] The above work songs certainly express that dissatisfaction.

Of course, this survey of the songs of northern Europeans cannot include all the themes in the repertoire of both folklife and entertainment. Sentiments concerning the changes and strains in family life, the role of women in the new society, community affairs, and local and national politics were also on the minds and in the lyrics of these people.[57] Because these groups were all white, literate, and heavily rural in the early years, and hence might have appeared to suffer little from majority discrimination, the bulk of their song literature still expressed a dissatisfaction with their new situation. Many songs of mostly young, potential emigrants speak of the strong desire to be rid of traditional European conventions. But those optimistic, emigrant lyrics were on the whole transformed in America to a generally pervasive and profound homesickness. This nostalgic pining was based heavily on the natural beauties of the old country. So, ironically, rather than finding the democratic and egalitarian Eden as they had expected, arrivals, especially those who came later in the movement, offered songs that told of a familiar class-based society.

4

The Eastern European Jews

Migration and the Family

It is clear that the Jews are one of the most familiar minorities in the United States. Their conspicuous position is because they began coming to America as a group in colonial days and continued in much larger numbers into the nineteenth and early twentieth centuries. Also, they have achieved significant social mobility over the years and prominence in a number of fields. In addition, until recently outsiders knew them historically as a homeless people, spread around the world, peripatetic in the Diaspora. But not being Christian and traditionally regarded negatively as a marginal people, Jews have always been on the move. Ever since ancient times, when they were forced out of the Holy Land, they had to move elsewhere, first settling in lands around the Mediterranean Sea and later shifting farther into Europe and then overseas. Historically, as much as any other people, the Jews experienced migration and marginality. While some countries did offer them sanctuary even with privileges, they always lived as outsiders, everywhere a minority in a world dominated by Gentiles of differing religions, particularly Christianity and Islam.

The Jews, then, have been a pariah group, generally insecure in their settlements yet always trying to establish permanent roots in an alien land. But their efforts were for naught as they often encountered intolerance and anti-Semitism, which eventually forced many to flee. Their initial appearance in North America in 1654 at New Amsterdam is a case in point, for they arrived as refugees seeking sanctuary.[1] It therefore is no wonder that so much of their culture and hence their musical traditions generally and even in America reflect that frequent displacement. In fact, as we have learned from African American history, oppression actually promotes the cultivation of music and song, not only as a psychic release from majority mistreatment but also as covert protest to maintain a group's dignity.

One would assume that coming to America, with its principles of freedom, democracy, and equality, the "land of milk and honey" that others had sung about, would also be the theme of the musical repertoire of Jewish arrival. Indeed, a good portion of their most popular songs do exalt America as a "Promised Land," an asylum. This New World sanctuary followed the famous lines of one of their well-known poets, Emma Lazarus, in her "The New Colossus," written in 1883 and inscribed twenty years later on the base of the Statue of Liberty. Yet most of the songs of Jewish immigrants are not a paean to the American sanctuary but rather a lamentation, a grieving over the more difficult prospects of life. Similar to that of other immigrant groups, their musical testimony is, in fact, mixed, for their lyrics also refer to both their discomfort as well as their potential opportunity in the New World. Yet again, as with others, their songs often tell of the unhappy tales of family separation, hard work, labor exploitation, and even disillusionment.

Like the Germans, whom some Jews accompanied to America, the latter continued to migrate here for two centuries after their initial seventeenth-century appearance. This analysis only treats the Yiddish-speaking element from eastern Europe. They arrived in the New World after the Sephardic contingent from the Iberian Peninsula and the Ashkenazim from western and central Europe. These latter two groups were pioneers, with generally assimilative goals in America, who brought with them either a small or much less distinctively separate musical culture than that of their later-coming Yiddish-speaking cousins.

Eastern European Jewish immigrants from Russia, Poland, and the Balkans flooded America quickly in the late nineteenth century, becoming the majority of Jews in the country. While numbering only about 40,000 of the 250,000 American Jews in 1880, the easterners numbered about 3,333,000 forty years later.[2] Largely working class and coming from more segregated eastern European communities, ghettoes, and shtetls than their wealthier Sephardic and Ashkenazic predecessors, these "Orientals" brought with them a rich folk-music tradition that continues to flower in America.

Since the Yiddish song repertoire was so prolific, extremely popular, and enduring in the new community, as one might expect, scholars have already given it some attention. The critical works of folklorist Ruth Rubin, Chana and Joseph Mlotek, Jerry Silverman, Fred Somkin, ethnomusicologist Mark Slobin, and Irene Heskes, among others, have so thoroughly and repeatedly identified and reviewed the vast corpus of Yiddish music and songs, one might question the need for still another assessment.[3] But while former studies have conveyed the wealth and scope of that musical culture, its origins in the Old World, the large number and variety of ballads and popular works, the extraordinary contributions of the Yiddish musical theater, and the large amount and influence of sheet music from publishers, one type of analysis still has been neglected. There has been little scrutiny of the *conflicting* themes in the musical repertoire or even any citation of a dominant subject among the more popular songs, not to mention comparison with other immigrant groups.

Slobin's fine study, *Tenement Songs*, comes the closest. His vast and intimate knowledge of popular Jewish songs are both wide-ranging and cogent, and he has made some significant observations about the easterners. One distinctive characteristic that he has attributed to Yiddish songs is that they show Jews as notably articulate in expressing themselves about their particular themes. His observation that they represent the Jews' characteristic excellence in linguistic communication is an important point, for it fits with the group's culture as a whole. While many of these later-coming Jews were poor, they still had one of the highest rates of literacy of all immigrant groups.

At any rate, Slobin's review of Yiddish culture does not identify any particular genre of songs and ballads as representative. He does refer to the great variety of topics in songs but adds that that plethora makes it difficult to arrive at any overarching synthesis. As he states the matter, one is hard put "to reconnoiter the bewildering array of topics and means of expression."[4]

Thus, still obscure in any assessment of this huge repertoire is how it may have reflected any particular mental or emotional conditioning of the people or what might have been the major, everyday pressures felt by listeners or expressed by performers. This chapter contends that many Yiddish songs suggest that migration had a painful and even deleterious effect on the immigrant's distinctive sense of family integrity. Once again, to be sure, the entire corpus of the group's immigrant music is mixed. Some songs do indeed herald America as a haven, a place of refuge for a people yearning for a receptive homeland they could call their own. But more pervasive are statements of unhappiness over the way migration put pressure on and did violence to a vital cultural value, traditional family roles.

Certainly, as previous writers have noted and as this work has already shown, Yiddish immigrant songs do express themes that were universal among all groups coming to America. These were feelings of discomfort and ambivalence over leaving familiar surroundings, fearing the dangers of the crossing, the difficulties at the arrival, and worry over not being accepted at the port of entry; despite their eternal wanderings, Jews even bemoaned nostalgic homesickness for the eastern European, Old World village from which they came. In their case, though, they romanticized their little Jewish village, the shtetl.

Admittedly, unhappiness over the weakening of family ties in the migration was universal among all groups going to America. But again, in the Jewish case the pressure and stress on the perceived parent-child relationship still appeared particularly heavy to bear. As a knowledgeable reviewer of a recent work on Jewish fathers and families puts it, "If the civilization of the Jews has one pre-occupation, it is with the family."[5]

The clearest proof of that assertion is the unanimous opinion of the sources that cite the four most popular songs among Jewish American immigrants. All of them express similar social concerns, either centrally or tangentially, about the maintenance of family integrity and happiness. These are a European cradlesong, "Schlof Mein Kind" ("Sleep My Child"), and three other Jewish American pieces: "Di Grine Kusine" ("The Green[horn] Cousin"); another cradlesong, "Mayn Yingele" ("My Little Boy"), which was a part of the repertoire of popular labor ballads that include the problem of raising children; and "A Brivele der Mamen" ("A Letter for Mother").

In addition to the heightened fear over family dysfunction and the upsetting effects of migration on family roles, the corpus of songs also suggest a lack of concern about their lives that should have been universally apparent. Not only is there a curious absence of feeling about family but also about Zionism. This neglect contrasts sharply with the developing sense of group nationalism that certainly grew in the minds of immigrant Germans, Irish, and many northern Europeans.[6] Yet Zionism did not even exist as a movement until the mid-1890s, and it never achieved mass support among American Jews until World War I. Thus, it is not represented in immigrant song. An emerging group consciousness did exist, but the Jewish immigrant concern was more reactive in lyrics than assertive. Since Jews were continually insecure about permanent settlement due to the real or potential hostility of the Gentile majority, their songs speak almost exclusively to personal survival, both as individuals and as a family. As Slobin has pointed out, in America anti-Semitism was milder than anywhere else, hence the group songs on balance do not concentrate on it. On the whole, he readily asserts that while most of the Jewish immigrant songs are in fact anti-American, that feeling came more from economic obstacles and was not based on anti-Semitism.[7]

Even before any left for America, conveying feelings about their lives in song had always been a common theme of Jews in eastern Europe. An enduring and universal hallmark of their vocal music was, as Slobin and Heskes have shown, its literacy and its polished communication through lyrics.[8] And as another authority puts it, "The folk song of the East European Jewish people is a true mirror of their life in the nineteenth century and the twentieth up to the Bolshevik regime."[9] Thus, while music for this group was, as with others, an integral part of their daily living, similarly traditional was a particular, spiritual, and modal pattern of tone, known as *ahavo rabbo*, that permeated Jewish folksong and offered heartfelt sentiment. This type of music allowed for strong emotional expression.[10]

Besides secular performances, formal religious services also provided an opportunity for singing. Synagogue song was led by a cantor who occasionally in solo and with the congregation offered prayers musically. The home celebration of the Sabbath and table songs provided additional opportunities for communication, for commonly Old (and New) World Jewish families would typically raise their voices in praise.

In addition, music was an integral part of more joyous lifecycle occasions such as weddings. The traditional *badkan,* for example, functioned in the community not only as a master of ceremonies but also as a promoter of entertainment that included dance and song. Still another opportunity for singing came with the regular appearance of small ensembles of traveling instrumentalists known as the *klezmorim.* These were players, normally string and woodwind instrumentalists, who roamed the Jewish settlements of eastern Europe like troubadours, bringing musically vocal accounts of happenings. Even in their nonvocal compositions, these musicians played instruments that "talked," the violin and clarinet producing sounds that approximated the human voice. Thus oral communication was evident in nonvocal, purely instrumental pieces as well.[11]

Communities welcomed the coming of these *klezmer* players not only as pleasant diversion but also as minstrels who provided musical therapy, an entertaining release and respite from the struggles of daily existence. Such diversion became ever more necessary in time as Jews were subject to increasing discrimination and an even more difficult life in nineteenth-century Russia and the Balkans. This was particularly true after radical Jews were charged with the assassination of Czar Alexander II in 1881. When the Russian government responded with the infamous 1882 May Laws as punishment, placing more restrictions on Jewish life, the action also released a wave of anti-Semitism that, in turn, led to pogroms. The hostility also produced the first major emigrant wave of these eastern Europeans, most of whom left for America.

Even before that 1880s exodus, the marginal condition of Jews had traditionally meant that it was common for male breadwinners to have to leave home and look for work. This departure of men and husbands created a particular song genre known everywhere as *agune* ballads, forms of which date back to medieval times.[12] Essentially, these musical works were the earnest cries of the deserted wife, the *agune,* whose spouse had gone off to work and had left her to shoulder the burdens of home and parenting. Her complaint of loss was additionally hurtful to those women who might seek another mate, for divorce in Jewish law was extremely difficult under such circumstances.

As one might expect, by separating family members, the massive movement to America in the middle and late 1800s made these *agune* songs much more common. They should be considered not only as *emigrant* but also as *immigrant* songs, for women did follow their partners to America. This meant that those Old World laments were sung on this side of the Atlantic as well. Thus a popular subject was the search for lost husbands.

Social workers knew that the hunt for wayward and neglectful husbands here was a common problem.[13] In one representative ballad, for example, the wife has become embittered over her desertion and complains that her husband has not written her as expected.

> Listen here you scoundrel
> Oh you rascal
> May you burn like a fire
> A curse upon your years
> For going off
> And refusing to return to me.
> The children beg for food
> And you have forgotten
> There is no bread to live on
> I have already pawned everything
> Even your prayer shawl
> And you don't want to send me a reply.[14]

A particular indication of the pervasiveness of this social problem is the attention the group's major immigrant paper, *The Jewish Daily Forward*, gave to it. It published photos in a section called the "Gallery of Missing Husbands" for abandoned wives in America. Other evidence of the abandonment problem is the common appearance of orphans in larger American cities. The *Forward* recorded the plight of wives and children in its famous "Bintel Brief," the popular column that contained letters of children and parents often looking for each other.[15]

One of the best-known songs on both sides of the Atlantic dealing with departure and its effect on the family is the lullaby written by one of the Jews' best-known writers, Sholem Aleichem, probably in the 1880s. When it appeared as a published poem in 1892, it had already been set to music and became so hugely popular that it had many variants. "Shlof Mein Kind" ("Sleep My Child") is a mother's explanation to her child as to why she, the parent, is crying. The reason is largely from anxiety about being alone; the husband-father is thousands of miles away. Yet as the woman states, as unhappy as she is, she does anticipate that her situation will improve. She reminds her son that she expects the father to call for them soon and looks forward to the time when the family will all be reunited in America, where they will live in comfort:

Sleep my child.
By your cradle your mother sits
Sings a song and weeps. . . .
In America is your father . . .
In America there is for all . . . real joy and a paradise
There on weekdays they eat Khale [Sabbath white bread]
[And there I will make broths . . .]
God bidding he will send us . . . letters . . . [and] twenty dollars
And his picture, too . . . he will take us . . . over there
He will hug us then and kiss us . . .
[So] Until the ticket comes . . .
Sleep my little son.[16]

Before reviewing further the most popular pieces sung by Jewish Americans in their adopted country, we must first indicate venues, particular places in America where songs were sung. To some extent, they were similar to the locations in the Old World: at home and at family gatherings as well as in more public locations at more formal times, when instrumentalists and singers gave performances.

The better-known sites were the social centers of Jewish American settlements, particularly in the group's major immigrant neighborhood, New York's Lower East Side. There in the 1890s and early-twentieth century around Delancey and Houston Streets, Second Avenue, and East Broadway arose Jewish restaurants and cafes like the Royale, Greenberg's, and Moskowitz's Wine Cellar. Some of these gathering places emerged as exchange locations for intellectual fellowship; they even provided space where song composers would write their tunes. There writers might play or work on and test their songs among the patrons. In addition, more-professional musical entertainers were often present to perform these and other works on formal occasions. A leading and famous habitué of these cafes around the turn of the century, for example, was the most popular star of the Yiddish theater and promoter Boris Thomashefsky.

In featuring music and dancing, some of these cafes developed a particular character and became known as hangouts of immigrants from particular regions or with special interests. As a personal observer described one place, "At Moskowitz's on Houston Street [founded in 1909], the Rumanian Jews sung at the top of their voices the songs of the country they left." Another popular social center in the area was a Polish music hall where Jews from that homeland would "gather and sing."[17] Still another was the cafe Zum Essex, where Jewish radicals welcomed their newly arriving refugee friends with drink and toasts.[18] Other venues for entertainers were at meetings of voluntary associations as well as simply out in the open with the more casual and spontaneous singing of street musicians.

Finally, another important place where popular immigrant songs were sung was the Yiddish theater. This vital and much-loved entertainment and social institution provided the ideal opportunity and house for composers to present their works. The various playhouses put on musical productions that allowed lyricists and musical writers to deliver their songs, some of which became standards in the Jewish American musical repertoire.

Aside from Sholem Aleichem's cradlesong mentioned above, it would be impossible to list or necessary to identify the most significant musicals among the Yiddish-speaking masses in America. Yet some general observations are possible. A good many dealt with life in the adopted country in which one can find a wide-ranging mixture of both optimistic and pessimistic attitudes about settling in what they called the "Goldene Medina," (the Golden Realm.)

One of the oldest songs expressing appreciation for the American asylum is a stirring 1892 satire. It is oddly defensive, protecting their adopted land from the criticisms leveled by some immigrants. This musical piece is in the form of a vocal response to those recent Russian arrivals who had expressed their dissatisfaction with the United States. They had so disliked certain *American* restrictions, and especially the extraordinary hardship in earning an income in the strange country, that surprisingly they built a yearning to return to Russia despite its harsh anti-Semitism. The narrator in the song, however, responds to that love of the homeland by reminding them, and hence all listeners, of their much-less-pleasant life under the czar and their subjugation to much greater oppression, fear, and pogroms.[19]

Similarly, other songs dwell on the greater freedom in the United States, as in the work of lyricist Solomon (Sholem) Shmulewitz and his "Song to America, Land of the Free" (1911). Its refrain reiterates the necessity of doing hard work in America, but it adds that such a difficulty is the only cost to the immigrant and certainly well worth the advantage of liberty in the new country.

> Let's honor this free land
> Especially when it comes to the Jew
> Who gains rights, happiness and freedom
> You have a voice when you are a citizen,
> Work and you will make money
> You will bring your children to a good situation
> Blessed be this free land![20]

More-positive expressions of gratitude appeared with the onset of World War I, when the pressure to demonstrate American patriotism required a greater assertiveness and supporting war aims in keeping with the Wilsonian goal of "making

the world safe for democracy." Jews could readily identify with that noble objective and produced songs that showed their support for the Allied struggle. One
entitled "Leben Zol Kolumbus" (1915) is a toast to the Great Discoverer for finding
this sanctuary. Another was written by Morris Rosenfeld, the major Jewish labor
poet who (as we will see) expressed an earlier dissatisfaction with American capitalism. His "My America: Our New Hymn" (1917) encourages Jewish boys to join
military service in order to repay the nation for its offering Jews asylum and providing democratic values.[21]

Nevertheless, while honoring America philosophically for the freedom it offered to a pariah people seeking a secure home, still on balance, as Slobin has
stated, the Yiddish American song repertoire and especially its most popular
pieces dwell on the unhappiness of the immigrant in his daily life, actually coming
to and living in America.[22]

A hint of the misgivings within the group is in one of the most enthusiastic
songs just mentioned, "Leben Zol Kolumbus." This Yiddish theater song of praise
for the explorer's discovery is really an open effort to counter pessimists. It concludes: "Be happy, don't listen to the grumblers. Jews shout together, 'Long Live
Columbus!'"[23] Common among the lyrics are such themes as the pain of being so
far from home, the insecurity of being accepted, the oppressiveness and exploitation at work, and above all the guilt about and concern for family members, loved
ones whom they had to abandon.

Both dramatic and musical examples of the profound awareness of being away
from Old Country relatives are found in other productions in the Yiddish theater.
That institution had developed in eastern Europe by Abraham Goldfadden in the
mid-1870s and was brought to America around 1882, when Baruch (Boris) Toma-
shevsky, as a young teenager, later its major star, but then acting as its initial promoter, developed the new land's appeal to immigrants.[24] He made many of the
Yiddish theater productions immensely popular on the Lower East Side by including American settings in his musicals. Many Jewish intellectuals and members
of the elite, however, criticized his efforts, for they considered many of these productions *shund,* trash. This was particularly true around the turn of the century as
other promoters of the Yiddish theater wanted to raise its offerings to the level of
the finest European drama.

In any event, the efforts of one well-known Yiddish-theater playwright are
further proof of the consciousness of Jews bearing heavy family responsibilities.
While purely dramatic and not musical presentations, two of the most popular
theatrical works by the famous playwright Jacob Gordin brought that weighty
concern over parent-child relations to the surface. Gordin came to America in
1891 and was largely responsible for trying to raise the quality of Yiddish-theater
productions. He regarded the institution not just as a place for entertainment but

also for instruction and uplift. His influence was powerful; he was referred to as a "central presence in the Yiddish theater" in the 1890s and 1900s.[25]

Two of his best-known efforts resonated profoundly among his audience. *The Jewish King Lear,* taken from Shakespeare, is a tale of an old, wealthy man who errs in his treatment of his daughters. The greater message of the play, however, is the plot, dwelling on the torment of parents and the ingratitude of children. The other was *Mirele Efros* (*The Jewish Queen Lear*), which also deals with ungrateful children. It and *The Jewish King Lear* both "spoke to the common Jewish perception . . . that the survival of a persecuted minority required an iron adherence to traditional patterns of family life."[26]

Two illustrations indicate the profound influence of Gordin's work. First, his audiences were usually made up of parents who took their children to see the performances. The parents viewed the stories as lessons for their offspring as to the proper filial duties in treating the older generation in the family. Second, a Lower East Side banker once commented on the beneficial effect that Gordin's plays had on his business. He said he knew when his two leading works were performed because, for some time afterward, a flood of sons and daughters, apparently with guilty consciences, came into his institution to send money home to their relatives in the old country.[27]

The Yiddish theater, of course, offered musicals as well as dramas, and both had an enormous appeal to the masses because of their sentimentality. Many were tearjerkers treating the tender relations between the generations, but all were of varying quality. Many leading critics referred to such works geared at the masses as trash. The creations of two prolific playwrights, Moshe Isaac Hurwitz and Jacob Lateiner, dominated the theater's offerings, setting the character and style of plays during its early years before 1900; their works were later referred to as "onion" plays for the tears they generated.[28] The plots were exceptionally sentimental, dealing particularly with the relations between parents and children, stories that the working-class audience grew to love.

One of Lateiner's most popular and enduring musicals was *Dos Yidishe Harts* (*The Jewish Heart;* 1908), which set a record for the number of performances.[29] It was the kind of domestic drama that the Yiddish theater began to assume generally in that decade. The story is a lesson in mother-son relations, particularly dwelling on the guilt of an emigrating child.

The protagonist is one of two sons of a mother who has deserted her for being a Jew, acknowledging only a Gentile brother. The heavily sentimental essence of the play is in its conclusion. At the finale the mother suffers from that abandonment when she is humiliated at the protagonist's wedding. As the formula for these soap-opera plots dictated, while she must suffer for her neglect, she is allowed to repent and find ultimate peace when seeing her son married and happy;

she expires there at the ceremony. One effect of the work on the audience was the heightened awareness of Jewish identity; also notable was the lesson of the durability of a mother's love regardless of her mistakes and sins.[30]

Another important part of the song genre often appearing in Yiddish musicals is the *brivele,* or "little letter" series. These songs had a profound resonance among immigrants, for they thematically represented typical immigrant correspondence among Jews. Their theme was the constant concern over the separation of family members in letters exchanged between the Old and New Worlds. In particular, frequently discussed were the roles of family members, most typically the obligations of children who had gone to America toward the parents they had left behind. It was difficult if not impossible to maintain those filial duties, with family bonds stretched across oceans, as the lyrics suggest. Among these works are "A Brivele fun der heym" ("A Letter from Home"; 1897), which offers the tragic news that parents have died in a pogrom, meaning the recipient has no hometown any longer; "A Brivele der Taten" ("A Letter for Father"; 1911), in which a son brings his father to America after the death of his mother, but the old man, sick upon arrival, is rejected at Ellis Island and has to return to the old country; "A Brivele fun Russland" ("A Letter from Russia"; 1912), which reminds children of their obligation to either bring parents from Russia to America or at least provide money for their needs; "Dem Pedlars Brivele" ("The Peddler's Letter"; 1922), in which a peddler asks his mother to pray for him so he could be assured of earning an adequate living in America; and "A Briv fun Amerike" ("A Letter from America"; ca. 1918), which presents a son's dilemma as he is torn between love for his wife in America and his duty to his mother in Russia. In this last piece, the son feels he must return to his birthplace to care for his mother and thus fulfill his filial obligation. But his wife forbids him to leave, fearing that he will be subject to Russian military conscription and the authorities will never allow him to return.[31]

The leading song in this *brivele* category, however, and one of the most popular Yiddish ones among eastern European Jews, is "A Brivele der Mamen" ("A Letter for Mother"). While this work was copyrighted in 1907 by the well-known lyricist Solomon Shmulewitz, who also wrote the music, it might well have appeared earlier.[32] In any event, it was as familiar to all Jews as "Schlof Mein Kind." Its story is another sad, classic tale of an American-bound child, in this case a son, leaving his old-country mother, her pain of missing him, and her ultimate passing at home, presumably never seeing him again:

> My child, my comfort, you are going away
> See that you be a good son,

This with tears and worry
Your devoted mother begs of you.

You are going, my child, my only child
Across distant seas
Oh arrive there in good health
And don't forget your mother. . . .

Yes, depart and get there in safety
See that you send a letter each week
To refresh your mother's heart, my child

A letter to mother
Do not delay
Write soon dear child
And give her some consolation
Your mother will read your letter
And will rejoice
You will heal her wounds
Her bitter heart
You will refresh her spirit.[33]

The mother, however, soon complains that after he left her eight years previously, sending him a hundred letters, she has yet to receive his reply. The story, as one would expect, ends tragically. While the son has achieved considerable material success, living in a "rich house" in New York with a "pretty wife and two attractive children," he has forgotten his mother. The news finally arrives that she has died. But her last wish is a plea that at least he console her in her grave; he could "heal her pain, her bitter heart and refresh her spirit" by at least saying "Kaddish," the Jewish prayer for the dead.[34]

The affective power of this particular song among Jewish Americans whenever it was presented is well known. According to one reminiscence, it always "called forth oceans of tears." Boris Thomashefsky certainly knew this, and his performance of the song must have contributed to the building of his immense following of *patrioten* (fans). He offered this "mama" song whenever he could find an appropriate scene and opportunity in *any* play. On such occasions, when rendered, the ballad, "with all the true Yiddish sentimentality, mothers and children—the whole audience . . . found it impossible to hold back the tears."[35] In addition, the song was recorded by Victor on November 30, 1908.[36]

The composer, Solomon Shmulewitz, also wrote a similar piece, and although it was not part of the "letter" series, it was still popular. Called "Ellis Island" (1914), it once again dwells on immigration's deleterious effects on family responsibility. The song's main complaint is that the denial of acceptance at that New York harbor entrance to "Free America" was devastating to some "poor souls." It uses one case as an example in which a father is rejected and cannot reunite with his American "sons and daughters here, [who] want to take us in!"

> Their children shed bitter tears,
> The children protest to Washington and are told
> The newcomers are of no great use to the country.[37]

A similar tune, "Lozt Arayn!" ("Let Us In!"), likely appearing about the same time, tells the same tragic story of a father at Ellis Island unable to meet his children. In this situation the mother had recently died in Europe, so the song uses that unfair denial of admission by officials to plea for acceptance of all Jews to let them in and not break their hearts."[38]

Besides the letter songs and musical references to the fears of not being admitted, another familiar, pessimistic theme in Jewish immigrant vocal works is the dissatisfaction over conditions at the workplace. Again, criticism of the evils of capitalist exploitation had been evident in eastern Europe as the emergence of a socialist movement and the Jewish Bund showed. The situation produced a labor-song repertoire in Europe among factory-working women in particular.[39]

The dissatisfaction in America came from not only Gentile employers but fellow Jews as well. When some Jews, especially those from Germany, had accumulated enough capital to start manufacturing enterprises in the needles trade, they hired and even sometimes exploited their poorer, incoming Russian "cousins," paying them very little and thus causing worker discontent and unrest. This was particularly true in the tenement "sweatshop" factories, where newcomers, both men and women, labored long and hard under trying working conditions. The result was the rise in America of a vigorous trade-union sentiment among the newly arrived Jewish workers and a musical literature that went along with it.

Early, even before the turn of the century, a number of labor "poets" appeared, offering appropriate lyrics expressing the sentiments of the workers. And like the *brivele* and the Yiddish musicals, the best known dealt with the effect of work on the family. The most famous composers were a quartet of songwriters, Joseph Bovshover, Morris Winchevsky, David Edelstadt (Edelshtadt), and the most famous "bard" of the Jewish proletariat, Morris Rosenfeld. Bovshover left Russia as a youth with high hopes for the American "flower garden," only to find more injustice in the sweatshops of New York. He joined the socialists in 1890, became acquainted with Edelstadt, and began writing increasingly bitter poems and prose in both Yiddish and English about workplace injustice. His best-known work was "A Song for the People," in which he condemns wage slavery and its durability.[40]

Better known was Edelstadt, who in 1882 also left Russia but avoided New York by going west to Ohio to establish a model farming community. But seeing the conditions at a Cincinnati button-factory workshop embittered him, and he began to write popular verse attacking the system. His poems became very popular as songs with titles like "In Battle" and "The Worker." The latter ends by expressing the unhealthy effects of excruciating labor: "My pain is so great, I can scarcely bend—and at night I cough without rest."[41]

The most famous and honored of these proletarian composers is Morris Rosenfeld. As one writer describes it, being "celebrated in the shops and [labor] halls," Rosenfeld was able to touch closely the "intimate experience of his audience."[42] He had always loved poems and Yiddish song as a teenager in Russia around 1880. Rosenfeld left Poland a few years later, working in sweatshops in both London and New York, where he had arrived in 1886. His compositions, his use of dialectic Yiddish, and his effective performances as a singer in New York and on tour made him enormously appealing to working-class audiences after the mid-1880s.[43] He achieved critical acclaim when a Harvard professor published his *Songs of the Ghetto* (in English) in 1898.

Rosenfeld's major song hit, as familiar and appealing to immigrants as Shalom Aleichem's "Shlof Mein Kind" and Shmulewitz's "A Brivele der Mamen," was "Mayn Yingele" ("My Little Boy").[44] It is an American ballad, written in 1887, a year after he arrived in his new land. It tells of what the songwriter saw firsthand, the miserable workplace of the needles-trade workers. Notably, this piece is similar to the two former ballads in that it concerns the maintenance of family integrity. Its speaker is an ordinary worker who, because he must labor so long, cannot carry out his proper fatherly duties. An abbreviated version of the lyrics in translation begins:

> I have a little boy, a fine fellow is he!
> When I see him, it appears to me the whole world is mine.
>
> Only rarely, rarely do I see him, my pretty little son, when he is awake
> I find him always asleep, I see him only at night.
>
> My work drives me out early and brings me home late;
> Oh my own flesh is a stranger to me! O strange to me the glances of my
>   child.

The wife tells her husband that their son plays and speaks well but always asks to see his "Papa." The father stands by the boy's bed at night after returning from work.

> I touch his eyelids with my lips.
> The blue eyes open then
> They look at me! They look at me!
> And quickly shut again.

The father concludes that sometimes the boy will not find him present.

> I watch him, wounded and depressed
> By thoughts I cannot bear:
> "One Morning, when you wake—my child—
> You'll find that I'm not here."[45]

The song is in the tradition of Rosenfeld's other, less popular works that simply attack the sweatshop and labor exploitation. One of the latter is "Mayn Rue Platz" ("My Resting Place"), in which the singer laments his slavery and asks his lover to ease his pain. Another is "The Tear Drop Millionaire," in which the singer is a wealthy figure whom workers can pay only with tears.[46] The Jewish musical repertoire is rich with songs of labor protest written by others, such as "Di nyu-yorker trern" ("New York Tears"; 1910), which once more refers to families, an eviction, and a murder; "Swing Days" (1908); and several ballads that came out of the major Jewish workers' tragedy, the Triangle Fire of 1911, like "Mamenyu! Including an Elegy to the Triangle Fire Victims." This song again alludes, in part, to family matters, such as the lament of an orphan who had lost her mother, or a mother grieving over her dead daughter.[47]

Likely the most popular song among Jewish Americans when it appeared around World War I was "Di Grine Kusine" ("The Green Cousin"). Despite its extraordinary, widespread popularity, its origins and the true identity of its original composer are exceptionally complicated and uncertain. The song's creators were likely Abe Schwartz or Jacob Leiserowitz, who wrote the music, and Hyman Prizant, the lyricist. The most solid additional evidence is that "Di Grine Kusine" first appeared in a newspaper early in 1917 and was performed as a theater song at the Grand Theater in New York. It was such an instant sensation that in the next few years it spawned a rash of other ballads about the innocent female "greenhorn cousin."[48]

Another certainty attested to by critics is the song's paramount significance, for it has been referred to as "the most famous of all Jewish immigrant songs," "one of the most popular songs of immigrant life of America," "the biggest song hit in the history of Jewish music," and "the most famous song of its time."[49] As Leiserowitz was a satirist, some might place the piece in the comic tradition of a greenhorn's life like that of the Swedish Olle I Stkatthult group. But a reading of the lyrics certainly does not indicate such a lighthearted or humorous characterization. The song is a serious comment about the vulnerability, exploitation, and lost innocence of a newly arrived working girl in American capitalistic society. It was a "bitter song of defeat" that "provoked tears" and became "an enormous hit."[50]

"Di Grine Kusine" tells of a fresh young maiden, full of life and optimism, who is ground down by her American job. It is in that sense similar to the labor songs of Rosenfeld and others in their criticism of the inhuman working conditions. And while not concerned openly with the parent-child bond, the song is rooted in a family connection. The narrator is kin to the unfortunate girl and apparently feels obliged to complain of her degradation.

> There came to me a cousin
> Pretty as gold was she, the green one
> Her cheeks were like red oranges
> Her little feet just begged for a dance. . . .
> She walked not but she skipped
> She talked not but she sang
> Gay and cheerful was her manner
> This is how my cousin once was.

The narrator then gets her a job in a millinery store, and in stating his gratitude to the "Golden Land" for providing employment, he expresses that ambivalence about America that affected so many other immigrants. In the end, though, her exhausting labor causes her ruination.

> Many years of collecting wages
> Till nothing was left of her
> Beneath her pretty blue eyes
> Black lines were drawn
> Her cheeks, once like red oranges
> Have turned completely green already
> Today, when I meet my cousin
> And I ask her: How are you green one?
> She'll reply with a grimace
> To blazes with Columbus's country![51]

More evidence of the song's enormous popularity is its publishing history and frequent appearance on records. After it had been performed on stage during World War I, at least three copyrights for the sheet music were granted between December 1921 and March 1922. In addition, at least ten separate recordings of the song, albeit differing versions, were made in 1922 alone.[52]

As the 1920s wore on, and while such songs as "Di Grine Kusine" were still on the minds of group members, the most popular themes of the Yiddish musical theater shifted away from concerns over family responsibilities. Possibly due to the end of mass immigration and the rise of an American-born second generation, the plays stressed more romance and a growing nostalgia and homesickness for the Old World. The new leading star of these Yiddish musicals was the ebullient comedian Aaron Lebedeff, who overwhelmed his audience with his vitality and zest for life. He became known as the Jewish "Maurice Chevalier," especially since his signature song, "Rumania, Rumania," spoke of the epicurean and hedonistic pleasures of that land. This was a suggestion to his listeners in the late 1920s, and for decades afterward, to remember the delights of other shtetl regions.[53]

Thus, despite an apparent upturn of anti-Semitism in the postwar era in America, the Jewish community prospered and began to feel more secure in the new land as the immigrant era began to fade. In any event, it appears that the immediate and painful effects of immigration, like the guilt over leaving relatives, were replaced by a more generalized nostalgia for the old home.

From a review of the themes of the most popular Yiddish immigrant songs, one must conclude that the overwhelming sentiment on the minds of Jewish arrivals upon their coming and settlement in America was predominantly one of discomfort. To be sure, the complete repertoire of the popular works was, as with the other groups, eclectic and covered a wide variety of opinions about the trip to America, from the most optimistic expectations and gratitude to fears about the future in the new land. As with other groups too, song subjects included such mixed feelings as young people's wish to be free of parental control and military service, a deep-seated apprehension about the dangers of the crossing, and hope for a better life.

Nevertheless, if one attempts to ascertain the major sentiment of most ordinary Jews from eastern Europe to be extracted from the *leading* immigrant songs, the overall attitude was a feeling of personal loss. Most prominent in the case of the Jews were the destructive effects of migration, including separation and exploitation, both negative influences on traditional family ties.

This is not to say that Jewish immigrants felt they should never have left eastern Europe. Certainly, the rather hostile economic and social conditions in the old country pushed them to the United States. But the transfer was certainly a disruptive one psychologically, and immigrants were always not completely satisfied with their move. It should be remembered that the backward tug on those who departed still was effective, for even with the more virulent anti-Semitism and pogroms in their Russian home, some who went to America still returned to their shtetl in eastern Europe.

Writers have paid lesser attention to Jewish re-emigrants. Possibly suggesting a corrective and new trend in Jewish emigrant historiography, one scholar has challenged students to remember the emotional tie immigrants retained of the Old World. Jonathan Sarna observes that at least in the early years before 1908, the statistics suggest the re-emigration of much higher numbers of Jews than formerly believed. The causes were several, such as economic failure and an inability to meet their expectations here, a general insecurity in a "Godless America," and "loneliness," which certainly included the fervent wish to restore sundered family bonds. Thus, one could say that the *agune's* (abandoned wife's) desperate need for restoration of the spousal tie may have been partially effective in returning the husband.[54] America, in other words, was not quite the "Promised Land" that earlier historians and mythology had proposed. Most immigrants, of course, never did go back, and while life in the United States may have been better than in Russia, it still was troubling remembering those left behind.

Finally, all immigrant groups suffered from the departure of loved ones, as the traumatic songs about an Irish wake have shown. Still, the Jewish immigrant-song record suggests that the damage to the familial tie was distinctive in its greater prominence in song and mentality.

5

The Italians

Uncertain Followers of Columbus

In numerous ways Italian immigrants to America had experiences and hence produced songs that spoke about themes similar to those of other newcomers. The Italians also produced a mix of optimistic and pessimistic songs, some of which glorified the attractions of the new land, such as several in thanking Columbus, their countryman, for finding the New World. They also lionized the Great Discoverer for his deed, for Italians, of course, had the greatest ethnic claim on the man. But recognizing him was not only done with praise; they referred to him in negative terms as well. Hence for this group as well, contradictory references blaming and lionizing their hero suggest a certain ambivalence about their emigration.

Once again, Italians echoed the concerns of other groups in their musical criticism of those emigrating, particularly stressing the perils of leaving. As in the case of northern Europeans and Germans, for example, some Italian lyrics commonly reject the whole idea of abandoning home and family. And as in the Irish case, much is made of the ominous threat of ship disasters. Generally with the others too was the pervasive theme of dissatisfaction and discomfort of arriving and settling in the new land. While these southern Europeans bemoaned the discriminatory treatment of the dominant Anglo-Americans, their accounts in song characteristically differ from the widespread unease by a particular unfamiliarity and confusion over a certain cultural norm of their hosts.

Particularly distinctive in the Italian case was their problem of language adjustment. As with many other groups, their encounter with English and the resulting Anglo-American assimilation of their speech were upsetting, complicating their communication and making more difficult their adjustment in the new land.

While, as expected, other immigrant groups also suffered from language contact, such assimilation in the Italian case seemed particularly upsetting, for its effects were serious, even threatening their other traditional ways of life.

Overall then, while Italian songs did express an optimism similar to that of other groups, appreciating their freer life and prospects of a better material existence than the one at home, their song repertoire also contained the problems and grievances that accompanied those advantages. The greater egalitarianism in America in the relations between the sexes, for example, was paradoxically a mixed blessing, endangering the revered values of the southern Europeans.

Even before any substantial number moved to the United States in the late 1900s, emigration was not new for them. Italians had been familiar with a large outflow of their people beyond their borders. Leaving one's hometown from the Apennines for work in distant locations had been common, at least as far back as the 1700s.[1] So by the middle of the next century, many had already forsaken their Mediterranean country in sizable numbers.

The earliest wave of emigrants in the 1800s left from the northern provinces for those places where they could make a better income. Their early destinations were the industrial centers of Europe and South America; only a few settled at that time in the United States. It was not until later, after the American Civil War, that a much larger contingent, chiefly from southern Italy, crossed the Atlantic for the land of Washington. The causes of that enlarged outflow were similar in general to the exodus elsewhere on the continent—that is, for economic reasons—such as agricultural crises, famine, and poverty as well as escaping disease, military conscription, and certain natural calamities. Further dissatisfaction leading to the departure of these later Italians was the role of unsympathetic authorities. The national government, controlled by northerners, generally mistreated and exploited southerners, and the other domineering group, the Catholic Church hierarchy, was unsympathetic to the plight of the masses.

This later emigration became massive by the turn of the twentieth century, and by the start of World War I, the total number who had left was nearly four million. (Some of course did return.) By that time four-fifths of all Italian immigrants in the United States were southerners, coming from the more economically depressed provinces of Apulia, Basilicata, Calabria, Campania (which included Naples), and Sicily.[2]

These people were notably not culturally homogeneous. Similar to but not fully like the Germans, they carried with them their distinct, highly localized, regional consciousness and ways of life. Italian immigrants, then, were initially fragmented as shown by the way they identified themselves, that is, as people from a specific small community or provincial town. As the Conte di Cavour, the leader struggling to achieve Italian unity, knew, few really considered themselves

"Italian." In addition to this exceptional fragmentation of place, these immigrant southerners in the post-1880 era had a high rate of illiteracy and hence communicated less in print than in oral forms. Thus possessing a rich folk culture, they brought with them a considerable corpus and practice of music and song.

The scope of the Italian-immigrant repertoire was as vast as any other group. Their music included lullabies and songs about many human activities, work, romance, social protest, and emigration. One Italian folklorist may have best justified studying southern Italian folk culture as a whole by stating that it "allows us new and varied perspectives on societies . . . with their mentalities and reasons for being, their own ways and traditions, their own expressions of identity."[3]

While the southerners all differed in their regional folkways, one can still generalize about the objectives of the Calabrians, Neapolitans, Sicilians, and others leaving for America. They normally departed as sojourners intent on earning enough money to resettle back home in comfort. Indeed, a particularly large percentage were re-emigrants in the decade and a half before World War I; estimates run to almost one-half or more of all Italian immigrants. Thus, clearly as in other group cases, America was not to be their permanent home, and with the Italians, many actually did return to the old country. Of course, one cannot know precisely why; it may suggest that most of these *Americani* (the term used in Italy for re-emigrants) went back dissatisfied with the United States or may have fulfilled their objective. It is certain that some undoubtedly crossed the Atlantic several times.

As for their music, the world is familiar with the many Italian vocal works, particularly the musical compositions from the famous bel canto operatic arias to Neapolitan songs that have been so enormously popular. In addition, folksong collections of the *contadini* (southern Italian peasants) for the 1800s are also popularly known and in print. But all of these songs, or at least those that deal with emigration, have yet to be integrated fully into academic scholarship.[4] Thus the works selected here are only a fragment of the group's entire immigrant repertoire. Nevertheless, they still offer some insight into the mentality of the newcomers. They include, as with the Jews, the most beloved pieces of the lively and popular Italian American musical theater.

As is the case with other groups, the thematic character of the songs concerning the overseas passage was an emotional mixture of feeling. They both heralded the promise of America as well as described the hardships in leaving and settling there. So in this case too, the internal disposition of the newcomers was conflicted, indicating once again a pervasive sense of doubt about the future.

It is true that the origins of the emigrant songs were, like much of Italian culture, fragmented, and hence, with a few exceptions, a reflection of the people's extensive regional variety. Nevertheless, since the emigration fever affected many

A young Viggianese (Italian) street harpist in 1876. From Thomas Smith and A. Smith, *Street Life in London* (London, 1876).

localities, most heavily in the southern Italy, it is possible that some of those localized songs were known beyond the region from which they came, particularly when they joined with others in the settlements, or *colonias,* abroad.

This extended diffusion of regional songs was also due in part to the ubiquitous nature of particular performing ensembles that became known throughout the Italian diaspora. These were traveling musicians who toured many areas, both at home and abroad, singing peasant tunes. Likely the best known of these troupes were children of Viggiano, who traveled not only throughout the villages of southern Italy but also around the world. From the late 1800s until the beginning of the twentieth century, one could find them on the city streets of Europe, Asia, and America, especially in Boston, New York, and Chicago.[5] All this suggests that some of the emigrant songs and ballads describing human conditions were sung by more than just emigrants of a particular region; they emanated from the entire Italian working class overseas.[6]

As indicated, some of the better-known vocal pieces speak eagerly of going to the United States. For example, one collection of works sung in the immigrant Italian dialect in the early 1900s gathered by two field workers in West Virginia in the early 1930s compared the differing attractions of the *Americas,* South and North. The songs specifically differentiated Latin America as the "poor America,"

Street musicians originally from Viggiano, Italy, were found all around the world in the late 1800s. From Francesco de Bourcard, *Usi e costumi de Napoli e Contorni* (Milano: Longanesi, 1970).

while the northern continent was "Great America," where in that "land of the free and the brave" opportunities abounded.[7]

For a close comparison between the Old and New World Italian cultures, another folklorist compared the folk traditions of two related ethnic communities with the same name, the Rosetos, one in Italy and the other in Pennsylvania. Her musical examples also affirmed the promise of America.

Italians had been going to Roseto, Pennsylvania, as quarry workers since the early 1880s. Their songs visualize the New World as an earthly paradise, a place that could provide relief from the arduous hardships and grinding poverty of the homeland. The references to the great deed of Columbus and the metaphor of America as a place of natural beauty, especially abundant flowers, are common themes:

> I bless Christopher Columbus,
> Who discovered the third part of the world [where]
> . . . we Italians are called to work there. . . .
> And America is long and wide and beautiful.

It is all made of roses and flowers, . . .
Long live America and those who go there.[8]

America's natural beauty appeared to be an important attraction in other Italian songs as well. Another, more-ambivalent example, for it includes the problem of the long journey westward, still refers to it as "a bunch of flowers. / I want to go there though it is a distant land." While welcoming the new land's providing a more adequate living, the singer further expects a positive outcome: emigrating will also change his identity for the better spiritually as well as materially. There he actually "becomes American [and] can eat and drink like a Christian [that is, human being]"; he also will become "as rich as a king."[9]

Still more expressed gratitude for America in some song texts in a body of works that vocalize a fervent patriotism for the adopted country. While these were collected in West Virginia in the early 1930s, some years after the mass immigration, since they dealt with the migration theme, it is likely that they existed during the immigration era. One representative piece is appropriately entitled "My Land of Adoption" and begins with the standard reference to Columbus as the Great Discoverer.

Oh, you beautiful vast land!
Which lies in that continent
Discovered by that unfortunate friend
Born in the sunny Italian land.

You have been and are a haven
To those who opportunity seek.

It then cites the establishment of the nation that provided political freedom and praises the Founding Fathers for building a sanctuary for those coming from the Old World. Its most appreciative stanza describes why the singer came and is devoted to his adopted land.

I as yet a child heard those who came
From America to Italy, telling of the opportunity
To work and gain knowledge of Uncle Sam,
And see the new land of youth and equal society.

It concludes:

[I] risked my life; for you my heart rent
For you I left the land which me begot.[10]

Two other songs in that collection express similar sentiments. One, entitled the "Fourth of July," talks about the holiday that teaches people to hate tyranny and love liberty. The other, "Fourteen Ninety-Two," once again cites Columbus as a hero, bonding Italian immigrants to America:

> Let's remember the year fourteen ninety-two
> To America is an old fact, not new,
> For we gladly under [the] USA's flag live
> And land of freedom which Columbus gave.[11]

Thus, expressions of the advantages of leaving home and living in America, both material and philosophical, are evident in these works. Yet as with the music of other ethnic groups, overwhelmingly the prospects for the future of the Italian emigrant were uncertain at best, ominous at worst. The kind of "parting" ballads, originally known as *partenze,* in which the bride leaves home, is a large part of and strongly influenced the traditional emigrant repertoire.[12]

The best proof of the less happy quality of Italian emigrant songs is the popularity of what is arguably the leading work in the entire group's emigrant-music literature: "Mamma, Mamma, Mamma, damme cendo lire" ("Mama, Mama, Mama, Give Me a Hundred Lire"). This song has special significance, for it was familiar to almost every Italian in the diaspora, regardless of regional origin, known and sung on every continent that had colonies of Italian immigrants. The work apparently is based on an 1888 publication of another ballad, "Maledizione della Madre" ("The Mother's Curse"), which in turn came from an even earlier tale in oral tradition. It tells the story of a young girl who, after eloping on horseback, drowns as a result of her mother's evil curse.[13]

In the emigrant version, the girl asks for money from her mother to go to America. Her brother adds his support to her petition, but the mother refuses to grant it. The girl willfully departs, but the ship on which she was traveling tragically sinks in midocean, and there, clothed in her wedding dress, she drowns. The implied moral of this mournful lament is, of course, a strong one warning of the fate of emigrants and hence asserts vehement opposition to emigration. In a restatement of traditional family roles, it warns all offspring to obey their parents and not leave home. By such a warning one can infer that prospective emigrants and those who *do* leave had to shoulder an additional moral burden.

Since it was so widely sung, numerous variants of the piece exist. The one popular in Pennsylvania reads:

> "Mother, mother, give me a hundred lire,
> Because I want to go to America."

[The mother replies,] "I will give you a hundred lire
But to America, no, no, no!"

The brother urges the mother to let her daughter go, and the young girl threatens to kill herself if she does not get her parent's permission. The mother answers,

"Go ahead, evil daughter,
May you drop in the deep, deep sea!"

The ship later sinks in midocean, taking the young girl with it.

Another version identifies the brother as the villain. In that song the drowned girl, now remorseful, blames her brother for encouraging her and blesses her mother for telling her the truth. That song concludes, in lugubrious detail, with fish eating the girl's eyes, hands, and other body parts. Still another version ends with the girl blaming the mother:

"These for sure must be the curses
That my mother put on me."[14]

That this song appeared in broadsheets is further proof that it was known widely among Italians abroad.[15] Thus, given the considerable fragmentation and heterogeneity of southern Italian culture during the immigrant era, the universality of this song in both Old and New World colonies is particularly noteworthy and cannot be overstated.

Other, more regionally based songs dwell on the certain fears that emigrants encountered. Similar to "Mama, Mama," another work about emigration causing family distress is the ballad of the ship *Sirio*, popular among northern Italians around 1900. It fits the more general genre of shipwreck ballads, the kind of transportation disaster that all travelers feared. In this case, soon after leaving Genoa, the vessel struck a rock, and many drowned. The song conveys the agony of frantic parents looking for children who had gone under the waves.[16]

Another regional song from Calabria, in a version published in 1908, likely had wide currency among emigrants since it came from a province that was a leading emigrant producer. It treats another sad characteristic of the exodus in referring to and condemning the hemorrhaging of the province's departing youth. In something of a reversal of the more positive ballads, it places much of the blame for the human loss on the nation's first emigrant: "Christopher Columbus, what did you do? / You spoiled our best youth as [they] went to sea in that black wooden ship." Another version of this ballad lays the responsibility for the depopulation on King Victor Emmanuel. The allegation had a ring of truth, for

escaping the government policy of military conscription was indeed a common
motive for departing youth.[17]

While the popularity of another song genre is uncertain, it too was likely representative since it came from a very old song tradition, known as the *villanella*.
It was in the style of a medieval madrigal and came from the town of Acri in the
province of Calabria. (The song was collected recently by Anna Chairetakis in
Brooklyn, New York, from a group of Calabrian emigrants.) Like the songs of many
other groups, it too stresses what those in America would miss by leaving the old
country.

Some might consider this song strange as offered by immigrants in America;
the text is a warning to those who are considering following others. It lists the
faults of the new land:

> I've heard that you want to go to America . . .
> You will find neither water nor wine, and the fountains will dry up
> You will find no church to enter nor even saints to worship
> You'll go far away, and then you'll remember:
> Beautiful Calabria, where [why?] have I left you?[18]

Still a third Calabrian song from the nineteenth century, "Chaintu d'emigrantu,"
follows that persistent theme of ambivalence. It refers to both the emigrant's insecurity over the future—"I don't know where fortune will lead me"—and the grief
of the one left behind—"Oh my Saint Anthony, make him return and don't send
me any more pain!"[19]

This uncertainty over the venture certainly played a significant role in emigrant
mentality despite the potential advantage of improving one's material condition.
As in other ethnic traditions, another song wonders how much of a sacrifice it
would be to live in America. Since most came to fill unskilled jobs that required
long, backbreaking labor, such as construction work, building railway lines, working in tenement sweatshops, rag picking, and mineworking, the lyrics of the song
warns that the benefits of America may be chimerical.

> Some say America is a wealthy land
> They do not know that one may also find weakness [or poverty there]
> Very heavy jobs, always and always hard work. . . .
> An honest person who wants to work is killed by this life and never gets
>   money
> I always work, all day long and then I sigh and say this land is not for me.

He, in fact, looks forward to returning home:

I want to leave [here] maybe to die.
I am glad to die [but] I say I want to see my Italy [first].[20]

Still another song from the Pennsylvanian Rosetans uses a metaphor to put the paradox of America succinctly and symbolically in religious terms. It is both a heaven and hell:

What can we find in America?
Mountains of gold and mountains of work,
A golden cross, but still a cross
A diamond cross is still a cross.[21]

Sensitive accounts have dwelled on the difficult psychological state and conflict that immigrants felt when situated in America. Robert Orsi has identified a source of that mental struggle in his description of the popular religious manifestations in one of the ethnic group's major centers, Italian Harlem in New York City. That inner discomfort came to the fore, he asserts, when newcomers celebrated their patron-saint days. That pain was the result not only from the fond memory of "Calabria bella" but also of the heavy and constant pressure newcomers felt to assure themselves that their sacrifice in leaving home was worth the effort. As Orsi puts it, they suffered from "guilt that they were not doing enough, pressure to work harder and faster, and fear that they would be unsuccessful . . . , all this haunted the early arrivals."[22]

Other evidence of the ambivalence of immigrants upon arrival is an autobiographical poem that a re-emigrant published in the early 1920s that reviews his overseas experience. The pain of marginality in the poem "A Hurried Man" has to do with the conflict of American vis-à-vis traditional values. In America there are fewer traditions for guidance than in the old country, and Americans are too absorbed with a spirited quest for progress. The new culture thus minimizes the warm old-country feelings of love and kindness. Thus ironically put, what is achieved in America causes an unhappy, permanent alienation from Italy. "America, you gather the *hungry* people and give them new hungers for the old ones."[23]

Another song that indicates the conflict in the mind of the immigrant is "The Disillusioned Immigrant." It is actually a work song that is an argument over the benefits and evils of American materialism. On the one hand, it heralds the prosperity and social mobility achievable in the new land, but on the other hand the immigrant engaged in the process of earning income is divested of the nobler human virtues. The song was recorded in Detroit after World War II but retains the sentiment of ballads from the era of mass immigration. It concludes that the speaker and his listeners ought not to emigrate.

Money, Money, Money!
Where is that money?
I dreamed a strange dream, I dreamed of finding it in trees
Money, Money, Money!
Stay right where you are
If this is what America is like,
I want to go back![24]

To recapitulate, the Italian immigrant songs reviewed here contain a repetition of those concerns found in most other ethnic groups—reflections on the hardships of leaving home and family, the dangers of crossing, the hard work necessary for income, and the general pressures to make a success of the venture. In seeking what may have been distinctive, any observer will note that absent, or at least minimal in the Italian repertoire, are songs that deal with what was a prominent feature of the Italian American experience, labor radicalism. Also missing is any song referring to Italian nationalism. This is understandable, though, given the intense regionalism evident among the group as well as the profound hostility toward the unfriendly government in the Old World.

The one feature that appears most distinctive of Italians in their musical literature has to do with the greatest difficulty in adjusting to Anglo-American culture, the issue of language. In fact, the gradual integration of the English language into immigrant speech in America and the difficulty of making oneself understood orally was one important result of majority discrimination and abuse. Italian American scholarship has cited the linguistic problem as a common source of cultural distress under which newcomers, especially greenhorns, labored. That concern over oral communication and the emergence of a new immigrant vernacular was certainly reflected in Italian American vaudeville, comedy, and song.

The newcomers' obstacle in adjusting their speech is suggested in the creation of a new argot, which some have referred to as "Italiese" or "Italglish."[25] It was speech that assimilated some of the expressions of the Anglo-American majority culture, eventually becoming the oral communication used by all Italian Americans, rich and poor alike. This process of speech Americanization was so important that at its height new, Italianized English words constituted one-quarter of an immigrant's spoken language. This hybrid language had its beginning early in the 1860s among ordinary immigrants. That easy acceptance of English words in the foreign tongue, which nevertheless retained the Italian linguistic structure, was further helped by adding word borrowings from other neighboring immigrant groups, such as the Irish and Jews. Italglish, then, was an "insider" language that was an authentic reflection of immigrant experience.[26]

The pressure for newly arrived Italian immigrants to modify and American-ize their speech was considerable, not only to avoid ridicule from their Anglo-American hosts but also from their more assimilated compatriots. The necessity and consequent pressure to acquire this new language was also natural. While many came with a regional dialect, the broader Italglish was developed to facili-tate communication with other regional Italians. It was simply a "practical way to carry on everyday affairs."[27]

Two good musical examples of that vernacular that reflect the difficulties of language modification are popular songs among both the Pennsylvania Rosetans and Italian Americans from West Virginia. The first example, popular on both sides of the Atlantic, refers to the familiar metaphor of America as a natural par-adise. But the lyrics include the problem of communication as well as the mysteri-ous paradoxes and unfamiliar egalitarianism found in the new land.

The attraction of America, the song narrator begins, is as "a little bunch of flowers." His steamship left Italy, and "when we got to the [New York] Battery, all people spoke and I didn't understand." The ballad goes on to marvel somewhat satirically at the technology of the New York subway, where "the train went down and the water on top," and also at the confusing social mobility both up and down, where "even the [poorer] peasants wear evening suits" and the formerly skilled Italian artisan with "a shovel in his hands . . . plows the asphalt!"[28]

The other song, from West Virginia, called "Nicolo [*sic*, Niccolo] Went to the USA," recounts the personal experience of an immigrant who describes his pain-ful encounters, partially linguistic, as he tries to adjust to the unfamiliar society. It begins with an implied regret over how the singer left Italy:

> My friend used to say, "Nico,
> America is a nice country,
> Tutti fanno planty money,"
>
> Like a stupid, I believed him,
> I gave him my goat and then embarked.
> You want to know the end of the story in America?

While generally a lighthearted narrative meant to entertain, it still reveals the prob-lem many compatriots had in dealing with local authorities. He recounts the trouble he gets into with the police because they do not understand his explanation.

> One night I was out on the street,
> Someone gave me a punch with his fist,
> Then I was afraid [there] was going to be more on the list.

I soon cried out aloud:

Police! Police! Help, help!

But when the police came, he arrested me.

They tell him that he would have to pay five dollars or be put in jail. He concludes that he will pay it to avoid incarceration and hopes that that will be the last of his "trouble." But that was not to be, for on a streetcar an ugly man calls him a "Wop!" and instructs him to give a lady his seat. Confused, he objects, but the reply is unexpected. "Suddenly I felt a big blow on my poor left eye[,] then everything went dark."[29]

Besides these examples of individual and private presentations of ethnic songs, another area of musical expression unfolded, of course, in the more public settings among Italians, in their saloons, cafes, and theatrical houses. It was there that entertainers offered their reflections on the life of their audiences. As one might imagine, the linguistic obstacle was again a major source of comedy, and actors made the most of it.

Probably the earliest venue for singing and performing Americanized songs of Italian immigrants was aboard ship prior to their arrival in the new land. One reporter noted that an immigrant ship leaving Naples about 1900 had both singing and musical entertainment on board. The travelers' first encounter with English took place on their way to America. About the time the vessel was leaving Gibraltar, the observer noticed the steerage passengers happily singing from time to time, but he also detected a difficult change in the nature of the songs: "the Italian provincial songs which had prevailed, changed to American airs, attempted by those who had been in the States."[30]

Nevertheless, the major performance site for music and singing was, of course, at various public social centers in the Italian urban colonies. Best known were the several establishments not only in New York City uptown around Harlem at the turn of the century but especially in the largest Italian concentration on the Lower East Side. One 1910 estimate of the number of commercial places where Italians gathered to hear their music is impressive. There at the height of Little Italy were forty cafes, seventeen saloons, and other places that offered entertainment. These were sites like the ubiquitous open-air marionette puppet shows and even barber shops, both additional places of song in Italy and America. Instrumentalists played their guitars and mandolins to give the Italian quarter an extraordinary musical ambiance. It is noteworthy too that all these venues were entirely male preserves.[31]

It is well known that Italian operatic arias as well as folk tunes were heard almost everywhere, even outside in the streets. In those settings pushcart peddlers accompanied the hawking of their wares with song, and there organ grinders added their tunes for whatever income passersby offered.[32] Popular songs could also be heard in the street, emanating from the several ethnic music stores in the Italian Lower East Side. In that neighborhood of Bayard, Mott, Mulberry, and Elizabeth Streets, as one visitor put it, one could listen to "clever ditties about the eternal subject of mirth [and] mothers-in-law" coming from those shops.[33]

While no direct reference is available as to what particular songs were heard in these outdoor performances, it is certain that these establishments provided musical entertainment that dealt with the plight of the new Italian arrival. Observers of these venues have referred to them generically as the "caffé concerto." Such restaurants, bars, and music halls playing Italian music arose in the 1890s and early 1900s to provide comfort and entertainment for the Italian working class seeking respite from their hard labor. These musical places were undoubtedly popular and certainly accessible to the poorest of workers. Their admission charge was as little as five to ten cents.[34]

The best-known cafe was the Villa Vittorio Emanuele III. It opened in 1892 and was located on Mulberry Street near Canal. Like other establishments, it regularly employed entertainers; its most famous was the leading Italian ethnic comedian of the time, and for decades afterward, Eduardo Migliaccio. Better known by his stage name Farfariello, the "Little Butterfly," Migliaccio was a huge favorite of Italian-immigrant audiences for his satirical interpretations of a wide variety of immigrant types; he eventually had a repertoire of five hundred different impersonations. Migliaccio's most familiar and beloved characterization was that of the greenhorn. He depicted this figure in the Italian tradition of the *cafone,* the naïve and unlettered peasant clod. Migliaccio drew that person in the immigrant context as a provincial Italian trying with difficulty to make sense of his or her new life in America.[35] By highlighting that *cafone* and his dilemma, he employed his humor to help his audience survive the psychic disruption of the immigrant experience.

Fortunately, much has been written about this comic genius and the tradition of the *cafone*/clown in Old World entertainment, so no lengthy review is necessary here. Suffice it to say that similar humorous characterizations were not new in America but had originated in several regions of the old country. The Campania area around Naples, for example, had its "Pulcinella"; Tuscany, its "Stenterello"; and Sicily, its "Pasquino."[36] While all were not totally alike, they were similar in their depictions of figures who were typical of the rural population. They were generally naïve, generous, and a bit thickheaded, with little formal education. Performers presented them in brief skits or character sketches known as *machiette.* The type was particularly popular in Naples, where the character had a hooked nose, a hump back, and big stomach.[37] The performance was all improvisational, a theatrical tradition known as Commedia Dell'Arte.

Italian musical drama came to America in the 1880s when Neapolitan and Sicilian songs and dances were performed in New York's Little Italy, first in non-group playhouses and later in the *café chantants*.[38] By his unequalled popularity as *the* immigrant clown, Migliaccio thus became the major contributor and promoter of the *machiette coloniale,* theatrical sketches performed in the American colonies.

As others have noted, as Migliaccio lived and observed his countrymen on the Lower East Side, the "Little Butterfly" developed an uncanny ability of discerning and presenting the problems that ordinary immigrants faced. He wove them into humorous and satirical sketches that he performed in cafes, restaurants, theaters, and on recordings that captivated his audiences for almost half a century after 1900. As one observer describes his treatment of the immigrant right off the boat, Migliaccio's *cafone* was "helplessly adrift in the New World . . . , [this] little guy, full of good intentions and ambitious but victimized by both society and his own ineptitude."[39] Thus, while presenting that character in parody, the comedian characterized the newcomer in an uncomfortable psychological state similar to that encountered by all the other new arrivals.

We not only know from Migliaccio, then, the various manifestations of that *cafone* condition but can also identify its roots. The basis of the distress of the greenhorn in that humorous characterization was the problem they encountered with language and adjusting to a new tongue. Ignorance of English was a central element in much of Migliaccio's repertoire. Spoken communication bedeviled the *cafone*/greenhorn.[40] One folklorist has referred to the generic difficulty as expressed in Migliaccio's songs. Such lyrics, she observes, concern not only "departure, alienation, nostalgia but also humorous misadventures, often bringing on cultural and linguistic misunderstanding."[41]

The difficulty of language adjustment, of course, was not unique to the Italians but was felt to some degree by every non-English-speaking arrival. Consider, for example, the hybrid "Yinglish" (Yiddish English) developed by east European Jews. The new immigrant argot among Italians, however, was clearly more problematic and uncomfortable. The Jewish depictions on the musical stage refer only marginally to the problem of communication, for the construction of American Yiddish went far smoother than Italglish. The reasons may have been the greater homogeneity of regional Yiddish in Europe and the Jews' far greater literacy among the eastern Europeans, around 90 percent compared to the southern Italian's 50 percent rate. For Jews, since their vernacular language had more of a literary character, it would naturally produce a generalized and homogeneous American Yiddish. The process of creating Italglish, however, being based more on oral communication, would be slower and more problematic. Italians simply had a more difficult time contending with more discrete and varied forms of their means of expression. In addition, the linguistic sources of the Italian-immigrant speech came from several more disparate sources, American English, standard Italian, as well as the several provincial dialects.

By focusing on that problem, Migliaccio identified the process of creating new language as a source of immigrant discomfort. According to Nancy Carnevale, his songs "suggest a sense of chaos . . . , a Tower of Babel where it is impossible to comprehend anything and easy to misunderstand or be misunderstood."[42] In several songs like "Che Suonno" ("What a Dream") and "Charley My Boy," he refers to America being a new Babel, a land that for the ordinary Italian was one of chaotic communication. In another song likely performed earlier than its recording in the late 1920s, Migliaccio directly compares the traditional language with that of the adopted country. In it he concludes that the old speech was superior to English, and thus he highlights a problem for those having to adjust to the new culture. The narrator in "A Lengua 'Taliana" declares that the very sound of English is "crooked," while the tongue of the homeland is "smooth":

> What a beautiful language Italian is . . . ,
> While the English or American language
> I don't understand it even if you cut my throat.

The speaker then adds that he has been in America over twenty years:

> And I haven't learned even half a word of English,
> Because me no like "crooked tongues" . . .
> I will never learn a word of English.
> It's not that it's bad, the American language,
> It would be a beautiful language . . . but it isn't Italian.

He adds that he has suffered for his linguistic ignorance. He was forced to wait two years to get his citizenship papers: "I didn't get them because the judge spoke to me in English." Farfariello concludes that a deficient knowledge of an oral language would never cause such pain in Italy because one "makes himself understood with his hands." English, therefore, "could never become Calabrese."[43]

Another rather serious social matter having to do with gender relations also arose from the language issue. It may appear as simply a superficial anomaly in the similar pronunciation of one word in the two languages, but for immigrants it masked a more important issue of cultural change that represented a challenge to Italian male dominance. *Uomini*, for example, means "men" in Italian but is close phonetically to the word *women* in English. Along with Migliaccio's frequent reference to America as being a strange "upside down world," this spoken-word identity of the sexes raised the ominous and upsetting notion of gender equality in this patriarchal culture. As Nancy Carnevale has succinctly put it, "Immigration presented Italian men with a host of challenges, not the least of which was the threat to traditional notions of masculinity . . . , [and] Farfariello expertly captures these gender and related tensions in his language humor."[44]

The pressures on Italian men in America thus mounted. They not only encountered the external dangers of travel and reestablishing their life in the new land but also found that the juxtaposition of Italian and English upset the traditional relationship between men and women.[45]

In another song Farfariello deals with still another problem for Italians resulting from language contact. This was the discriminatory and hostile expressions of Anglo-Americans who used bigoted epithets in denigrating Italian immigrants. In Migliaccio's "U Figlio d'o Cafone che ragiona" ("Son of a Thinking Greenhorn"), the group narrator objects when an American calls the immigrant a "dago[.] I say for what reason do you offend Italians?" since Italians have contributed much both morally and culturally to civilization with their "masters of science [and even] teachers." Yet the Italian can criticize Americans as uncouth, lacking polish, and having a "reproachful life style." They are also hypocritical. "They blow their noses with their hands right in the street . . . and [still they call us] ghinneys? . . . [T]hey say we are sons of macaroni, [yet] they fill up their bellies with coffee."[46]

A final example of the language problem is found in one of Migliaccio's most frequently performed skits and characterizations, "Crazy Patsy," recorded in 1916. While commenting generally once again on the "upside down world" immigrants had to face in America, the "Little Butterfly" refers specifically to a heralded, but actually confusing, meaning of a word that American natives use as a democratic virtue. American "freedom" as expressed was, of course, a highly praised feature of the host culture, but it was also an evil in immigrant eyes since license should not be absolute. The nation's great symbol, the Statue of Liberty, does indeed proclaim that word for all, Patsy observes, but unfortunately that also means "a roughneck . . . can do whatever he wants." But "if you [spit] on a trolley . . . , whoever is there won't let you leave."[47]

In conclusion, with his long list of immigrant troubles, one must admit that Migliaccio's overall influence on his audience was likely beneficial. While he did highlight in various ways the painful effects of language adjustment, by identifying the problem in a humorous context, the comedian helped his listeners deal with it. Humor, of course, has that therapeutic effect.

Overall, then, as for other immigrant groups, Italian immigrant songs reveal a certain duality on the act of emigrating. They, in part, express a positive rationale for leaving home, which was to achieve a better and freer life in America. But emigrants also retained misgivings about their going. These latter doubts concerned the hardships of leaving home and the uncertainty of earning an adequate living in an alien, even hostile, society. Most characteristically for Italians, though, was encountering the greatest difficulty of their various subcultures, the rather basic problem of communicating even with other Italian immigrants, not to mention with their Anglo-American hosts.

A final, particular song that compares the two lands, Italy and America, reveals the awkwardness of trying to identify with both. Entitled simply "L'Italia e l'America" ("Italy and America"), its message on the surface states that the immigrants' bonds with both lands are mutually compatible. Nevertheless, the lyrics are defensive and demonstrate a certain self-consciousness about this Italian's marginality. The dual loyalty is evident but, from the assertion in the opening stanza, certainly a difficult condition. At the outset the speaker seems resigned to his uncomfortable fate:

> I haven't seen my home country in ten years,
> I've been in this land for [that time]!
> Actually sometimes I'm homesick
> But then, I calm down and I must accept it.
> Once destiny has wanted this
> You cannot fight against it.

A typical chorus expresses an admiration for both countries but, as one might expect, for Italy above all.

> Those of us in America
> Cannot despise it
> But [also] against Italy,
> Nobody can talk.
> America, I love it very much
> For me, it is just like a lover
> But Italy is in my heart
> Forever, like an affectionate Mom.[48]

6

The Poles and Hungarians

Industrial Hardships

Eastern Europe has always been a region that is unfamiliar to most Americans. And from that lack of general knowledge of the area, it is also true that all the groups who made up the immigration to America in the nineteenth and twentieth centuries, certainly the non-Jews, have been an enigma to most outsiders. An added reason for this lack of understanding is that these particular foreigners possess cultures that are rather unlike and distant from that of the Anglo-American majority. Furthermore, they comprise a great variety of ethnic groups and hence are very heterogeneous; they include a bewildering variety of cultures, some of which differ greatly from one another in language, religion, customs, and the like. For example, they represent a wide spectrum of faiths, Roman Catholicism, Orthodoxy, Islam, and even Protestantism, extending ethnically from the Slavic majority to the Finno-Ugric Lithuanians and Hungarians to the Latin Rumanians. Even though the members of the largest ethno-national group in the region, the Poles, who came here were quite sizable in number, constituting about 2,500,000 in the pre-1920 era, their experience in America too is little known and has until quite recently received little attention from historians and other scholars.

Probably equally as important as an explanation for the lack of knowledge about the Poles is the fact that their culture, while certainly a rich one in the fine arts, is lesser known, neglected, and even denigrated at the folk and popular level. Unlike the better disseminated cultural life of the Italians or Jews, that of eastern European Americans still is little covered by the public media outside of occasional negative stereotypes.[1] And internally, the Polish American immigrant past appears to be even little known to descendants. It is no wonder, then, that a major Polish American historian titled one of the few group portraits *And My Children*

Did Not Know Me. Recent scholars have begun to fill in this significant lacuna, but even with these contributions, the aesthetic interests and expressive culture of the masses from eastern Europe remains obscure.[2]

The songs that two of these groups, the Poles and Hungarians, composed and sang about their American experience reflect an internal clash of opposing sentiments about settling in New World society. These two of the many groups coming from Eastern Europe are selected jointly because of two main reasons. One is the accessibility of sufficient musical evidence, which itself suggests the other, that is, in sum their vocal repertoires imply rather strongly similar attitudes about their living conditions in their American colonies. But a problem in surveying these groups' musical offerings compared to the others is determining the specific venues where they were performed. Although some references to those places are made below, here the major emphasis is on what the pieces say. As expected, what they do tell is a complex of sentiments about the immigrants' lives in a new society.

Both Polish and Hungarian immigrants came from the same regional and sociological origins, largely as peasants from the predominantly agrarian heartland of Eastern Europe, and with similar motives and goals. That was to supply the great and continual need in the burgeoning American heavy industry for unskilled labor in the mines, steel mills, meatpacking plants, oil refineries, and the like. This commonality of social class among the vast majority of Polish and Hungarian immigrants can also be applied to the other central and eastern Europeans, such as the Slovaks, Lithuanians, Rumanians, and other South Slavs, heading for the New World.

But while all these immigrant groups were much alike in the types of jobs they held and their economic goals, one must be careful not to describe each of the groups internally as sociologically homogeneous. Admittedly, the well-known depiction of Jurgis, the Lithuanian immigrant in Upton Sinclair's famous proletarian novel *The Jungle,* rightly indicates that getting work at a Chicago slaughterhouse was apt for many, even perhaps most, Eastern Europeans. The muckraking author, in fact, based his novel on his experience living in the Yards section of the city. But his drawing such a figure undoubtedly contributed to the creation of the unflattering stereotype of the "Hunkie" in later years.

The generalized picture of that suffering, muscle-bound, unintelligent, naïve clod obscured an accurate picture of those peoples' communities. They all had differing cultures, religions, and ethnic roots, and more importantly, while they were largely working class, they all had a stratified social structure, the Poles likely more so than the Hungarians. This more accurate and more complex profile that included a non-working-class contingent of well-to-do farmers, small businessmen, priests, and intellectuals is necessary to note here, particularly for the Poles since their elite, while small, did contribute to the group's song repertoire in America. They, similar to the Irish and Germans, cultivated and expressed in music a strong cultural pride and ethnic patriotism.

This upper class, which promoted those kinds of musical works, was largely descended from the earliest number of Polish arrivals, who made up one of three major regional contingents of that group's immigrants. These first immigrants were from Prussia, later the western borderlands of the German Empire, and came mainly in the 1870–1900 era. Poland had lost its independence in 1795 when its three neighboring empires, Prussia, Russia, and Austria, each carved out sections of the country for themselves. Poles in the German sector differed from their countrymen in the other two areas. They were somewhat better endowed, possessing greater literacy; were more skilled in occupation; and had a higher standard of living. In addition, as a whole, they were more nationally conscious.

While a few pioneers left home earlier, economic and social conditions in the Prussian-held areas caused the initial mass movement of Polish emigration to begin in the 1870s. The early pressure on peasants to consider leaving was caused by agricultural consolidation, military conscription, and a hostile anti-Polish, anti-Catholic campaign in the early 1870s known as the German Kulturkampf. This not only produced an outflow of peasant and artisan families but also motivated some Polish intellectuals to broadcast national consciousness more widely than ever before.

That national sense among Poles had not died of course with the breakup of their state in the late 1700s. Outbreaks of hostilities aiming at freeing the suppressed people had occurred in 1830, 1848, and 1863; but all had failed, producing émigrés in the various sanctuaries of the West, Geneva, Paris, London, and New York. In any event, it was clear by the later decades of the century that the greatest mass support for what was called "organic work" in the home area came from Prussian Poland rather than the later-coming, less nationally conscious, ethnic masses of Russia and Austria. That certainly included song.

The Poles' great literary nationalist, Adam Mickiewicz, had stressed the importance of maintaining native song in his early-nineteenth-century writings. His plea along with the burgeoning of German singing societies that promoted cultural nationalism affected the establishment and popularity of Polish choral singing in the Prussian sector.[3] The trend there was so widespread and was supported especially by Polish artisans and the upper classes in the mid-1800s that German authorities considered the situation a serious subversive threat from the Slavic population in the cities.[4]

Thus when these German Poles began to arrive in America, settling and organizing in early colonies in Texas, the Upper Midwest, and the Northeast, their communities established choral groups to preserve Polish culture and aid in the resurrection of the Polish state. The founder, organizer, and leader of what would be a national organization in America, known as the Polish Singers' Alliance, formed in 1889, was Antoni Małłek.

Małłek himself had come from Prussian Poland, where the level of Polish ethnic consciousness was highest. His father had provided him with a musical education, and he became imbued with Mickiewicz's idea that music and song ought to contribute to a heightened cultural nationalism. He was, in a sense, a refugee himself, for he fled from his involvement in the Franco-Prussian War in 1871 and went to live with his brother in Chicago.[5] The very next year he organized a choir at the city's mother Polish parish, another in Milwaukee the year following, and several others in the surrounding states throughout the 1880s. He showed his strong ethnic loyalty at this time as an active officer in the newly formed association dedicated to ethnic nationalism, the Polish National Alliance (PNA), which had begun in 1880. He occupied then two important group roles, as a PNA leader and director of the national Polish Singer's Alliance in America (PSAA), which was formed at the end of that decade.

We do know part of the repertoire of the PSAA, whose constituent groups (like the German singing societies) would perform at local civic and patriotic ethnic events. Their programs were eclectic, including both religious and secular pieces, but dominant were heavily patriotic and folk selections along with art songs.[6] Such presentations during this time rarely included Polish American compositions, but one can assume that, again similar to the German festivals expressing their culture in traditional songs, it was an implied statement of Polish gratitude to their American hosts for allowing them the freedom to present their patriotic melodies. And like the Germans and the Irish, the Polish concert programs included patriotic American pieces around the turn of the century.[7]

Additional expressions of this Polish immigrant elite about the appeal of American democracy appeared in the years around the turn of the century. That time coincided with the ethnic community's centennial commemoration of certain patriotic group events, such as the promulgation of the liberal Polish constitution in 1891 and the heroism of its two American-Polish heroes. The best known was Thaddeus Kosciuszko, who led his people's European struggle for freedom in 1794. He along with Casimir Pulaski, both of whom fought in the American Revolution, were the personal symbols of the common identity of both American and Polish liberal values. The notable celebrations of Polonia's (Polish American community) commemoration were the dedication of several statues of Kosciuszko in three locations, Chicago, Milwaukee, and the nation's capital, Washington, D.C., in 1910, where a similar replica of Pulaski was also honored.[8]

Immigrants who came from the sections in the Russian and Austrian Empires dominated the influx of Poles during the 1890s and 1900s; they, however, were less educated and poorer as a whole, making their departure and adjustment more difficult and problematic than those arriving from the German Empire. Thus less literate and poorer, they sought employment most often as unskilled laborers in American industry. While in some cases similarly motivated politically, they departed more as single individuals; hence, more so than the German Poles, they had to leave behind more of their closest family members. The transition for these emigrants was likely to be as upsetting or worse. In any event, theirs too was certainly a difficult exodus.

Intimate evidence shows, like all the other European groups, the psychic strain on Poles of being connected to both Old and New Worlds, needing to go west for practical reasons but still reluctant to leave home and family. The decision-making process for these emigrants too was not an easy one.

Admittedly, many of those considering leaving did have sources of information that indicated the attractive potential for achieving success and prosperity. One source of the freer life and higher wage rates in America was the correspondence from earlier emigrants whom villagers knew, thus the importance of "chain" migration. Perhaps even more important as a prod to leave was the re-emigration and presence of returnees themselves. In her outstanding ethnographic study of the eastern Europeans in Johnstown, Pennsylvania, Ewa Morawska identifies in particular the dramatic and hence major stimulus for emigration as simply the personal appearance in the village of the prosperous, returned migrant. That personification of success was, more than any other evidence, proof of the possibility of achieving the ultimate and much desired status of the eastern European peasant, becoming *kmiec,* a yeoman farmer.[9]

Another observer, writing about the poorest Polish region, the province of Galicia in Austria, has also suggested that potential migrants idolized America as an economic "paradise." That, in a peculiar way, confirmed the power of the well-to-do returnee to motivate even more emigration. This source notes that one emigrant back home was actually reluctant to show his accumulated wealth because such ostentatiousness would lead to the breakup of families and thus antagonize some village neighbors.[10]

In any event, one must remember that for most, the appeal of the quest for economic betterment in America was not an ultimate goal but rather a means to an end. Their original intention was not to stay permanently overseas but to return home in a few years with their earnings and become landowners in Europe as the model re-emigrants had done.[11] While some did leave permanently for the lure of modern life, buy farmland in America, and escape unhappy personal and family situations in the Old World, status advancement at home was likely the greater goal for migrants, especially for those from Russia and Austria.[12]

Yet even with regular correspondence with relatives and friends abroad, that appealing prospect of betterment remained mixed with a troubling insecurity. One cause of the reluctance was the anxiety over the ship passage itself, despite its technological improvement by the time most eastern Europeans left. Certainly, the overseas trip was less threatening for them by the 1890s than for earlier emigrating Europeans. The trip by steamship was much shorter than earlier in the century, taking as little as five days. A published collection of over 350 letters of Polish travelers writing back home at the time listed only two complaints about the voyage. But while music and song did relieve some of the tension about the future, the improved conditions did not totally eliminate the discomfort of leaving a life that the emigrants knew and loved.[13] This insecurity evident among Lithuanians is similar to all the other groups. Their most popular emigrant song in both America and the Old World is "Is jau vandravot, sau laim s pajieskot" ("I went off on a journey to seek good fortune").[14]

About 1970, one migrant recalled his ambivalent feelings traveling by rail and by ship fifty years previously: "When the boat moved, I moved among my tears thinking of my family, companions and friends. My regret began to return at the thought of my undertaking and with this I left the threshold of my family home and perhaps . . . forever? . . . I moved with father . . . to the train station among tears and wishes. I went through a terrible struggle."[15] Similarly, an entry in a diary of another Polish emigrant in 1924 recalled his troubled mental state as he contemplated leaving and used even the same phrase: "The thought came to me of going out into the world[, but] I was undergoing a terrible internal struggle. . . . At the thought of leaving my parents' home, I felt strange and unhappy."[16]

Even in Galicia, where economic conditions were the most miserable around the turn of the century, Polish peasants still did not welcome easily the idea of departing from that benighted land for much better income abroad. A farmer's young son still felt leaving was risky: "For a long time I was deliberating about America—what a strange country it is. . . . After long deliberation I decided to risk my savings for a ticket . . . and try my luck there. Were I to fail . . . I was planning to return to Poland.'"[17]

For the Poles as for the others, their songs dealt with both the hopes for success as well as the fears of failure in America. On the positive side, as one scholar familiar with conditions in eastern Europe puts it, song was not just a representation of the optimism, it was also a stimulus for hopeful anticipation in leaving. Without defining the appeal more specifically, she points out, "Songs circulating among the [Eastern European] villages at the turn of the century" encouraged the peasants to view America as the "'incredible land.'"[18] But other thoughts about abandoning the familiar environment expressed in lyrics, like other group emigrants, pulled them back to their home.

An example of that dilemma can be found in a particularly important musical piece that was known throughout the Polish diaspora as the informal "national anthem." Entitled "Góralu, Czy ci nie Żal" ("Mountaineer, Are You Not Sad"), it purportedly came from the culture of the Górale, a distinctive subcultural group with a fierce regional loyalty living in the mountains of southern Poland. The piece, in fact, was *not* a part of that group's folk tradition but was performed and sung by Polish Americans generally; they apparently used the Górale tradition to articulate the uncertainty of their departure. They echoed the circumstances of the Scandinavians by basing their ties to the home country on its natural beauty. The song originated as a familiar poem written in 1866 by a Polish writer, Michał Bałucki, in Austria who referred to the power of poverty as the major cause of emigration.[19]

Thus "Góralu" reiterates an expression of nostalgia for the home country setting similar to that among the Scandinavians. The lyrics tell of a highlander who, when asked if he intends to leave home, replies affirmatively but with regret at rejecting the "coniferous forests, and high meadowlands and the streams so pure." After looking fondly "at the mountains, and with his sleeve [wiping away] his tears," he utters that he has to go; it is "For Bread, Sir, For Bread."[20]

There were, of course, other drawbacks for emigrants in addition to leaving with a love of their traditional setting. Letters suggest these added disadvantages, for example, the risk emigrants felt about not being successful economically. One man leaving about 1912 was generally optimistic about his chances, but suffering too was expected. A sister, aunt, and uncle in America would help him get settled. But he still harbored doubts about the trip. "I thought a long time about what that strange country would be. I wanted to try my fortune overseas and see with my own eyes this [touted] paradise of workers. In case of failure I [still] planned to return wealthy at least [from the] experience."[21]

A more tragic situation is that of the emigrant who lost touch with relatives, resulting in the sundering of family ties. The problem of leaving behind loved ones was not just a Polish one: the cutting off of communication between a male emigrant breadwinner and his wife and children was not uncommon generally because the man was either unable to obtain the expected income or simply anxious to shed an unhappy marriage. After initial contact the emigrant was not heard from again, and the spouse and progeny had to fend for themselves. The point here is that certainly for some, the pressure to succeed in America had unfortunate results.

As a Polish observer in the early 1920s pointed out: "Not everyone is successful. Many who write at first . . . after are silent, [and] do not return or send anything. Wives remain at home, need help with dollars [and] when these are broken off they are entirely anarchic."[22] Of course, some male immigrants stopped old-country family connections happily, for the trip meant freedom and escape from a bad marriage. But no researched song expresses that sentiment. Rather, a musical work known in both northern New Jersey and Detroit tells of the immigrant's need to return home after years working abroad, but describes his distress resulting from the alienation of his children that his long absence has caused.[23]

Another song composed in the 1890s is as noteworthy as "Góralu, Czy ci nie Żal" since it too was popular among all Polish immigrants. On the surface, its title, "Ameryka To Sliczny Wolny Kraj" ("America, That Beautiful Free Country"), also known as "Piosenka O Ameryce" ("Song about America"), seems to glorify the United States.[24] It is a composition, not a folk song, though with a disputed authorship. The writer was either Jozef Bernolak, a musician who came to America in 1883 and then wrote both fiction and music, or more likely Dr. Julian Czupka, a lawyer who arrived here about 1890 and later became editor of a Polish Baltimore newspaper and author of various literary works. In any event, the song is actually a satire critical of America. Czupka cites the lure of new land; but the reality is unpleasant. The United States is a nation with many inequities, such as favoring wealth and the rich over the poor.

Since the song was so universally known among Polish immigrants, it requires careful review. It opens touting the supposed advantages of America over the homeland:

> When things are bad and you want your freedom
> Leave that ugly home and come over and join us,
> Here is a blissful fate, a money-bag filled with gold
> That wonderful country; there's enough for everyone
> It's heaven on earth!

But once here, one finds injustice a rampant materialism and official corruption.

> If you steal a crust of bread, to quiet your hunger pains
> They'll lock you up for a year and throw away the key.
> But steal a golden purse [make money illegally] and fate will smile on you.
> Just post your bail and they'll let you out of jail
> Because this is America.

The opportunity and employment for workers proves either illusory or a misuse and waste of an immigrant's work qualifications:

There's money to be made and lots of work to do
You will look for it till you're blue. . . .
And if you have [college] degrees . . .
You will get a job . . . milking cows
Because this is America.[25]

It is, of course, possible to view this song as simply a lighthearted, humorous attempt by the composer to entertain his audience. Thus it may not have represented any deep-seated dissatisfaction. One cannot know for certain, but other evidence suggests that such complaints about life in America were serious.

Fortunately, one is able to verify such criticisms from a review of the rich song repertoire of musical presentations sung in informal Polish American social centers and venues, such as in cabarets, amateur theater, and vaudeville. These musical works were a genre of pieces known as *kuplety*. Two recent Polish compilers of such works stress the salience of this musical evidence. They point out, "While reflecting Polish reality in America, [*kuplets*] were really a kind of inverted mirror created by the Polish community . . . for the needs of the community itself."[26]

The two Polish researchers embarked on their project not only to locate and collect these kinds of songs but also to analyze them.[27] While it is difficult to know the popularity of particular *kuplety*, the investigators were able to arrive at significant generalizations about some themes that helped explain Polish immigrant feeling. Since almost all appeared in print before 1920, these works qualify as expressions of the immigrant generation. Of course, even the few published after that date may qualify too, for they may well have been known and performed before World War I.[28] The songs were similar to the *machiette* and skits of Eduardo Migliaccio for the Italian Americans. Some of the Polish pieces did differ, for they appeared in songbooks and printed collections without ascription to any particular composer or performer.

The topics they deal with are eclectic, more than just the conflicting feelings over the appeal of America contrasted with nostalgia for the homeland. The songs offer some insight on a lesser-known subject that has been only been lightly covered by historians, the views *between* immigrant groups. While there has been some early scholarly interest in the relationship between Poles and others around the turn of the century, on the whole the matter remains obscure. While *kuplety* on this subject exist, the examples are fragmentary. Still, they constitute some suggestive evidence of how immigrants considered other minorities.

For example, a few refer to the sensitive matter of anti-Semitism. While that feeling did exist among some Old World Polish peasants, based in part on the stereotype of the Jewish financial conspiracy, the *immigrant* suspicion of Jews was not evident in the *kuplety* in America. In fact, the Polish immigrant reference to

Two popular Polish American songbooks published during World War I. (Courtesy St. Mary's College Archives, Orchard Lake, Mich.)

those non-Christians was one of toleration and even admiration. The conclusion of the *kuplety* song collectors is that immigrant opinion toward Jews was a "cheerful human attitude devoid of anti-Semitism." These songs largely praised the Polish Jewish work ethic. "Because they worked [hard]" for their income; the lyrics of one state that their known practice of accumulating wealth "is not shameful." Polish opinion, the song says, was that such Jews achieving entrepreneurial success were "honest and good."[29]

The attitude toward African Americans was more mixed but still in a few *kuplety* largely an accepting one, on the whole "amused tolerance." The initial sight of black women did cause consternation, probably because of their dark skin, but they still were viewed generally as having positive qualities. For example, songs state that blacks even might make superior wives to Anglo-American whites because they did not indulge in using cosmetics.[30]

Again, these musical examples of Polish immigrant relations with other minority groups are fragmentary and not abundant in the *kuplety* collection; rather, the dominant theme of these songs is disillusionment over the expected but dashed promise of America, expressed chiefly from a working-class point of view, a criticism related to the Górale. It seems to stem from the immigrants' rural origins as they compared the simple, natural beauty of their Old World home to the unpleasant filth, smoke, and modern technology of the American industrial city in which they lived. Also expressed in song was dissatisfaction over the lack of steady work, resulting in poverty, homelessness, and hunger; a corresponding generalized hostility toward those of great wealth; and a bitterness over the venality and corruption of local officials who administer the law. All these criticisms resulted in an occasional appeal in the songs to immigrants to abandon their older, typical code of humility toward power. The aim of the lyrics seems to be to raise workers' consciousness in America and unify their resistance to injustice.[31]

A related but often expressed charge in these cabaret works is the insidious influence (told by men) of the new American environment on the traditional place of women. The threat had appeared subtly among the Italians in that group's immigrant language; the Polish immigrant *kuplets* refer to the actual changes that were taking place in their women's role, particularly an increase in their status and independence.[32]

A few other songs hint at other subjects. Some dwell optimistically on expectations of the benefits of American life. A closer look at the *kuplety* themselves reconfirms not only the theme of great expectations immigrants had for America but also great disillusionment over that supposed reality. Not only was the previously described "Song of America" by Czupka popular in the cabarets but also another work in print around 1909 reiterates the expectation that America was a "paradise" with "lots of coin"; yet one *kuplet* on "Chicago" criticizes the drive for riches as demoralizing, for those who gain wealth are "unafraid of" and "scorn the law," while ordinary citizens who do more-honest work "decay in prison."[33] This song is significant also in its representativeness. Since Chicago was the leading industrial city in the post–Civil War era of mass immigration as well as the major center of Poles in America, all its promise and problems resulting from its meteoric growth conditioned the content of that group's songs in particular.

That Chicago Polish repertoire, then, is instructive, for it offers a complex of immigrant opinion, mainly dissatisfaction. "Chicago's Krakowiak" (a Polish dance form emanating from Galicia) condemns the law's arbitrary treatment of immigrants. Be careful, it says, for one will find deception in the smoky Chicago stockyards—if one gets into a quarrel with a neighbor, a policeman will put you in a patrol car, you will go to jail, and you will "not see the world for a long time."[34] A more bitter piece, ironically titled "No Place Is Better than Chicago," says: "If you go out into the street from your miserable cell, then my brother [I am not lying], the policeman will shoot you straight in your head," with the refrain, "O let's dance, the policeman is always triumphant." Even when trying to romance a woman on the street by telling her she is lovely, "you can surely expect an arrest and immediately you will be in court."[35] Politicians are no better than the police, for they punish simple people and, as city council members, "have glue on their palms."

An exceptional song is "Joe from Noble Street." "Joe" admits that he must work very hard, and his difficulty with English is frustrating, but he is able to save money. He even drinks in a saloon with a policeman and overall "likes his fun on Sunday when his pocket is full of money."[36] A similar but non-*kuplety* work also expresses the pleasure of enjoying the higher American standard, even as a lowly immigrant, better than that in the old country.

Still, that achievement too had pitfalls. While one long ballad, "Jechał Jeden Polak" ("A Pole Was Journeying"), traces one man's trip to America and finding a job, the narrator concludes, "American life was fine" but only "when there are jobs for all," and even if one can have beer and cigars, "life can be most lonely."[37]

A notable exception to the dominant pessimism about life in the United States are a few songs about women, that is, songs that welcomed the freedom and independence for those who were single. The model of this genre is a cabaret song simply titled "Kuplet," in which a young woman characterizes her transition to America and her emancipation in the change of her name, from Kaszka to Katie. In Poland, Kaszka used "to tend geese, hungry, barefooted, and dirty all over." But in America, after being employed at several jobs where she earned money, Katie ultimately attains the status of "lady" as a saleswoman in a store. Not only did American employment help Katie's social mobility, but its laws were also an ally and protector. While men's songs criticize the police and the courts for mistreatment and corruption, the Katies welcome them as a defense against spousal abuse and violence, even forcing suitors into marriage when called for and assuring wives and divorcees of sufficient financial support.[38]

That new female assertiveness also showed up at the workplace, if only on occasion. Since there is only one musical example of this, it is still not possible to know how widespread workforce assimilation was for females. But it certainly demonstrates a new spiritedness among immigrant working women. This *kuplet,* "Na Przyzbie" ("At the Home Conversation Bench"), which appeared in 1916, tells of a strike by women in a cigarette factory who then attack their boss after he has mistreated them and referred to them as "cattle."[39]

This song introduces another genre of musical work among Poles, immigrant workers' songs. In essence, the question arises, if immigrant songs are mirrors of how newcomers felt, can they also relate how Poles and eastern Europeans in general thought of their jobs? Did they consider themselves as naïve, passive employees, as early labor historians have concluded, or, as more-recent historiography has suggested, as militant resistors and protestors against employers' abuse and exploitation?

It is certain that most Poles, Slavs, and other non-Jews from the region came as unskilled manual laborers. Obvious as well was the arduous nature of their employment. Placing themselves in jobs in heavy industries like steel, coal, meat-packing, and textiles meant encountering workplace conditions that offered little security or union protection because of strong employer control and little interest by organized labor in mobilizing the industrial proletariat. As a result the jobs themselves were exploitative and incredibly difficult, with long hours, low pay, and a high incidence of accidental injury and death. That immigrant workers en-dured the horrendous conditions was due, according to recent analyses, to their dogged peasant stoicism.[40]

The preponderance of songs, however, indicates that while they did earn and save under such difficult conditions, immigrants reached their goal of added in-come at a considerable psychic price. Particularly noteworthy is a desperate yearn-ing to return to Europe as soon as possible as well as self-criticism of their desper-ate need for money, which often resulted in excessive materialism.

Before reviewing particular musical examples, the body of songs in the Hun-garian immigrant experience can be introduced here as well. Joining that group's repertoire at this point with the Poles is justified because the two groups' im-migrant labor history and concerns about earnings were generally similar. The Hungarians' differed minimally in that their immigrant numbers were smaller, about a 500,000 in the two decades after the mid-1890s; they were socially more homogeneous, with a larger percentage coming as single males or without fami-lies; and their percentage of unskilled industrial workers was greater than that of the Poles, who had a higher proportion in the middle class.[41] Still, on the major points Poles and Hungarians were alike. They left Europe for similar reasons, mainly due to economic problems, and thus found employment in heavy indus-try, coal, steel, and the like with common objectives of earning enough to return home and live there at a more secure and higher socioeconomic level than when they left. An important subtle difference expressed in Hungarian American song (and hence more on the minds of that group) is a more universal complaint over the arduousness of their work environment.

Fortunately for researchers, the Hungarian immigrant community created a considerable written literature that concentrated heavily on the unfortunate lot of their working class. The shock of laboring in American industry caused "an an-guish of the immigrants," and hence the writings, especially of poets like György Kemény and György Szécskay, tell of the "strong feeling of alienation . . . loneli-ness, [and] helplessness, caught up in the [ruthlessness] of an acquisitive society." Those majority values made many feel like outcasts and promoted "a yearning for community comradeship" that their typical boardinghouse arrangement, the *bur-doshaz,* and mutual-aid societies only partially ameliorated.[42] The general prob-lems of immigrants were expressed in a long, bitter poem published in 1911 in Budapest by a Hungarian writer in America. Entitled simply "America" and written in the immigrant vernacular, it tells of the arrival's uncertainty of being rejected for medical reasons; the exploitation of rapacious agents, fellow country-men, and employers; the prospect of unemployment and vagrancy; and the pres-sure on immigrants to fabricate their success in correspondence home, thus causing more misery for later arrivals.[43]

More specifically in song is the feeling of an intense longing among both Poles and Hungarians for home, where the pursuit of wealth was much less frenetic. Also causing discomfort in America was these groups' general marginalization by the Anglo-American majority. Hungarian songs in America actually raised a di-lemma for the immigrants. In "Why Did I Come?" the speaker condemns the pres-sures of working for that "cursed gold," while others express unhappiness with some Old World conditions too. The result is feeling like "eternal wanderers."[44]

A Polish American counterpart concerning return is another rejection of American materialism, as well as the lack of spirituality among the majority, as told in another worker's song. "W Żelaznej Fabryce" ("In a Steel Mill") was a widely known musical piece sung by Polish workers in Chicago factories and col-lected by Alan Lomax in the 1930s. Here the speaker finds work, but despite being abused by the American foreman, he will stay on the job apparently until he earns enough money. Then, because in part "in America there is nothing but unbeliev-ers," he concludes, "if God grants him good health, I'll return to the homeland."[45]

The desire of Hungarians to go back was again similar to the Poles and other new immigrant groups, but it was likely more powerful and originated in the rather distinctive ambience of the group, the industrial employment itself, espe-cially the mines.[46]

Two songs brought back to the homeland suggest that yearning for return. One that appeared in 1893 refers specifically to the unrealistic hopes of Hungarians. Entitled "Amerika Aranybányák Hazája" ("America, the Land of Gold Mines"), it advises listeners to reject the hyperbole that the new land has gold mines and pro-vides roast duck for all; it suggests that the speaker's dashed expectations will cause him to return home the following summer.[47] Another, from an informant who emigrated in 1910, urges the ship captain to sail carefully back to Hungary, where, with a "sad homesick heart about to break," the narrator knows "his wife and chil-dren are waiting."[48]

Of course, as with the Poles and others, not all the songs express such misery; one humorous work, in fact, welcomes the increased income. It expresses thanks to the local saloonkeeper for allowing the worker to elevate a mineworker's status to "gentleman." This is achieved by the tavern owner giving him credit for his liquor tab; greater alcoholic consumption was apparently a sign of a wealthier patron![49] All of these selections, however, even those that tell of accomplishment, still depict the everyday difficulty of adjusting to a new society.

The New World optimism over social mobility was still counterbalanced by the appeal of the homeland, which overall still seemed attractive. A distinctive source of that idolization of origins among Hungarians in a number of songs is the especially intense comparison made between their American and European living and working settings. The songs that tell of the unpleasant contrast between the rural life they left and the work environment they found in America are especially numerous and graphic. A large segment of the Hungarian immigrant population lived in the depressing sections of coal-mining country in Pennsylvania, Ohio, and Illinois, with the ubiquitous culm (waste) coal piles and coal dust that exuded a kind of gray pallor throughout the environment. Also, the physical task of mine-working itself, especially laboring in the shafts underground, meant doing tasks in constant blackness. The songs of the Hungarians reflect that grim atmosphere, a daily setting that was both dangerous and virtually devoid of color. Workers had little opportunity to view blue skies and sunshine or to smell the sweet odor of their old-country acacia trees.[50]

The musical examples of this depressing situation are numerous. One work composed in 1918 after a cave-in in the area of McKeesport, Pennsylvania, was entitled "Temet A Bánya" ("The Mine Is Burying"); another, says the speaker, would stay in the United States to do the hated task of "hew[ing] coal in the mine," which was better than being a "servant to a Jew at home." The lament over darkness underground was evident too among the Poles, though it appears less intense than among the Hungarians. A 1910 Polish song, for example, refers to the awful fear of placing the bodies of deceased immigrant workers "in a dark tomb."[51]

To be sure, included in all this Hungarian and eastern European melancholy in song are a few musical examples that either take satisfaction in the earning of income or otherwise reject complaining and oppose abuse. Polish American working women, for example, were particularly enthused about fighting injustice, and the aforementioned "Song of America" called on the group to organize collectively.

These musical examples are consonant with the now accepted view that eastern Europeans were not simply naïve, passive operatives vis-à-vis their employers. Incidents of protesting "Hunkies," as they were called pejoratively, in fact were common in the American industrial heartland in the 1890s and 1900s, in Milwaukee, Chicago, Pennsylvania, New York, and the Northeast textile mills, even without much support from the AFL or other organized labor.[52]

Admittedly, however, despite the pervasive dissatisfaction they expressed about their working conditions, eastern Europeans certainly did not go to the kind of radical extreme in song that Jews and Finns did in openly attacking the capitalist system. A particularly popular musical work suggests that "Hunkies" did support organized protest. That song, though, "Me, Johnny Mitchell Man," is a strange anomaly for several reasons. It came out of a particular dispute, the epic anthracite labor strike in Pennsylvania in 1902; it was composed by a non–eastern European outsider who wrote the words in a faulty immigrant dialect that makes it seem patronizing; and it idolizes the Anglo-American union leader, who typically was unacquainted with his immigrant supporters.[53]

The ballad was written by Con Carbon of Wilkes-Barre, who composed it to dispel the innate suspicion that the older Anglo-Americans had of the newer eastern European mineworkers. The song was sung widely throughout the region at labor rallies during the five-month-long work stoppage and, according to the leading folksong collector in the region, was an apparent success in bonding the two communities. It attacks the leading coalmine operators for refusing to raise wages and concludes, "Un shtrike kin come, like a son of a gun / Me, Johnny Mitchell Man." In short, while not a folksong that emanated from eastern European workers, it assuredly expresses their devotion to their Anglo-American union leader and his cause.[54] Thus in this case and even in general, Hungarian American workers often supported unions and sought to improve their workplace conditions. Overall, their songs certainly condemned their unhappy employment, but few seemed to want to abolish the established economic system.[55]

A recent recording of Hungarian folksongs, appropriately entitled "Kivándorlás/Emigration" and based on turn-of-the-twentieth-century folklore sources, offers works that touches on almost all of the emotional conflicts felt by these eastern European peasants-turned-American-industrial-workers. The most dramatic piece, "In Fiume," a common emigrant port on the Adriatic for many Austro-Hungarians, like so many other songs, repeats the mixed feelings of hope and fear. It expresses a man's lament over leaving his sweetheart and includes blessing his homeland as the ship departs and his fears of shipwreck, drowning, and being eaten by "big fish" on the high seas. Yet included too is his reassertion, upon arrival in America, of why he left home, the possible end of his Hungarian identity, and finally his uncertain hope that his stay in this country "will not hurt."

Another ballad in the collection tells of the awful life of a miner who is out on strike, "embittered . . . [and] does not even feel like singing," because of the abuse of his mine boss. While "America is a gold mine . . . The hell wanted it! . . . be cursed!"

A third song, once again typical of many other groups, expands on the baleful effects of living, as its title states, "In an Alien Land." The narrator is "so sick," in this strange country, neighbors tell him he may even die. "In [this] alien country," the people are strange, and "I walk the streets and I don't know anybody."

> I would talk to them but they do not understand me.
> Because of this, my heart is very bitter.

He concludes realizing he is torn by dissatisfaction with life in both rich America and "beautiful" Hungary. On the one hand, he hopes in the end to return to his ancestral home, which he has not seen "for a long time."

> If I ever see it again,
> I will stay in it,
> I never again want
> the treasures of America.

On the other hand,

> It is not good at home, either.
> Taxes are high, tax collectors,
> Notaries, sheriffs, there are many of.

But in the end,

> I will take my cane
> And cross the waves;
> I will go back.[56]

Clearly, then, Polish and Hungarian immigrant songs also fit the pattern of other groups, expressing that mental dilemma of all arrivals. Some works herald the attractions of America, its freedom, social democracy, and economic opportunity. But these musical statements also include serious reservations about those advantages. Living in the States also meant unpleasant excesses, such as the loss of traditional codes of conduct and an overemphasis on obtaining income. In addition, the works suggest the more sophisticated notion that the touted attractions were more theoretical than real and often not evident in everyday life.

But the greatest concern is one stated by others: the agony over leaving home and family. Eastern Europeans in song showed their particular dissatisfaction. With an immigrant society consisting of largely ex-peasant, unskilled workers living in grimy American industrial cities, these peoples in their more intimate songs continued to wonder why they had left, particularly as time passed after their arrival. The simple agrarian life and home that they left behind (whether it was true or not) seemed more and more attractive, and they continued to question their decision to emigrate.

The outbreak of World War I seemed to accentuate that psychic ambivalence. In addition to the personal ambivalence over leaving relatives in Poland, the conflict itself caused more guilt over leaving the homeland in its time of national need.

The more generalized obligation of many immigrants to fulfill their ethnic and national obligations must have weighed on their conscience.

This rise in group and national consciousness had been taking place among ordinary immigrants in Polonia in the early years of the century.[57] The situation is treated in a particular Polish *kuplet* from 1915, "Polak I Amerykanin" ("The Pole and the American"), in a conversation between an immigrant and non–group member. The Pole expresses his obligation to go back home, fight to free his homeland, and live there. To the American's question of why he was so "sad [and] pale" when he already admitted that he left home and made money here, the immigrant replies, "I prefer to bear poverty and hunger [in Poland] to living in a foreign palace," for "there I have my mother, there I have land," and "Here I have nothing, nothing, completely nothing."[58] Many, of course, did not return, but this song, like so many others, does question the attractions of America.[59]

7

The Chinese

Struggle on "Gold Mountain"

As one might readily imagine, the effect of the dominant Anglo-American society on the nonwhite immigrants from Asia and Latin America was clearly more devastating psychically than that on newly arriving Europeans. The basis of the difference was, of course, the racial one, a much greater hostility by whites toward others. That such prejudice and discrimination caused considerable pain and anguish among Chinese and Mexican immigrants hardly needs much debate. While the hope and dream of achieving financial success in the United States, or "Gold Mountain," as the Chinese referred to it, among Asian arrivals may have been undiminished down to recent times, certainly the mental and emotional distress in trying to earn income was well articulated in the songs and lyrics that both Chinese and Mexican immigrants sang.

Likely influenced by postmodern thinking, some Chinese American historians have urged their colleagues to add a new perspective and expand the previous approaches of research. That was to go beyond traditional generalizations concerning topics such as macroeconomics, politics, and legislation to a more innovative treatment and study of the personal feelings of their predecessors, especially among the lower classes.[1]

Actually, a few writers have already taken up that kind of study "from the ground up." Particularly significant in covering the more intimate sentiments of people's lives have been Asian Americanists such as Marlon Hom, ethnomusicologist Su de San Zheng, Him Mark Lai and his team of oral interviewers, and historian Madeline Y. Hsu.[2] The first three in particular compliment the expressive culture of ordinary Chinese immigrants, particularly their musical and literary activities and compositions, to understand their mentality and personal concerns about coming to and settling in America. As communication, that type of evidence was reflected in particular in the effect of Anglo-American discrimination on arrivals from the Celestial Kingdom in the years before and after the Exclusion Acts of the late nineteenth and early twentieth centuries.

The purpose here is not simply to identify the variety of personal expressions in song but to indicate that the list of examples is quite extensive. Hom in particular has already provided a comprehensive survey of the various kinds of songs that made up the immigrant repertoire. On the surface, they appear to be generally similar in topic to all the other groups covered, suggesting mainly the uncomfortable anxiety over the emigrant experience. They include the usual ambivalence over leaving, the typical concerns about the need to earn income, and the intention of returning after acquiring some wealth. The list also tells of the problem already found in almost all the other cases attendant to emigrating, such as the pain of family separation expressed by both the emigrants and those left behind, the potential dangers of the passage, and the nostalgia, loneliness, and suffering from Anglo-American mistreatment. But the repertoire of this group too, as with the others, necessitates closer attention because their particular situation, again like the others, did differ. Chinese immigrant songs also reveal a distinctiveness in three ways on these subjects in comparison to other groups.

One is the special importance of the musical tradition itself in those areas from which most of these Asian emigrants came through the 1920s. Perhaps more than that of any European group, the Chinese folk and popular songs of the emigrant-producing region in particular conveyed for centuries the most heartfelt feelings about life. That tradition came in two musical forms: one was the *muk-yu* (wooden fish) song, and the other, the Cantonese opera. Both were types of oral expression brought over to America.

A second distinctive feature of these songs concerns the musical message regarding the different migratory experiences of these Asians vis-à-vis the Europeans. Coming from a much greater distance, both spatially and culturally; encountering more virulent social and political discrimination in America, with greater obstacles in bringing over wives, lovers, and families; and barred from becoming citizens, the male Chinese arrivals soon suffered from intense feelings of inadequacy, loneliness, and unhappiness. Third, the two characteristic features of this exodus of greater distance and discrimination created in the lives of these arrivals a musical and literary genre not just of melancholy and pain but also of memories and sentiments of anger, bitterness, and protest against authorities.

To be sure, again as elsewhere, the immigrant songs are not universal expressions of injury. Following the historical and sociological research of Madeline Hsu and Paul Siu among the Chinese, a few works (as I will suggest below) are positive about the Chinese prospects and even excited about the potential chances for material success. But overwhelmingly the songs consist of statements of dissatisfaction in America, directed at not only their Caucasian hosts but also on occasion at representatives of their own government for its failure to adequately protect its people. Overall then, Chinese American song does offer evidence of that "immigrant voice" that the newer historians, Wong and Chan, have asked for.

As usual with other groups, examining the context of their historical experience is necessary to fully understand the importance and meaning of their songs. Above all it is important to recognize the highly localized origins of Chinese immigrants to America up to and after passage of the Exclusionary Acts (also known as "Exclusion") in 1882. The emigrants came from a surprisingly small, concentrated region in southern China around the port of Canton in Guangdong Province. That city was the logical departure point for emigrants to the east since it was historically the first one open to foreign shipping.

The major geographical source of Chinese emigrants was the Pearl River delta area that includes the Sze Yap districts, particularly Taishan (Toisan).[3] That region provided almost three-quarters of all the immigrant laborers going to America up to the 1880s and even to about 1930.[4] This was probably due to that section of China having been the locus of maximum Western influence and penetration.

Still other factors motivated people to leave as well. These were the rather adverse living conditions of the mid-1800s caused by such natural disasters as floods, drought, and famine along with the political instability from local wars. All these circumstances forced almost 2,500,000 people from the area to go abroad to other areas of Asia and the Pacific, including South America, during the last half of the nineteenth century. The discovery of gold in California in 1848 and the need for labor for economic development directed part of the outgoing stream toward the United States. Just over 250,000 went there in the period before about 1890. That was the reason departing Chinese referred to San Francisco, the major port of entry and hence the United States in general, as *Gam Saan* (Gold Mountain).[5] The emigrating wave at that time consisted of mainly peasants but included some merchants too.

An indication of the great value of song as communication among these arrivals is that the Guangdong area was also the region that traditionally cultivated the *muk-yu* folksong tradition. These musical offerings were vernacular, rhymed narratives that originated in the early seventeenth century. They were at first conveyed orally but later began to appear in print in the early nineteenth century. Their content was similar to other folksongs and included texts from history, folk tales, religion, and personal experience. They were either sung unaccompanied or recited by the lower classes at both public and private ceremonies. They were especially common at community or village gatherings, which typically formed at the end of the workday. The songs varied in length, melody, and even language while conveying the same text. Even among a minority group of Hakka-speaking peasants who inhabited Guangdong Province, some of whom also became emigrants, it was common for men and women to sing to each other as they worked in the fields.[6] In any event, songs were without question a popular folk tradition for the people of the region around 1800 and later.[7]

It is important to note that over the entire century and a half of Chinese emigration before and after Exclusion, *muk-yu* songs not only came to America but also returned and crisscrossed the Pacific. So not only did emigrants actually bring those songs from Asia, but some were also composed or altered here and then taken back to China. All this took place despite the major cultural upheavals there of recent times. The songs have continued to be performed among the overseas Chinese and have provided a means of social contact, mutual aid, and popular interaction.[8]

While certainly different in form as staged musical drama, with arias instead of songs, Cantonese opera was somewhat similar to the *muk-yu* tradition. Originating as early as the 1400s, it also long predated emigration and over the centuries became a popular form of entertainment. More specifically, it also became a means of uplifting and educating the illiterate peasants. The opera plots treated themes that were similar to the *muk-yu* songs, with myths, historical narratives, and involved stories of family and conjugal relations. Cantonese opera was, of course, a more formal kind of presentation than *muk-yu* and further differed by combining both song and spoken dialogue. But overall, it too was a means of reinforcing traditional moral standards.[9] Again, the important consideration for these two musical traditions is that both were forms of social communication representative of immigrant sentiment that were carried across the Pacific.

Music was as much a part of Chinese immigrant life in America as it was for all the other groups. While musicians themselves held a low status, instrumental performances in the American settlements were common as early as the formative days of the group colonies. Noting the initial warm acceptance of these Asians in white society during those pioneer days in California, one historian has dated the first performance of a Chinese band to an 1852 parade, presumably in San Francisco for all the inhabitants. The musicians comprised a six-piece ensemble playing and joining the white inhabitants to help celebrate Washington's Birthday. This early participation in Anglo-American civic observances was apparently exceptional later, after anti-Chinese discrimination intensified. While immigrant playing and singing of music was popular broadly, these activities over time became confined to internal group settings, likely as a result of the isolation and segregation of Asians by the majority community. In any event, singing was still common in the most informal Chinese American quarters, rooming houses, and apartments as well as outdoors at banquets, funerals, and festivals during the last half of the nineteenth century.[10]

As for the *muk-yu* songs themselves, Marlon Hom has translated and commented on a comprehensive list of "Gold Mountain" works from original Chinese sources that were published from about 1910 to 1929. On the surface, they again appear very much like the works noted in other group traditions. The lyrics, for example, weigh the various pros and cons of emigration, such as the attraction of earning money in America over other, closer opportunities in Hong Kong or the region and the loss of contact with family members, rationalizing that the absence would be temporary.[11] But while the subjects may appear to be similar to say the Irish, Italian, and even Jewish cases, there are subtle but notable differences.

The most obvious technical distinction in the Chinese immigrant repertoire, according to Hom, is the unusual way that the hopes and fears of women left behind are expressed by the *male* arrivals in America. Emigrant men would perform in gender reverse as wives or other females lamenting the loss of family members in works sung abroad. Overseas, males vocalized those female roles not only because few women had left home but also because cultural convention dictated that men could not speak openly about spousal affection. Thus they could do so only in disguise. This genre of song is important since by openly expressing themselves as women in song, men used the latter "as a vehicle of their own feelings."[12]

Overall, more specific subjects covered by the immigrant songs in Hom's list are the standard ones of hoping to gain income abroad to buy land at home, the debate over whether one should marry a prospective male emigrant, and the difficulties of family separation. The particular concern among the Chinese was the inordinate length of time that husbands as sojourners were expected to be away. A work exemplifying these worries is one where the "wife" sings:

> Poverty leads to desperation:
> My husband took off to Gold Mountain
> You left home for Gold Mountain.
> Five years have since passed; I haven't seen him come home.
> Many times I write and ask geese to deliver my messages to him.

She no longer cares for the added money.

> How can I get you back to cheer me up?
> Just come home; rich or poor, I simply don't care any more.[13]

Another Hakka folksong, "A Young Bride Calls across the Hills," concludes:

> Also I beg you that your heart won't change
> That you keep your heart and mind in taking care of your family.
> Each month or half a month send a letter home
> In two or three years my wish is to welcome you home.[14]

From another Toishan *muk-yu* collection is a work known as "Xiu Hua Ge" ("The Embroidery Song"). It is another song that tells about a wife who thinks of her absent spouse while she sews.

> You said you went to Gold Mountain because of poverty at home.
> You promised to return in just a few years.
> But now I am left all by myself, solely accompanied by loneliness.[15]

Again, these songs are similar to the unhappiness of Europeans about the straining of family ties, but the conditions of departure and absence put a sharper edge on the disruption among the Chinese.

Besides the problem of separation, transportation to America was also exceptionally difficult for emigrants in particular. Unlike those coming from Europe, the greater length of the passage created more concern about personal security and even survival in the minds of the Asians.

To about 1870, crossing the Pacific was almost entirely by sail and normally would take as much as three months or more to arrive in San Francisco, certainly longer than an Atlantic passage. Steamships began to replace sail in the 1860s until the Exclusion Act of 1882.[16] The Burlingame Amity Treaty of 1868 between the United States and the Celestial Kingdom encouraged Chinese labor immigration so the number doubled from the 1860s to the 1870s to over 120,000; but it halved again as a result of legislative restrictions in the 1880s.

Economic growth and the demand for labor in the American West was the magnet for these arrivals. The initial attraction was the search for gold and employment in silver mines in the 1850s and 1860s; later, it was the lure of jobs in railroad construction, various urban needs, domestic service, commercial agricultural, the fishing industry, and light manufacturing.

Unfortunately, personal accounts of the early decades around midcentury are rare, but some inkling of the immigrants' inner turmoil has appeared in song. Su de San Zheng lists two particularly sensitive ballads of self-conscious expression that were a part of the repertoire of the folksinger known as "Uncle Ng." He had learned his songs about immigration from a schoolteacher in the Toisan district in the 1920s. Fortunately, some can be dated from context. One offers a brief account of the journey done under sail, hence from the era prior to the 1870s. Its value is not only in offering a glimpse of the immigrant's concern about ocean travel but also a description of one route followed.

In the first musical example, the initial leg of the journey for one emigrant is his trip to Hong Kong. He records it as actually pleasant, for he is accompanied by "fellow villagers" and "family members" who had joined him, possibly to see him off. The next leg is on board his ship, which goes along the coast of Fujian Province northeast from Canton toward Japan. On that journey, certain climatic elements make the voyage much more problematical. As the narrator puts it, winds whipped up "the high waves [that] hit the boat's front. I couldn't sleep, I was really worried." After arriving in Japan and proceeding across the Pacific, the ship has to traverse other obstacles for "many miles."[17]

The other song also dates from the years of sail, the mid-1800s, as the narrator leaves to work the American gold mines. Since it covers almost all the experiences from departure through transportation, employment, mistreatment, and the narrator's concluding wish to return home, it is worth an extended review. Its title is appropriately "Jinshan Lun" ("Discourse on the Gold Mountain"). Overall, while he too, like the singer in the previous work, is comforted by being accompanied on his journey by village compatriots both across the sea and in the gold fields, he remains particularly fearful of and vulnerable to "bandits" and "foreign devils," apparently rapacious whites.[18] Such concern about discrimination here was more pervasive among Chinese than in the case of Europeans.

This musical tale unfortunately opens with no reference as to why the emigrant decides to leave. He does not indicate his going is a result of chain migration, that is, communication from relatives or previously emigrating villagers who informed him about opportunity in America. But whatever his source of information, he seeks to gain a better income overseas. He proceeds to borrow money for the trip, which he expects to repay soon after his arrival. Prior to leaving his village, he visits his Buddhist temple to ask for divine help. Still insecure, he also consults fortunetellers, who inform him that he will be successful. Despite these preparations and assurances, an indication of the inner turmoil and ambivalence about his plan is the translated word he uses for his departure. He confesses that he has "abandoned" his clan, ancestors, wife, and parents who did not want him to leave.[19]

The generally cool reaction of townspeople to his leaving may have had some additional influence on his state of mind. Their attitude is mixed: some are jealous, others more hostile. In any event, clan members urge him to write back if he were successful. He promises his friends and loved ones that he will be away no longer than a year before returning with several hundred dollars.

While being somewhat comforted by other villagers with him on his trip, he still is fearful about being robbed or exploited, encountering rough weather, and inadequate food, all of which do make the experience a "hardship." He is much relieved to finally arrive at the American port, but when he goes off to work, he finds the quarters at the mining site primitive, uncomfortable, and beset with hostile animals, "foreign devils [that is, Anglo-Americans]," and Indians. Thereafter, his greatest concerns in his search for the precious metal is both his lack of success in finding it as well as repeatedly encountering "ugly devils" who squat on his land and "would loot when they want to loot" and "beat and curse [him] without any mercy."[20] His remedy is to escape by moving south, but that solution turns out to be fruitless. He knows that some Chinese are lucky and return home with money, but he also knows that these cases are rare. And he is also aware of others who are unsuccessful. They become dissolute either by gambling, drinking, or visiting brothels, and if any of them decided to return home, they would simply sell their stake and go back empty handed.

The narrator continues to seek his find by borrowing to buy more land. But again he encounters adverse living conditions, bandits, savages, and "the devils" who continue to humiliate . . . and bully me." Now heavily in debt, he cannot sleep with the thought of not being able to pay back his loans. He ends his woeful tale by ascribing his suffering to an inherent weakness, "I didn't cultivate my virtue in my previous life." If he would be able to endure all his difficulties, he could return to China "to praise prosperity."[21]

Such detail about the immigrant experience when once settled in America is unfortunately rare in song, even in the collection upon which Hom drew for his valuable compilation. Of the approximately sixteen hundred original works he found, Hom translated just over two hundred that "best illustrate the lives of the early Chinese Americans and [San Francisco] Chinatown."[22] He breaks down his list into eleven categories. The most valuable are the lesser-known songs about the taboo themes of men's sexual appetite, marriage, and prostitution, a subject one might expect from an immigrant community that had few women and was throughout so heavily male. Overall once again, the dominant theme of Hom's collection is one of disillusionment, alienation, and misery. But as important as they are, the songs are difficult to identify as distinctive of the group. They are uniformly brief and largely hard to place in any specific time period during the era prior to the 1920s.

It is not that these closely personal musical reflections among Chinese immigrants did not exist particularly about their working in the new land. Imaginative written evidence on the subject, like the literature of writers on other groups, is extant in the case of these Asians. The dean of Chinese American historians, Him Mark Lai, has suggested that such literary evidence may offer an insight into the feelings of the community as a whole; "most of the Chinese in America did not express themselves in belles-lettres, nonetheless, there were always a few inclined toward creative literature."[23]

Lai cites, as one example, a well-known poet, Wen Yiduo (Wen I-to), whose literary philosophy about writing was to identify closely with the lower classes. Influenced in the early 1900s by a general rise in Chinese nationalism, Wen developed an even stronger national loyalty based on his outrage at the American denigration and abuse of ordinary Chinese immigrants. Using an innovative technique of employing the vernacular, he attempted to give voice to the feelings of these lowly workers in one of his best-known works, "Xiyi Ge" ("Song of the Washerman"), or "The Laundry Song." It was written during or as a result of his visit as a student in America between 1923 and 1925. The work transforms the low esteem that Americans held for the typical Chinese workman into a process that ironically ennobles him. Wen I-to does this by reminding the Anglo-American majority of the deeper meaning of the menial task it is asking him to perform, not just to clean and make clothes presentable but also symbolically to wash away the sins of his patrons, hence affecting the moral purification of his hosts and those of all Asian Americans.

In the song the laundryman first responds to the low status ascribed to him by reminding his Caucasian patrons that their own Christian tradition, in fact, honors manual labor:

> You say the laundry business is too base.
> Only Chinamen are willing to stoop so low?
> It was your preacher who once told me:
> Christ's father used to be a carpenter.
> Do you believe it? Don't you believe it?

Wen concludes by depicting this allegedly base, hard-working Chinese immigrant as morally superior to Americans, for by working hard he is able to clean and purify what they have dirtied.

> Year in year out a drop of homesick tears
> Midnight, in the depth of night, a laundry lamp . . .
> Menial or not, you need not bother,
> Just see what is not clean, what is not smooth,
> And ask the Chinaman, ask the Chinaman.

And the refrain:

I can wash handkerchiefs wet with sad tears,
I can wash shirts soiled in sinful crimes.
The grease of greed, the dirt of desire . . .
And all the filthy things in your house,
Give them to me—I'll wash them, give them to me.[24]

That the song was familiar to Chinese Americans, at least those in the laundry business, is suggested by the writer Maxine Hong Kingston. One of her semi-
documentary accounts of the life of a New York washerman has him singing the
piece to alleviate his struggle for existence, probably in the 1930s.[25]

Even though the historian Madeline Y. Hsu stresses the doggedly held immigrant belief over the years in viewing America as *Gam Saan,* she still admits that
maintaining family integrity was hard. Migrant separations "did require emotional
and practical adaptation and sacrifices. Loneliness, alienation, uncertainty, and
self-denial were but a few of the costs."[26] And she refers to the sociological research
of Paul Siu on the feelings of the laundrymen whose hopes of making money were
tempered seriously by the necessity of unremitting toil in America. As he puts
it, "Some laundrymen are so dissatisfied with their mode of life that they try
to discourage the coming of their relatives." As one of Siu's respondents reported:
"No, I don't like it here. In China . . . I was dreaming, too, about coming over.
Now I am here. What I see in this country is just like this: working day and night."[27]

Another similar song, in this case firmly in the *muk-yu* folk tradition, also
merits attention since it too deals with the problematic work situation among the
Chinese. It recounts the fears of emigrants from the time they left home to their
lives as miners in America. This song probably appeared after the 1882 Exclusion
Act, which barred working-class Chinese immigrants, since it refers to the kind of
official American inspections that took place after 1880. It is included in a recent
Chinese publication with other collected materials that condemns America's legal
discrimination of these Asians.

*A Collection of Literature against the United States Treaty Excluding Chinese
Labor* lists the same concerns raised by emigrants in the two previous ballads
offered by Zheng, particularly the difficulties aboard ship. Added in this account
is the mistreatment of American immigration officials in their examination of
arrivals. Further, it expresses the consequent feeling of indignity and shame as
well as a criticism of the Chinese imperial government for not adequately protecting its citizens. Finally, it shows the tension that existed between the immigrant
and native American miners.[28]

The narrator begins by saying that he had expected that earning money in
America would be easy, "For that I left my home village." But the rough seas and
the lack of adequate food cause both physical and mental discomfort.

From the time I got on the boat, I could not look at food,
The waves were huge and continuously crashing,
That was so frightening, I had to tolerate that for several tens of days,
So half dead and half alive, I could hardly crack my [eyes] open
My belly was hollow; my head dizzy because I could not eat; I was half
    starved
I could hear muffled words but I buried my head
Afraid that I would not survive to set foot on land again,
The fearsome harsh inspection terrified me
I was . . . asked my name and after having documents checked,
I was allowed to proceed
I felt humiliated by this.

When he finally lands, the inspection process adds to his discomfort.

Those with disabilities or contagious illnesses
were sent for further inspection.

He is ashamed of his country and ruler.

We have a so-called [Chinese] Emperor and whatever happens he is
    willing to
accept being insulted
Going on like this is causing his decline and decay.

He concludes with the tensions workers had toward Americans and supplies a
proffered remedy in action:

The Chinese workers have endured so much but have survived
They have come so far [at] such great risks
Suffered so much that our hair is falling out
And nonetheless not [having] money
How can it be that despite all this we are so poor?
We have [cut out] our hearts and guts seeking money
Beautiful gold and silver is all stained with blood and sweat
If you look closely you can see fresh wounds because we have competed
    with
American workers and aroused their heartless jealousy. . . .
If you are talking about trying to make a living, I want to try again
You can resist only as a group and display the spirit of our people.[29]

And there was resistance. The rising nativism and more virulent anti-Chinese racialism at the end of the 1800s certainly affected the group's mentality and hence song repertoire. Increasingly, as discrimination and violence against the group mounted in the last quarter of the century, similar to what African Americans had suffered previously under slavery and the Jim Crow system afterward, the Chinese expressed in song their dissatisfaction over their mistreatment. That outrage reached a high point among all overseas Chinese colonies in their worldwide boycott of American goods in 1905.

To understand that people's shift in music to a more aggressive mentality requires a brief review of the increasing anti-Chinese hysteria in the United States around the turn of the twentieth century. As the earlier song about the immigrant miner indicates, the abuse and exploitation of these Asians began almost as soon as the group arrived at work in the minefields. Along with those injustices were discriminatory local ordinances aimed particularly at them for not showing sufficient assimilation. These laws, for example, levied taxes designed to deal with particular Chinese street laborers, scavengers, and other local enterprises. Communities also passed other legal restrictions to compel Asians to assimilate culturally, attacking their customary practices, such as limiting their hair length and thus doing away with their well-known queue.

By the early 1870s, along with the denial of their ability to be naturalized as U.S. citizens, was the rising hostility of organized American labor organizations, particularly in the West, against these "coolies." The result was the passage of anti-Chinese laws at the state level in the 1870s. The nativist movement achieved national sanction for this mistreatment with the passage of federal exclusion acts in 1882, 1892, 1902, and 1904 that permanently barred further entrance of working-class Chinese to the United States. The only exempted groups were close relatives of immigrant families already here and a few members of the upper classes, all of whom had to prove their status with documents. In addition, new arrivals had to pass a rigorous oral examination.

Meanwhile, as the statutory laws over time made it increasingly difficult for Chinese immigrants to enter the country, social discrimination against them intensified. In a number of western towns and cities in the 1880s and 1890s, violent attacks on "Chinatowns" and other Chinese quarters took place along with expulsions of the inhabitants, similar to the Jewish pogroms in Europe. The result was enormous property losses by Chinese Americans, with physical casualties and killings too.[30]

Important to understand here is that the victims did not accept such mistreatment passively. Not only did particular individuals bring up cases in the courts testing the constitutionality of these various laws and immigrant procedures, but Chinese American organizations also took action occasionally with the support of

Chinese diplomatic officials.[31] All contended that these depredations violated previous agreements, such as the Burlingame Amity Treaty of 1868 between China and the United States, and other arrangements that were supposed to protect that immigrant group in America. Adding to the Asians' dissatisfaction was the discriminatory provision of the 1888 Scott Act that barred the return of Chinese workers who had previously been in the United States.

After the 1892 Exclusion Act, which stripped the group of certain civil rights, the weight of punitive and prejudicial laws caused massive protests among Chinese Americans by the turn of the century. By the 1890s they also directed some of their complaints at Chinese governmental representatives. While on occasion that country's diplomats did assert their opposition against the inequitable immigrant policy, the immigrants themselves still criticized their homeland for not taking advantage of a renewal of a 1904 agreement between both countries to ameliorate American policy. Rather, the United States took that opportunity to institute a still more stringent administration and to make exclusion permanent.[32]

So the years around the turn of the century saw a heightening of dissatisfaction and protest among Chinese and Chinese Americans. Particularly important in their complaints was the callous treatment of newcomers at port facilities by immigration officials who applied their regulations harshly. This was especially grievous in the case of female arrivals, who were subjected to exhaustive and embarrassing interrogation at that time.[33]

Other developments occurred to further fuel the protest, such as broadening the exclusion policy to incoming Chinese workers in the newly acquired territories of Hawaii and the Philippines in 1898; the officially sanctioned burning of the Honolulu Chinatown in 1900, ostensibly for health reasons; and the renewal and permanent extension of exclusion laws in 1902 and 1904. Undoubtedly, yet another factor opposing the United States and the West was heightened Chinese nationalism at home and abroad resulting from the Boxer Rebellion in 1900. The stage was set, then, for a call to take broader action, which would be manifest in a worldwide Chinese boycott of American goods in 1905.

Begun in Shanghai that year, the appeal against the purchase of American products spread quickly among all Chinese overseas communities, *including* those in the United States, where the idea had already been considered. This anti-American furor became so pervasive that it assumed the character of an international crusade. One historian has specified an important element in the heightened emotional feeling in China; it was a time when many "anti-exclusion songs were composed and sung."[34] Thus, if the campaign in the homeland included music, it is plausible to assume that some form of protest in song took place in America as well, particularly in light of later developments.

The boycott itself ended late in 1905 and was partly successful, resulting in some amelioration of the harsh federal law. Yet while the organized refusal of Chinese Americans not to buy goods may have ended, their dissatisfaction over the mistreatment of immigrants did not. This was partly due to a spirited campaign that mobilized the community in condemning the wretched conditions at the processing facility in San Francisco. While the U.S. government did agree to move the reception area to another location, Angel Island in San Francisco Bay, local Chinese Americans still objected, for when Angel Island opened in 1910, it was less accessible to them and more isolated than the former facility.[35] In addition, the examinations and detention on the island were also little better than those in the original shed back on the mainland.

The anger of the immigrant community manifested itself in these years not only in *muk-yu* but also in the other popular form of musical expression, the Cantonese opera. As mentioned earlier, this latter genre was part of the tradition of carrying on and conveying the folk legends and myths of the past as both entertainment and uplift for its semiliterate audience. The opera had arrived in the United States almost with the earliest immigrants; as early as 1852 a troupe had come from China and was performing its repertoire in San Francisco. Thereafter, other companies traversed the circuit of Chinese American settlements, not only in the West but also all over North America, before and after the Exclusion era. Supplemented often by local talent, these ensembles grew in popularity, particularly as a result of rising discrimination. Chinese immigrants needed the reassurance of the exploits of their heroes that the plots recounted. Role models were welcomed among a group that sought a bolstering self-confidence. In fact, as one critic has put it, the plays were not static performances of the classics; actors deliberately modified their repertoire to fit the overseas Chinese's "own mythologies."[36] The companies' presentations, then, were altered to fit the emotional needs of their audience. As one student observes, especially in the era of Exclusion in the immigrant bachelor community, the "Cantonese Opera [in America] became the favorite pastime as an alternative to gambling and other vices, and the opera houses became 'clubs' and 'community centers' as an alternative to the bunk bed 'homes' the men were normally confined in."[37]

Fortunately, the content of one Cantonese opera relevant to Chinese immigrants' life in America is extant. While this work by itself may be insufficient evidence of the mentality of all immigrants, its theme certainly reveals the dissatisfaction recounted in other performance media. One must remember that Chinese opera was not only performed but also disseminated in print. The "libretto" of this production appeared serially in one of the better-known Chinese-language newspapers in San Francisco, *Jinshan Geji* (Young China), February–April 1911, all of which suggests more-extended popular exposure.[38] Called "Huaqiao Xue Lei" ("Blood and Tears of an Overseas Chinese"), it highlights the physical and mental abuse immigrants were subjected to.

It is the story of an American doctor who aggressively asserts his position as medical examiner of Chinese immigrants; in fact, he takes pleasure in insulting them. Despite the objections of a Chinese physician and other educated group members, the American insists on examining the most sensitive areas of the newcomers' bodies, justifying his action by asserting that he has to check for parasitical diseases. If any of his subjects refuse to submit, he subjects them to both physical and psychological abuse and threatens to label them ill with contagious diseases, thus forcing them to return home. He gets pleasure out of such mistreatment, while the immigrants only feel shame and disgrace as a result of the examination. They internalize the abuse and in such a state consider themselves criminals.

It then refers to the immigrants' disillusionment as a result of their experience. While having sacrificed much to reach their overseas "paradise," their hopes are dashed by the brusque way immigrant officials treat them. They also feel the degradation of their country, humiliated in the eyes of the world.

But the tale is not wholly depressing, for it does have a hero in the form of a Chinese immigrant physician who arrives in San Francisco. He is a Dr. Guan, who since he was trained in England, has the ability to function easily in American society. Seeing the injustice in the processing of his countrymen, he vows to combat it. First he learns that those who do have some diseases are wrongly deported since their affliction is not infectious; thus they should be able to enter the country. Both he and a local Chinese consul complain to the American doctor about his decisions. The latter rejects their petition and insists that he is merely following official rules. Not getting satisfaction, Guan goes on to New York to get the help of the Chinese consul there, but unfortunately he refuses to provide any assistance. Clearly a corrupt official, he wants only to keep his position and his wealth, which is based on ingratiating himself with the American authorities and his friends.[39]

That the grievances inherent in this opera, the unhappiness with both the American authorities and Chinese officials, continued for decades down to World War II is supported by recent, additional, and unusual evidence, further illuminating the immigrant mentality. These are the poetic inscriptions on walls written by Angel Island inmates during the operation of the facility between 1910 and 1940. It is important here to remember that, especially in Chinese literary tradition, the relationship between poem and popular music and folksong has always been close. New poetry forms developed from the latter, and the most popular literary works were often sung to familiar tunes.[40]

These poetic inscriptions were discovered about the 1960s and found to provide some insight into the feelings of Chinese immigrants hurt psychologically by both the officials and their long detention. They poured out their frustration in verse, some of which did appear in a song collection published about 1911. There is even an aria written in Cantonese opera style from the early 1920s entitled "A Chinese Traveler Imprisoned on Angel Island."[41] Researchers recently translated and published a number of wall poems along with oral testimony of former inmates.[42]

Just how representative these expressed sentiments of detainees were of *all* arriving immigrants is uncertain. One source states that some ship passengers were never detained or examined at the island, while another, an inmate in 1914, has observed that "all" arriving immigrants were ferried there.[43] Whatever the proportion of total immigrants the fifty thousand Chinese who arrived at Angel Island in the thirty years after 1910 comprised, many did go through the harrowing process of examination. So some attention to the poems does illuminate the lament of those detained, and again, it is consonant with the unhappiness conveyed in the Cantonese opera piece above and other musical forms. The occasional separation of families by immigrant officials, the limited time allowed for visiting relatives, the unfamiliar medical examination, and the shame over deportation all made the experience that much more traumatic.

These discovered poems numbered about one hundred. Most were unsigned, some "were meant to be sung as Cantonese opera," and from their vocabulary obviously written mostly by peasants.[44] One inscription, apparently composed in 1920, seems to be a representative evocation of the thoughts of the other inmates, including the great expectation of wealth many carried to America and the dashing of those hopes by the difficult passage and the long detention, for some up to several years, while their case was adjudicated. The processing made one immigrant feel like a criminal and resulted in the writer's expressed wish to return home. He once admired "America as a land of promise," but after an uncomfortable trip by boat, he was now "trapped in this prison place." From his island confines he could even see his destination, but having been denied the ability to reach it, he now only wished to return home and resume farming. With a heart full of sorrow, he could not sleep, so he wrote "these words to express his sadness."[45]

A more aggressive, dissatisfied writer returned to the familiar theme of criticizing his own country's weakness and of urging a more vigorous protest. After he "abandoned" his village and parents, he became "A wanderer longing for the wealth of merchant Hou Gee" but "unexpectedly [found himself] a prisoner of Angel Island." He cries "bitter tears . . . for China, a nation in shame," as foreigners have drained it of its "wealth and power." But he concludes with an appeal, urging "countrymen [to] be resolute. Dare to conquer America and avenge past wrongs."[46]

As the first immigrant group to suffer legally racial discrimination and prejudice, Chinese immigrants found their reception both immediately and over time increasingly uncomfortable. Their songs reflect that change. While their experience in some ways was similar to European emigrants in their initial hopes to win wealth and return to a better life in the old country, along with much homesickness for family, loved ones, and their ancestral home, these Asian arrivals encountered a much more hostile reception. The longer distance from their village, both culturally and psychically, than those from Europe; the greater intensity of majority discrimination; and the more formidable legal barriers to their immigration all distinguished their settling here.

But the group did have a compensation: Their musical compositions provided not just an outlet for their emotional distress but also some insight into how they felt about their mistreatment. The songs not only bemoaned the discomfort of male loneliness and victimization but also offered a basis of action through united resistance. Thus, strangely enough, this music of pain and powerlessness also provided a sense of self-confidence, moral strength, and even ethnic identity.

8

The Mexicans

The "Hero" as Anti-American

The last major immigrant group that appeared in the United States through the 1930s was the Mexicans. The proposition that song would indeed convey their mentality is perhaps least contentious in their case; many Americans have long recognized and admired Latino culture for its rich musical content. In fact, the assertion is widely accepted that the musical artistry of those groups, including dance, like African American jazz, has had an enduring influence on American popular music over the past century. The popularity of Latin American and especially Mexican music has been so obvious that Anglos would have to agree that it must be an important part of the lives of Mexicans and Latinos.

Leading students of Mexican songs in particular have shown that that repertoire does sensitively reflect on the lives and thoughts of that ethnic group. Serious studies of the subject over the years by a number of aficionados, early collectors, and academics, such as anthropologist Manuel Gamio, labor economist Paul Taylor, and more recently folklorist Américo Paredes and literary scholar Maria Herrera-Sobek, have shown that the vocal pieces of the group were not only prolific in number but also, more importantly, vehicles that expressed the most intimate thoughts and feelings of the immigrants.[1] As a recent academic chair of a La Raza studies program advised: "Those of us who are English-dominant would learn a great deal of the needs—aspirations of our immigrant population, of their frustrated hopes, their frustrated dreams. In these songs, it's all there."[2] Hence the conclusion must be that these works, especially those of the Mexican folk-ballad genre known as *corridos,* certainly offer a good reading of the mentality of the newcomers.

This vocal music, as in the other groups, expresses the concerns of those who left home, hence their attitudes about migration. They tell about universal feelings that were similar to the thoughts of every other group, including the presentation of psychic problems. Thus these neighbors from beyond the southern U.S. border also experienced that general ambivalence and emotional tug-of-war that afflicted overseas travelers from more distant places.

But the prospect of achieving a better life for themselves and their loved ones was quite appealing and a driving motive; yet, as was the case with other groups, that was accompanied by the unhappy abandoning of what was familiar and cherished, even if the trip of these Latino travelers was shorter and their destination nearer. There were then, for them too, similar uncertainties about the future, particularly the expected difficult encounters of living and working in an alien society. More particular in their case were the barriers to achieving their goal of a better life: the hostility of the Anglo-American majority toward them, the loss or weakening of their traditional culture, and the deleterious effects on their vulnerable youth by the forces of modernism.

The more distinctive and specific Mexican concerns stemmed in part from the differing nature of the circumstances of their migration and reception. One must be reminded that most immediately obvious is the fact that not all Mexican Americans were *immigrants*. Some, of course, were indigenous to the area, the natives whose ancestors had settled *before* Anglo-Americans arrived in Texas and the Southwest. They then viewed the Anglo-Americans as the newcomers. While Spanish-speaking inhabitants did predate "gringo" settlement in the early 1800s, the interlopers soon turned the tables by becoming hegemonic by force.

Anglo-American discrimination against them was somewhat different from that against the other nonwhite aliens in the region, Chinese Americans, because unlike the Asians, for many Mexicans the land had been theirs first. The result of this incursion by alien Anglos, their domination, and the ensuing isolation, segregation, and abuse of Mexican Americans that endured into the twentieth century was an indigenous resistance that was more intense than that of Asians in the area. Their opposition to such injustice was more evident and enduring in its expression, both in deed and in song. Oddly, that hostility toward Anglo-Americans also had a beneficial effect on the Mexicans. The mistreatment unified the group in the United States, homogenizing disparate Mexicans who had come from various regions.[3] The waves of immigrants who left central Mexico at the end of the nineteenth century joined those who were native to the lower Rio Grande borderland in a common feeling of opposition to Anglo injustice.

Besides the general resistance to American mistreatment, another distinctive feature of Mexican Americans was the constant reinforcement and retention of their traditional culture in the United States, which has also continued to the present. Being much closer to their home than the Asians across the Pacific, and thus more easily able to cross the border, Mexican immigrants have constantly strengthened their ethnic culture in their U.S. communities. That cultural reinforcement, in turn, has brought about a more heated condemnation in sentiment and song of those who have assimilated. The result has been a greater intolerance to those, such as young people, some women, and others, who have been more willing than others in the group to quickly change and conform to Anglo-majority ways.

These features of a durable culture and a profound condemnation of assimilators produced substantial protest hostility to the hegemonic power of their English-speaking neighbors. Hence the most characteristic feature of the Mexican American musical repertoire and the factor that sets their songs apart from other immigrant groups is the anti-Americanism in their vocal works. Their heroic songs, therefore, have lionized their men of great courage who resisted the *norteamericanos.* Mexican immigrants created these musical memorials in their folk tradition from the first contact with their oppressors in the early 1800s through a century of discrimination to the Great Depression of the 1930s. Mexicans expressed these attitudes in their *corridos,* musical recountings of the noble exploits of brave individuals who fought against the dominant power of the "Colossus of the North" and its Anglo-American representatives.[4]

Certainly, the history of relations between the two peoples and their governments in the nineteenth and early twentieth centuries shows a general atmosphere of ill will and conflict. This clash began before the middle of the nineteenth century with endemic individual and group disputes over land title. The beginning of European settlement in the Southwest took place in the 1500s in what would become the state of New Mexico; the peopling of Texas came later in the early 1800s, and that of Arizona and California afterward.

The connection between these northern reaches of the Spanish Southwest and the central government in Mexico City, both before and after Mexico became independent in 1821, remained distant. This regional isolation from the governing authority would exacerbate conflict between the indigenous Spanish-speaking inhabitants and the later-coming Anglo-Americans who filled the region in the early days of Mexico. The borderland areas, including what would be south Texas along the lower Rio Grande, were to be places of protracted and bitter interethnic conflict.

The character of the population in the region would also be a potential trigger for conflict as the area's economic development in ranching and agriculture produced a highly developed sense of individualism among the inhabitants, similar to what was then occurring all over the pioneering American West. The situation became even more explosive as the Mexican government initially encouraged the coming of Anglos in the 1820s and early 1830s to help develop the region. These arrivals, who became trappers and merchants in New Mexico and California, were in a sense a vanguard, like the soldiers of the Trojan horse. When the Mexican authorities began a policy of administrative centralization, Anglo-Texans particularly objected, all of which led to violent clashes and eventually their independence in the mid-1830s. The young Texas nation later joined the United States in 1845, and after a dispute over the boundary territory, in which the U.S. government sought to acquire Mexican lands, the Mexican American War began in 1846.

The Treaty of Guadeloupe-Hidalgo of 1848 honored old land titles and granted legal guarantees to the Mexicans who remained in Texas, but the agreement hardly solved disputes over these matters. Resentment still festered in the borderlands even after monetary compensation was given to Mexico, and the United States added to that sum by the Gadsden Purchase of more land in 1854. Troublesome afterward too were ensuing legal battles over land titles and heightened anti-Mexican discrimination by Anglos, many of whom had fought in the war. Regardless of the number of Mexicans who had originally sided with the Anglo-Texans in their struggle for independence, clearly a hostile attitude arose between the two groups of inhabitants.

Inflaming the relationship further was the fact that many of the Anglos were American southerners who had come with heightened racialist sentiments. The impressions of the soldiers in the Mexican American War and other Anglo-Texans later looked upon Mexican men as "greasers" and a people with filthy habits. Although Latino women did possess some attractive romantic and exotic characteristics for male Anglos, overall the continued adherence of the Hispanics to Catholicism indicated to most that the "peons" were priest-ridden, hence undemocratic and unprogressive, lazy, lacking initiative, and typically criminal.[5] The extraordinarily popular dime novels published by the Beadle brothers, describing the romance and adventure in the American West, helped fix a stereotype of the Mexican vaquero (cowboy) as generally vicious and untrustworthy.[6]

That rising racist hostility toward these Latinos, however, did not inhibit more Mexicans from other areas from entering the United States for almost a century, first as immigrants in modest numbers to 1900 and later in much larger waves from then until the Great Depression. The particular magnets drawing them varied, but like other arrivals, better economic opportunity across the border dominated supported by dissatisfaction with unstable political conditions at home.

From 1850 to the end of the century, the discovery of gold in California, the demand for mineworkers in Arizona, and above all the agricultural expansion in Texas and the rest of the region pulled in a modest number of Mexicans from not only the northern provinces but also from those farther south. By 1890 about 75,000 immigrants were living the United States. Another cause for emigration was the harsh dictatorial regime of Porfirio Díaz, which lasted from 1877 until his deposition in the Mexican Revolution of 1910. The brutal internal conflicts during that era pushed out many ordinary Mexicans seeking a more stable existence in the freer political system of the north. This movement into south Texas occurred despite the ongoing deterioration of order and near anarchy along the border. There, as a result of discriminatory laws that weakened them politically, Texas-Mexican leaders clashed violently at times with local, state, and even federal authorities in the persons of sheriffs, Texas Rangers, and occasionally the U.S. Army. Vigilantes and guerilla bands from both sides roamed widely in the area with impunity during the 1880s, a condition that resulted in a virtual civil war along the border. These clashes would resonate in Mexican folk legend and song.

Still, in the midst of all this violence, Mexican immigration continued and enlarged in the early twentieth century, drawing workers north particularly after the enormous expansion of commercial agriculture as a result of the Federal Reclamation Act of 1902 and consequent labor needs in the region. The Mexicans generally increased not only as a result of the political chaos and the revolution in 1910 but also by other general "pull" factors, such as the growth of American heavy industry, particularly the steel mills, in the Midwest; the labor shortages caused by World War I; and the restrictive policies sharply limiting European immigration in the 1920s. Mexicans largely filled the vacuum of unskilled workers that resulted from the near barring of Europeans in that decade.

It is important to keep in mind the character of these Latino arrivals. Just like most Europeans before them, most Mexican emigrants originated from a concentrated region rather than from the country broadly. About three-fifths of the Mexican immigrants in the early 1900s came from just three provinces near Mexico City, Michoacán, Jalisco, and Guanajuato.[7]

Citing the incoming numbers by decades indicates the growing influx over time. The census numbers of Mexicans in the United States more than doubled in 1920 from its 1900 figure of 100,000 and reached almost 900,000 just before 1930. The sizable wage differential was largely responsible; the average pay of an unskilled worker in the United States in the 1920s was six times higher than that in Mexico, and the amount of immigrant remittances sent back home amounted to a sizable sum of over $8,000,000 in 1927.[8]

As with every other group, the emigrant psyche was one of ambivalence, wanting to leave but with some hesitation. Mexicans poured out that clash of impulses in song, especially the *corrido*, which developed during the mid-1800s. The essence of that form had actually appeared centuries earlier in a musical rendering known as the *romance*, a sixteen-syllable line work with no refrain, similar to an epic poem. The *conquistadores* had brought it over from Spain in the 1500s.[9] By the

time of Mexican independence in 1821, this musical genre had developed into another song form, the *decima,* an eight-syllable verse; a half century later it became
in turn the *corrido.* One could define both *decima* and *corrido* as ballads or popular poetry that dealt with news, events, and comment, not just descriptive tales,
particularly about national heroes. These songs have generally been described as a
"genuine product of sincere feeling; an outlet for the sorrows and joys of the
common people" and a "narrative viewed through the eyes of the people."[10] In
a thorough review of the *corrido,* another folklorist has carefully defined it as the
musical offerings that interprets known events. It modifies history as "a powerful
statement of community values and orientation."[11] Finally, while this song genre
as fully representative of the people may have the weakness of a patriarchal bias,
an observer has also viewed this musical form as "a valid social document" on
Mexican women.[12]

Musical performance became a widely practiced form of social expression for
these immigrants from the nineteenth century to the present. For the purposes
of this study, of most interest are those created to the end of the 1800s, during the
large-scale immigration through the 1920s, and the era of the Great Depression,
when hundreds of thousands of Mexican immigrants and Mexican Americans
were repatriated back to Mexico in its early days. The character of these immigrant ballads, according to major published collections, suggests how this group
felt about their lives, the conditions in their homeland, and their American destination. Of course, most significant in these musical messages is the opinion
expressed about the two societies, Mexican and American, on both sides of the
border.

Before a review of these immigrant vocals, it is important to note the context
of the presentation, how the songs were presented, their performers, and the venues. The circumstances in New Mexico were somewhat distinctive because
troubadours would sing *canciones,* essentially popular romantic songs at taverns;
if performed at home, these sessions were social gatherings called *tertulias.*[13] Such
works were common in that part of the American Southwest, for singing helped
lighten the work during the long mule trips of traders and along the trails of cattle
drivers.

One would find *corridos* sung outside of New Mexico, usually in Texas, California, and the rest of the Southwest, beginning in the late nineteenth century.
These ballads would be performed mainly by males at public places, in cantinas,
open-air plazas, barbershops, poolrooms, and later on radio programs. Women
also had a role in singing, for they were the main transmitters of the genre at
home, where they accompanied their household tasks with song or led the family
choruses in the evenings.[14] Both *decimas* and *corridos* were in that time either

Mexican Americans singing inside a chili stand in San Antonio in the 1930s. From liner notes, *Corridos and Tragedias de la Frontera*, CD 7019–7020 (El Cerrito, Calif.: Folklyric Records, 1994). (Courtesy San Antonio Light Collection, University of Texas Institute of Texan Cultures at San Antonio, no. 1433-E.)

unaccompanied or occasionally delivered with a guitar by *guitareros*. The musical pieces usually appeared in print and were widely available to the public as broadsides for a few pesos (or about five cents in the United States) in the 1920s and on record in the later years of the decade.[15] The subjects of these songs could be humorous or satirical as well as more serious political commentary or considerations of difficult life decisions like emigration.[16]

One representative and early collection of the Mexican song repertoire about the decision to leave is that of labor economist Paul Taylor, who indicates that the dilemma of the emigrant was similar to the ambivalence of the other ethnic groups. Three works, likely dating from the major migration of the 1920s, typify the enduring clash of motives of necessity and reluctance. One, "Defensa de Los Norteños" ("Defense of the Emigrants"), is a plaintive plea of a Mexican in the United States who defensively responds to criticism from others for leaving home. He concludes:

Many people have said that we are not patriotic
Because we go to serve for the accursed *patotas* [Americans, derisively]

But let them give us jobs and pay us decent wages;
Not one Mexican then will go to foreign lands.

We're anxious to return again to our adored country;
but what can we do about it if the country is ruined?[17]

Two others add what is likely a distinctive reference to religious sentiment in the minds of prospective travelers, returnees, and those left behind. "Despedida De Un Norteño" ("An Emigrant's Farewell"), for example, refers to the "Virgin" or "Mother Guadaloupe" and other saints as well as the "Holy Child." The singer voices his frustration about leaving, suggesting a guilty conscience:

Goodbye, my beloved country,
Now I am going away
I go to the United States,
Where I intend to work. . . .

I am not to blame
that I leave my country thus;
the fault is that of poverty
which keeps us all in want. . . .

Goodbye, fair Guanajuato,
the state where I was born;
I'm going to the United States
far, far from you.[18]

A related *corrido* is an unusually revealing dialogue between an emigrant returnee and one who never left. "A Conversation between Two Ranchers" again shows the rationalization that emigrants had to make to others for leaving as well as the importance of religious symbolism. The emigrant first brags about his success, his fine clothes, his "pockets always filled with plenty of silver," his winning "classy" women, and the higher standard of living in America, while

Here [in Mexico] for twenty-five cents
one works from sun to sun
there is nothing else to eat
but tortillas and beans.

I grant that Mexico is very pretty,
but it's down and out;
one works day and night
and never ceases to be a *pelado* [Indian].

The stay-at-home is especially outraged by his protagonist's criticism of his faith
and threatens him with a knife. The emigrant then feels remorse for his bragging
and in the name of a saint asks to be forgiven, to which the other replies that he
is a hypocrite: "Since you don't believe in saints nor even in the devil, then why
do you invoke glorious San Antonio? It seems to me your bravery is just a loud
mouth; that's why I am sorry for you."[19]

The conversation identifies and exposes a basic cultural difference between
American and Mexican values, or better, a conflict *in the minds* of the emigrants
themselves. Americans stress and uphold a forward-looking, acquisitive ethic that
places money and material wealth in defining self-worth while Mexicans treasure
their more humanistic culture based on tradition and the past.[20] That difference
may have festered *within* the mind of the immigrant. A recent and apparently
singular critic of the dominant school of Mexican and Chicano historiography
has reminded scholars that they should question the orthodoxy of heavily stressing oppression by the "gringos." Most Mexican Americans, he argues, did cross
the border into the Colossus of the North without coercion by Anglo conquest or
due to a lack of free will.[21] While I do not support fully this revisionism nor ignore
the victimization of immigrants in the United States, it is necessary to recognize
that their movement north included an earnest desire to achieve a better living
standard for themselves and those they left behind. Songs help to show this.

The principal *corrido* scholar, Américo Paredes, has referred to a number of
ballads that reveal the discomfiture of the migrant. In one that is critical of the
Americanized returnee, referred to as the *pocho,* in the era between the 1910 revolution and the 1930s, the *corrido* illustrates the mixture of sentiments on the
subject's mind as in "Bonita esta Tierra" ("Beautiful Is the Land"). While the narrator welcomes his income of gold and silver and the beautiful girls he has met,
having left his parents in Toluca near Mexico City and being now a prisoner in
jail, he wants to flee back to "my land."[22]

Besides the concern over the decision to migrate, another topic in song was,
of course, the difficult working conditions that immigrants found in the United
States. While worker dissatisfaction over employer exploitation certainly existed,
causing labor protest and strikes, such grievances before the Great Depression
hardly entered the folk or popular music that spoke about work on the railroads,
in the mines, in the steel mills, or in the fields picking fruit and vegetables. Complaint in song was common about the job, the long hours, the physically tiring

effort, and the difficult working conditions, but again any blaming of Anglo-American or employer exploitation is rarely evident in the more popular songs before 1930. Most express a clear preference for working in manufacturing over agriculture, likely because of the higher income in industrial rather than farming employment.

One of the earliest and widely known "labor" *corridos* was "Kainsis," with its several variants. It came out of the Texas border region in the late 1800s and refers to the dangerous work of the Mexican vaqueros. The labor of these men on horseback leading cattle drives north was an example, in song, of their superiority over the less experienced American cowboy. The narrator thus complains only mildly about Anglo denigration of his work.[23] Other labor ballads, such as the "*Corrido de Texas*" and "La Pensilvania," express workers' great reluctance at leaving their families in Texas for jobs elsewhere.[24] They feel they have to leave them and get away from the hated task of picking cotton for more preferable and profitable industrial employment in the mills of Indiana, Chicago, and the East.

Two other songs also illustrate the dislike of the kind of employment, again without blaming the employer. In "Corrido de Robstown" the prosperity of the 1920s apparently deflects any animus directed at an agricultural employer. It is a complaint about the backbreaking labor of picking the bolls on a Texas cotton farm. Yet in this case the speaker feels the hated effort is worth it because, in that community, income and employment at least are secure: "He who knows this town [Robstown] never can deny that lots of money can be earned because there is much work."[25]

The other example is from a popular *corrido* "El Lavaplatos" ("The Dishwasher"), which appeared about the same time in the years after World War I. It refers to one immigrant's dream of working in the burgeoning film industry. Aside from its wide appeal, the value of this ballad is in conveying the attitude of the singer in the variety of jobs he obtains after crossing the border, such as railroad laborer, construction worker, dishwasher, and farmhand picking tomatoes. He concludes by offering a lesson to his listeners that they be more realistic than he was in their hopes for material success, for "I return to my dear country / Poorer than when I came."[26]

Another certain theme of twentieth-century Mexican songs is the profound concern about assimilation. It was, of course, a subject discussed in other immigrant repertoires, condemning the loss of the old way of life, such as language change as a result of Americanizing pressures. But for this group, the criticism in song of such an assault on tradition was more pointed and was especially directed at the assimilative affect migration had on women. The matter may have assumed such intense concern among Mexicans because of the greater intolerance

toward any change in their new American community. As stated, the barrios
maintained the ethnic culture of Mexicans longer than other groups here due
to the proximity of the homeland and the easy and constant access of new immigrants.

Gamio, Paredes, and Herrera-Sobek all refer to a particular derogatory term
used for the partly assimilated, American-born Mexican as *pocho,* or *pocho-
agrinado,* a "gringoized" Mexican American who, having settled outside the areas
of intense Anglo-Mexican conflict along the border, was particularly receptive to
Anglo-American culture. By anglicizing their speech, quickly assuming American
clothing, and generally buying into the pervasive consumerism of the majority,
they encountered bitter criticism from homeland Mexicans, particularly upon returning to Mexico during the Depression repatriation.[27] Representative of this
theme is the comment in "El Renegado" ("The Renegade"): "he who denies his
race is the most miserable creature. . . . [A] good Mexican never disowns the dear
fatherland of his affections."[28]

But the most hostile criticism in the ballads over cultural decline is leveled
at Mexican women in general, both immigrants and American born. The songs
describe *Mexicanas* as particularly susceptible to adopting Yankee ways. In the
Herrera-Sobek and Gamio lists of pre-1930 acculturation *corridos,* most of the ballads condemn the deleterious assimilative influence of modern, urbanized American fashion on Mexican females.

"Las Pollas de California" ("The [Anglo] Chicks from California"), for example, urges immigrant men in that state not to marry any women there, for they
want only American clothes and food; "Los Mexicanos que Habla Inglés" ("The
Mexicans Who Speak English") and "La Pochita" ("The Americanized Mexican
Woman") refer derisively to those women who respond to Spanish questions only
in English; and others like "El Rancho" ("The Ranch") and "Las Palonas" ("The
Bobbed Heads") lament the destructive affects of the model American "flapper"
among ethnic women. With her cosmetics and revealing dress, that gussied-up
figure was hastening the demise of the old, noble feminine demeanor, a modest
and restrained style of traditional attire and appearance.[29]

More specifically, in another ballad, "Las Abolilladas" ("The Americanized
Ones"), the up-to-date dresses make the woman in the song look like a "monkey"
and the latest hairstyle makes her a "fool":

> You go out, showing your legs
> With your skirts up to your knees,
> God protect you because you have no modesty . . .
> [they] soon forget their native land

And use skirts in place of pants. . . .
They chew gum, try to speak English
And are even ashamed of being Mexicans.

"Las Pajamas" ("The Pajamas") calls the new dress fad "mannish," on the one hand, and too alluring, on the other, while "La Parodia de la Vergencita" ("The Parody of 'The Little Virgin'") condemns the "false eyebrows"; the "short skirts" that exhibit bare arms, legs, and feet; and the painted faces, which make women appear ugly—they "look like victims of tuberculosis already in the tomb" when they wash off the makeup.[30] Clearly, then, these works suggest the tensions that must have been felt in the families and homes of barrio inhabitants, especially in the conflict between male and female members.[31]

To this point, little has been said about Mexican-American conflict. The songs heretofore have revealed opposing cultural values between the Mexican minority and Anglo majority, as in the controversy over acculturation. But none of these ballads have conveyed specifically any complaint over the mistreatment of immigrants by American authorities or the psychic sense of outrage and protest of Mexican Americans against the kind of majority discrimination that was evident in the Chinese case. Such complaints did exist in the Mexican American repertoire, to such an extent, in fact, that the subject was always evident and likely even uppermost in their minds. The current scholarly consensus is that the *corrido* "suddenly burst forth [as early as the 1860s in a less developed form] as a dynamic expression of intercultural conflict."[32] The rise of this ballad tradition provides certain evidence of a deep-seated and enduring hostility toward Anglo-American authorities that extended over the entire history of contact, down to the Great Depression and beyond.[33]

Ballads demanding justice constitute a distinctive character of the Mexican immigrant sentiment, for unlike the protests of all of the other immigrant groups covered, these songs concentrate on individual heroes and their exploits, responding courageously against heavy odds to social injustice, exploitation, and mistreatment. The leading authority on this ballad genre, Américo Paredes, explains the Mexican American idolization of these figures as celebrated in the *corridos*. Their heroism was not the result of any superhuman ability; they were merely ordinary individuals wanting to correct injustice. Their actions provided an important aspect of the group's "long struggle to preserve [its] identity" and, more particularly, "to affirm [the peoples'] rights as human beings." The hero risks "life, liberty, and material goods *defendiendo su derecho* [defending their rights]."[34]

While the setting for most of these songs is the border area of south Texas, *corridos* played a significant role too in the wider immigrant experience, for most of the later newcomers who originated in Mexican provinces farther south traversed the region on their way to California and north into the central plains and the East. This suggests the ballad repertoire of the borderlands was known in many barrios of the Southwest.

As noted, the borderland was the locale of the bitterest Mexican-American conflicts, beginning after the Mexican American War and continuing later in the century with constant guerrilla clashes between Mexicans and U.S. authorities. The result was general chaos to the end of the century. To Mexicans, the principal villains of their mistreatment were those who enforced the repressive laws and discrimination—the hated *rinches,* the Texas Rangers.

Even before the Mexican-American conflict of the 1840s, the area had never really been pacified. It had been a center of rebellious Indian bandits, celebrated in *decimas.* So it was understandable that after the war ended in 1848, musical works appeared that sang of the courage and martyrdom of Spanish-speaking opponents to the American army. One was a Father Jarauta, who was executed by the Anglos for leading a guerilla band that refused to accept the provisions of Treaty of Guadaloupe-Hidalgo.[35]

Another hero in the Mexican pantheon, Joaquin Murrieta, was even more popular and legendary in song, with many versions of his exploits recounted. It is unknown if the man ever existed, but songs about Murieta were known throughout the borderlands. He supposedly went to California during the gold rush and, as a Mexican, suffered many inequities. In particular, he found that he was denied the ability to own land. Outraged, Murrieta assumed the role of a social bandit similar to Robin Hood, taking from the rich and giving to the poor. In one stanza Murrieta describes his empathy with the poor:

> I came from Hermosillo in search of gold and riches,
> The Indian poor and simple I defended with fierceness
> And a good price the [American] sheriffs would pay for my head.

After his wife is raped and his brother hanged, he proclaims, "I went punishing Americans," and charges one of them: "You must be the captain who killed my brother. You grabbed him defenseless, you stuck-up American."

When one of his American enemies is found dead, a sheriff tracks him down and engages him in a gun battle in which he kills the lawman. After he is charged with killing another American military officer in California, the Texas Rangers claim to have finally cornered and killed him, but according to legend, no one can be certain it was Murrieta who died. It is noteworthy and ironic that his story was popular among *both* Mexicans and Americans. The former saw him as anti-

American and fighting injustice, while American popular literature accepted and depicted him as a romantic. This *corrido* was composed in the late 1800s and sung during the 1910 revolution, especially in Mexico and Arizona.[36]

The stories of Father Jarauta and Murrieta were followed by those of a living anti-American hero, Juan Nepomuceno Cortina. In 1859 Cortina shot a Brownsville sheriff who had mistreated and arrested one of his mother's employees. He freed the *vaquero* from the local jail and then led a successful guerilla campaign against Anglo town leaders, the local police, the Texas Rangers, and even the U.S. Army; the soldiers eventually drove his band into exile across the border. The tale is told in "El General Cortina," which is a series of ballads that date back to about 1860 and to which other musical accounts were added until about 1890.[37]

The anti-American theme was maintained in even the balladry directed against the Mexican dictator Porfirio Díaz, who ruled from 1877 to 1910. Since this despot willingly worked with the hated Texas Rangers by returning Mexican fugitives to them, a number of songs blamed him too for Anglo-American mistreatment.[38] The suppression of the popular Garza Rebellion in Texas in a joint effort by Diaz and the *rinches* and the arrest and conviction of a Mexican gang of train robbers, both in 1891, characterized the pervasive anti-American sentiment in other *corridos* in that decade.[39]

By far, however, the most popular songs and the "epitome" of hero-*corridos* in the entire Mexican American repertoire heralded the exploits of Gregorio Cortéz. Over the entire last century, from the first incident in 1901 until now, "El Corrido de Gregorio Cortéz" is commonly sung in cantinas and at social gatherings by *guitarreros.*[40]

Cortéz's actual encounter with gringo officials largely followed the pattern of the Murrieta story. The hero once again was charged with the killing of an American sheriff in an exchange of gunfire after the latter tried to arrest him and his brother for a horse theft they did not commit. He and his wounded sibling escaped just ahead of an American posse. Cortéz was finally captured after a Mexican traitor, attracted by the reward money, identified him.

The hero was then tried on the horse-theft charge as well as the killing of another sheriff. At first declared innocent by the court by reason of self-defense, he was eventually convicted in 1905 for murder. The governor of Texas later pardoned him for the crime in 1913.

The *corrido* text stresses Cortéz's innocence in his confrontation with the sheriff. "'I don't regret that I killed him / A man must defend himself,'" he says, and the ballad ends with his escape from the three-hundred-man posse and its bloodhounds, his condemnation of the "cowardly rangers," and his ultimate decision to give himself up. But in true heroic style, Cortéz tells his captors, "You take me because I'm willing, but not any other way."[41] Again, this kind of popular song suggests the ambivalence Mexican immigrants had in moving to and being in America. Others followed.

The years up to, during, and after the Mexican Revolution of 1910 were, of course, ones of great instability for Mexicans and a time of continued hatred toward the Texas Rangers. Thus the dissatisfaction toward Anglo-American abuse continued to find its way into the Mexican song repertoire. Examples of these include the recounting of such incidents as the shootout in Brownsville in 1911 between the Trevino brothers and sheriff deputies and Rangers in the heroic *corrido* "Jacinto Trevino"; the Rangers' massacre of farmworkers after two heroes attempt a Texas Mexican uprising to establish a Spanish-speaking republic in 1915, as described in "Los Sediciosos" ("The Seditionists"); and the appearance of another legendary hero in the anti-American pantheon of song just before World War I, Pancho Villa.[42]

The canonization of Villa in popular Mexican literature was a complex process, for the historical facts, as usual, differed from the actual content of the *corridos* about him. While he did engage in fighting factions of his *own* people, the most popular songs made him a nationally unifying figure partly because of his struggle against U.S. authorities. As Villa's major biographer succinctly puts it, the myth of his struggling against the powerful Colossus of the North was "expressed above all in *corridos*."[43]

Villa's musical lionization was based on a variety of traits, some contradictory and even fictional: as an ordinary man who became a military genius; a seeker of revenge for a family injustice; a model of Mexican machismo; and a philanthropic Robin Hood who helped the poor.[44] But his most important legacy in several ballads was his one famous encounter, where he displayed his courage and cleverness, against a much more powerful force of Anglo-Americans. That was during the famous 1916 Mexican Punitive Expedition led by Maj. Gen. John Pershing, who was out to capture Villa for raiding an American town in New Mexico. One well-known song, in fact, depicts Pershing's soldiers as simply another group of Anglo oppressors, lumping together sheriffs, posses, immigration officials, prison guards, and, of course, *rinches*.[45]

"La Persecucion de Villa" opens by describing the massive U.S. force whose aim was to catch and kill the bandit. But after contact is made with skirmishes followed by a two-hour-long battle, the soldiers, tired and frustrated, want to return home. A second encounter proves even more disastrous for the Americans, the song noting that Pershing lost two hundred men dead. The narrator observes:

> What did these cowardly *rinches* think,
> That making war was like a fancy ball?

With their faces all full of shame
They returned once more to their country.

The *corrido* concludes triumphantly with a rhetorical question: "Didn't these big-footed Gringos know that they were no match for Pancho Villa?"[46]
Another version describes the vaunted American power as simply ineffective:

It doesn't matter that the "blondies" have
Battleships and vessels by the score
And airplanes and armored cars,
If they don't have what it takes.[47]

Villa's major biographer offers additional proof of his popular image among the Mexican populace. From the revolution to the early 1930s, the deliberate neglect of the hero by unpopular Mexican authorities for political reasons seemed to deify Villa even more among the masses.[48] At any rate, the ongoing popularity of anti-American ballads suggests the continued animus Mexican immigrants had for their hosts across the border.

In the 1920s that hostile relationship seems to have ameliorated somewhat, both in reality and in song, as huge numbers of Mexicans poured across the border to make up for the decreased immigration from Europe. No new major Mexican-American clashes took place along the border, only an ongoing dissatisfaction with the Border Patrol for its continued mistreatment of arrivals and their arrests of Mexican bootleggers trying to enter the United States during Prohibition.[49] Also important to note is the surprisingly widespread possession of phonographs among even the poorest of Mexicans, according to a survey done in the mid-1920s. Folk music was apparently as popular as ever.[50]

The end of the decade in 1929 and the start of the Great Depression renewed a flurry of anti-American sentiment and balladry as a result of repatriation efforts. Almost immediately after the stock market crash and ensuing distress of unemployment and hard times, the entire nation, particularly its poor, suffered economically. The waves of incoming Mexicans reversed as hundreds of thousands returned across the border, some voluntarily, most likely by force. Seeing the enormous burden of providing welfare support for these foreign poor, U.S. community and city leaders encouraged and often compelled their Latin American neighbors to go back home. To the loss of jobs and income was added more social and ethnic conflict by, in many cases, an unconstitutional removal of immigrant families, many members of which were already citizens. The critical situation undoubtedly exacerbated ethnic hostility on all sides.

Two types of *corridos* arose out of the early years of the Depression. One group simply recorded the misery of hard times; the other dwelled on the increased Anglo discrimination of particular immigrants. Of the first, the predominant sentiment was one of shock and the dashing of expectations about earning good income. These latter recorded the sufferings of immigrant families without blaming anyone. Some ballads even express gratitude for the help provided Mexicans by American welfare agencies prior to their reluctant decision to return home. Other songs, however, lay the misery of the expulsion largely at the hands of U.S. authorities for the immigrants' unemployment and later expulsion from the barrio.[51]

It is difficult to know which of the two causes, economic or social, was uppermost in the minds of most of the re-emigrants. One source says organized group protest was lacking because the repatriates were intimidated by the abuse. It adds, however, that music provides a key, "only the informal record—for example, of *corridos* . . . , suggests the depth of the distress."[52] But more-recent students, also using vocal music as evidence, suggest that the mistreatment by Anglo-American officials was the common psychological complaint among departing Mexican Americans.

One of their most popular Depression ballads was "El Deportado" ("The Deported One"), which refers to the immigrant "round up," their expulsion as "bandits," and their return to a now peaceful, "beautiful" homeland.[53] In addition, a heightened anti-Americanism arose once again in "hero" *corridos* similar to those about Cortina, Cortéz, and Villa. These include such songs as a 1930 ballad about a New Mexico sheriff shooting a Mexican teenager charged with killing an American deputy; another about one Juan Reyna, who died in San Quentin Prison in 1931 under suspicious circumstances after a controversial trial over the death of a local policeman; one about the killing in that same year of two Mexican students by an Oklahoma sheriff; and finally one about the controversial 1933 execution of the Hernandez brothers in Arizona for killing an American.[54]

Besides these works representing a deep resentment toward American injustice, additional evidence of that popular sentiment is the extraordinary appeal of a group of musicians who broadcast performances of these heroic ballads and others during the Depression's early years. These were Los Madrugadores, especially their founder, Pablo J. González. González had begun to sing on a Spanish-language radio program around Los Angeles in the late 1920s, and in 1929 he teamed up with two brothers named Sánchez to become the most popular group in the Southwest at that time. They ran an informal, two-hour, seven-day, early morning program (*madrugadores* means "early risers") over Los Angeles station KELW and in two years "became a household word in practically every Spanish-speaking home."[55] Besides singing all the best-known traditional and contemporary *corridos,* a good part of the group's success was its homey closeness to its audience, taking requests and dedications from working-class listeners in the early hours of the day as they went off to work.

More important, though, was González's guiding philosophy and purpose for his ensemble. His aim was not only to entertain but also to politicize his listeners. He sought to instill and maintain a strong ethnic identity and consciousness, and as the Depression deepened and discrimination intensified, he used his program to protest the forced expulsions and the persecution of Mexican Americans during those deportations. Among the best-known pieces performed (and recorded) by the group were some of the more anti-American *corridos* like those about Murieta and the Hermanos brothers. Since González "was feared as a rabble-rouser by the Anglo establishment," Los Madrugadores was also known for another controversial ballad about the unjust conviction in an U.S. court in 1934 of González himself.[56]

Once again, similar to that of all the other immigrant groups covered, the songs of Mexican Americans reflect a conflicting complex of attitudes about their migratory experience. Great hopes were combined with great fears; the attractive prospects for emigrants buoyed by the examples of successful returnees were balanced by a hesitation about leaving home and family as well as the social obstacles encountered once they crossed the border. In sum, as in other cases the group's ambivalent mentality was largely made up of uncertainty and even pessimism. Other sources of dissatisfaction also found their way into balladry, such as the hard work required on U.S. farms and in mines, railroads, and factories as well as the dangerous pressures of a too-rapid acculturation. The modernizing influences on the dress and appearance of vulnerable women and second-generation Mexican Americans were especially threatening to old-country tradition.

But above all in the case of these Latinos was the problem of Anglo discrimination and mistreatment. Over the entire course of contact between Mexicans and Americans, the *corridos* decried the abuse of local officials especially and the *rinches* in particular. This popular balladry, characteristically glorifying particular heroes, first emanated from the areas of initial encounter in the lower Rio Grande in the nineteenth century. Later in the 1900s, these songs spread over the entire Southwest, continuing into the Depression, telling of difficult economic conditions, and increasingly heralding the pantheon of group martyrs to social injustice.

Finally, this review of Mexican immigrant songs certainly questions the recent generalization of two students of Mexican American culture who take a more elitist view of the making of that group's culture up to the 1930s.[57] They conclude that it was the ethnic upper classes who set the tone of that society. Certainly, as they point out, some middle-class organizations like the League of United Latin American Citizens, formed in 1929 to promote democratic ideals, did contribute to creating a more homogenized ethnic group. But the popular *corridos* suggest that the shift from a Mexican to a Mexican American mentality that occurred in the 1920s and 1930s did not mean a complete acceptance of all of the values of the host society. As the eminent Mexican American historian George Sánchez has recently pointed out, the Americanization process involved immigrants who "negotiated the most critical decisions regarding their cultural future." But, he adds, they did so under the delimiting pressures of socioeconomic realities.[58] Their most popular songs before 1934 certainly substantiate the point.

9

Conclusion

The challenge of trying to generalize at this time about the innermost feelings of the tens of millions who arrived in the New World in the century after 1830 is certainly daunting. Even with the recognized importance and thus developing interest in the phenomena of ethnicity and race in America since 1960, determining the psychological conditioning of the vast and diverse multitudes who transited national boundaries is a difficult task to say the least. I have already indicated that music and song are important sources for a comprehensive and profound picture of how these alien individuals felt about their transnational experience. Having also referred to the general neglect of the immigrants' expressive culture by most previous scholars seeking to understand lower-class ethnic behavior, I will here review the historiography more closely, noting its more recent, occasional treatment of the newcomers' state of mind. This retrospective is necessary not only to place this study in its proper scholarly context but also to show that that shift in scholarly attention over time also has a bearing on understanding the immigrant mentality itself. I also offer a generalized summary of findings of this survey of immigrant songs and ballads, cover one generally outstanding feature as shown particularly in the Japanese experience, highlight comparisons in the various song repertoires of the groups, and finally suggest how the conclusions may apply to the general issue of ethnic identity and even the mentality of some recent and contemporary immigrants. Some of the emotions of immigrants are enduring ones built into the very process of transnational migration.

Looking at the entire scholarly literature on the subject suggests that the approach of American historians concerning the mental state of individual immigrants has been somewhat cyclical over the last half century. That treatment can be divided into three stages. The first is pathological, as told in the pioneering synthesis of Oscar Handlin, *The Uprooted* (1951). His work stresses the devastating psychological effect on aliens of their move to the United States.[1] That emphasis on cultural shock in the transfer, however, was criticized during the 1960s by a new generation of younger historians, some of whom came from particular groups, in a second stage. They generally tell the migration story from a particular, ethnic group, hence pluralistic group perspective. They largely reject the view that the social assimilation of immigrants was seriously dysfunctional.

Most recently, a few practitioners in a third stage covering the last decade have synthesized to some extent the two previous interpretations and perspectives. They have accepted that assimilation had, to some extent, done its work on the groups, but they still recognize the salience of America as a multicultural, multi-ethnic, and multiracial society. Most important of all for this study is their return to a focus of the earliest writers, on individual, psychic behavior.

In particular, with the exploding numbers of new immigrant peoples in recent decades from other parts of the world, the latest observations have extended beyond the experience of European arrivals. Most recently, their view that even the most beleaguered non-Caucasian arrivals also welcomed and accepted Anglo-American norms obviously has been controversial. In any event, these three stages of scholarly study require closer attention.

Handlin's study was a beautifully evocative excursion into the mentality of the migrant beset by the power of a hegemonic, alien culture. A sympathetic portrayal of psychologically injured foreign arrivals, this largely tragic rendering of their suffering was well received by the nostalgic, general reading public.[2]

Later scholars, however, led by Rudolph Vecoli in the early 1960s, rejected Handlin's universal picture of intense mental anguish.[3] While accepting the hard conditions of movement and settlement of these "strangers in the land," these newer historians opposed the Handlinian description of alien masses rapidly assimilating and quickly abandoning their cultural traditions. In their view immigrants were not the naïve, passive objects of cosmic forces but rather actors, assertive people who over several generations preserved and reconstructed, in fact, mediated their changing cultures. This process occurred over several generations, from immigrant arrivals to native-born descendants, their children, and beyond.[4]

With the rise of the "New Ethnicity" in the 1960s, followed by the huge growth of a new nonwhite immigration thereafter and the promotion of and debate over multiculturalism, later reviewers particularly chafed at *The Uprooted*'s Euro-centricity. They contended that, while he purported to cover all peoples in the mass immigration era, Handlin actually simply ignored other incoming streams from all the other parts of the world, especially from Latin America, the Middle East, and Asia.

Indeed, the experience of these nonwhite emigrants to the United States differed markedly from their Euro-American predecessors as recorded in *The*

Uprooted (which did not account for the factor of race). For example, the encounters of the Chinese in America were far more harsh and severe than those of the Scandinavians. By the earliest scholars' omission of race and racial difference, later research indicated that the original assimilation model as described was faulty and woefully inadequate. The newer view highlights the general refusal of all whites, immigrants, and natives to the integration of nonwhites. This most recent recognition in scholarly literature of the 1990s of the unifying consciousness of "whiteness" among *both* natives *and* immigrants spawned a whole new interpretive theory that stresses the European newcomers' wish to identify themselves as having a common racial identity with the Anglo-American majority.[5]

Another position shared by second-stage ethnoculturalists as well as the most recent racialist-minded scholars was that the description of the peasant heartland in *The Uprooted,* even on its own terms, was static and oversimplified. The transfer of people was not one way across the Atlantic but rather part of a larger worldwide movement. It was a massive exodus that included re-emigration of a largely regionally conscious people caused by the intercontinental forces of industrialization, urbanization, and political oppression.[6]

The result of these strictures was an outpouring of particularistic studies concentrating on more-localized group histories along with a few more recent ones that view such peoples comparatively. Yet despite all this half century of disapproval of Handlin's synthesis, a few recent writers in the current third stage paradoxically have not rejected the approach of *The Uprooted* entirely. They have returned to Handlin's focus on the power of the assimilative process in the mental conditioning of immigrants. The shift once again, then, has been to the issue of homogenization of group culture that was on the minds of *individuals.*

This handful of recent observers have demurred from what they have felt was an overemphasis on cultural persistence. One of these third-stage scholars, basing her judgment on her research on Johnstown, Pennsylvania, eastern Europeans and the transformations of small-town Jews in small U.S. towns, is Ewa Morawska. She urges a closer monitoring of exactly how *individual* assimilation has occurred. That kind of review, she asserts, has been heretofore neglected.[7]

A few other studies have begun to narrow the focus on personal and psychological reactions of immigrants, noting a certain homogenization. An important immigrant historian of one trend has dealt with the concept of historical memory, the psychological and tangible ways in which individuals, particularly ethnic-group members, memorialized historical events and personalities. This approach into the mentality of immigrants and their descendants has stressed the ways they may have bound themselves to the group and has introduced the various means for doing so. These were through various forms of festivity, artistic and cultural presentation, and the imagination. That bond thus was not necessarily based on an objective attempt to recapture the true past but was rather the result of subjective feelings influenced by upper-class and governmental efforts to assure national patriotism and loyalty.[8]

Another theme that contributes to exploring the psychic attitude of ethnic-group members is the emphasis placed upon the growth of group pride in America. Works in all stages convey an emerging sense of ethnic nationalism and a heightened homeland consciousness. That greater attachment to the old country the longer they were away obviously was paradoxical. That sense of working harder for group ideals and homeland independence was to some observers a part of their Americanization, rebuilding their country based on U.S. political principles. An outstanding example of this analysis is the work of Matthew Frye Jacobson. Influenced by historian Kirby Miller's depiction of Irish arrivals as exiles rather than mere immigrants, widely conscious of their refugee status from British oppression, Jacobson has also sought to approach the "inner world" of his subjects; in his work Jacobson includes the case of the Irish, the Poles, and eastern European Jews similarly. The emotional term he uses in describing the feelings of members of these three immigrant groups is their developing "special sorrows," that is, a feeling of displacement. Theirs was a lingering sympathy with the homeland that developed into a greater attachment at the very time of their Americanization.

Ironically perhaps, Jacobson readily admits that his portrait of the immigrant mentality is close to Handlin's description of withdrawal and isolation among the aliens.[9] While his study does not cite specifically the older historian's view of a dysfunctional immigrant adjustment, he does assert that nationalist sentiments are a part of that awareness of self. But in any event, even these internal associations individuals made of both homeland and American identities were "sorrows" and thus did not always sit comfortably in their minds.

Jacobson's study is also a model for this work from another standpoint, that is, in its methodological approach, particularly the evidence he uses to show immigrant sentiment. Many of his sources come from and appeal to the imagination. These are in the form of literary and artistic expression, in the written word, in the press, poetry, theater, music, and various types of outdoor festivity, including songs.[10] And as he points out, the public occasion of such demonstrative ceremonies referred to the "political obligations of the emigrant and to his or her place in the broadest tapestry" of the group's national history.[11]

In covering that generally cyclical shift in the literature on the immigrants' conceptualization of their place in America, from an individualistic, assimilationist position to one of group pluralism back to a personal perspective, I wish also to raise the point as to whether the two initial and apparently conflicting approaches, assimilation or pluralism, actually are as dichotomous as they appear.

Both can be situated in the *mind* of the immigrant, as uncomfortable and con-flicting as that condition may be. Any mentality, of course, could include emo-tions that are at odds with each other.

In fact, the entire trend of recent historiography increasingly concentrated on the history of ordinary people has begun to recognize the internal complexity of the human condition. One state-of-the-art review has observed that one of the major advances in historical analysis since the 1960s has been to show the irra-tionality of thought and feeling among people past and present. In a sweeping inventory of historical scholarship that appeared in the early 1980s, the editor of the work, Michael Kammen, quotes other historians who had noted that tran-sition. One, writing over a decade earlier, had trenchantly stated, "'If there is a single way of characterizing what has happened in our historical writing . . . , it must be . . . the rediscovery of complexity in American history: an engaging and moving simplicity . . . has given way to a new awareness of the multiplicity of forces.'" A later, related comment is the assessment of another scholar, "namely, the growing appreciation of *non-rational* elements in man's [and woman's] history and behavior."[12]

The study of the past, then, has come to accept that the human mind is subject to a variety of impulses, both rational and irrational. If we recognize that such in-nermost feelings do not need to be consistent, they can also be contradictory. In addition, a further complication is that that complex mental conditioning need not be static but dynamically changing over time. The immigrant mentality is cer-tainly no different, and again, as I have suggested, while admittedly music does have the property to motivate listeners in a certain direction, such as attacking op-pression and achieving social justice, it (as well as songs that express feeling) can also reflect a psychic morass, elements of which are at odds with each other.

Another distinguished scholar has provided an explanatory theoretical basis for the complexity and pathology of immigrants in particular. Robert K. Merton has suggested that as outsiders, or "others," they suffer from a psychological am-bivalence in contemplating their place in the world. This mental conditioning is a result of what he terms "sociological ambivalence." That feeling is normative but still involves conflicting expectations that society has assigned to individuals. The most obvious examples Merton offers are the varying roles society has placed on members of certain professions, such as doctors, teachers, administrators, and the like. He says that they are similar to marginal figures. Not only are they ex-pected to function appropriately in their professional positions, but they are also expected to have other personal responsibilities that may indeed conflict with or impinge upon their professional duties. It is these varying demands on their time that result in psychological difficulties.[13]

Again, a particularly appropriate example of this sociological and hence psychological ambivalence is found in societies that have substantial numbers of immigrants. Merton's views do, of course, echo the discomfort of the "marginal man" described by the earlier sociologists Robert E. Park and E. V. Stonequist. Like them, Merton too depicts the migrant as one who is forced to live in two different societies and therefore suffers from the pressures of differing values and conflicting demands.[14] He differs from Park and Stonequist, however, by elaborating on the recognized internal distress of the immigrant. Certainly, the songs that here reflect immigrant concerns do show that kind of marginality as well as the complicating pressures and stresses any ordinary person is under.

At this point, it would be appropriate to review broadly those emotional pressures recounted in this work that immigrant songs expose. Certainly the most evident, universal, and least surprising of all the known immigrant songs surveyed among all groups are those sung with lyrics about the departure. In most cases these musical pieces include the motives for leaving. Besides the expressed causes, the reasons expressed are also a listing of both the positive and negative concerns of relatives and friends, especially the reactions of those left behind. The emotional state expressed for most of those about to go off is a mixture of enthusiasm and sorrow. These people undoubtedly held conflicting and even painful feelings about their leaving. Over and over again from almost every emigrant source, one can hear the musical statement lamenting that act of "desertion" or "abandonment" as well as the rationalization for it.

It is extraordinary yet instructive that the most often sung and certainly best-known examples in most groups' song repertoire are similar on the point of conveying a certain reluctance or hesitancy about leaving. Nevertheless, while many songs are alike in that respect, they also express thoughts that are more distinctive. The Swedish "Halsa dem Darhemma" ("Greet the Folks Back Home"), for example, well known and sung by other Scandinavians, dwells nostalgically on missing the natural features of the homeland villages. The Polish "Góralu, Czy ci nie Żal" ("Mountaineer, Are You Not Sad") does the same, and while narrowly referring to a specific place, the Tatra Mountains, it contains an appeal known to all group emigrants. The very famous Irish "Skibbereen" has a decidedly political character, justifying a father's departure and stay abroad on his intended contribution to that land's freedom. The German "Muss I denn zum Städtele N'Aus" ("Must I Go Away from the Town?") is simply an emigrant's intensely personal lament over leaving his lover and ignores the danger of any cultural loss. The Jews' *agune* tradition lamented the damage emigration inflicts on family integrity. The Italians worried over the disruption of gender roles and the confusing language differences. The Chinese stressed the inordinate length of separation and the mistreatment by border officials. The Mexicans, more aware of the obstacles to living in the United States, likely expressed the least enthusiasm for crossing the border and included anti-American heroes in their repertoire, but the prospect of these Latinos earning a better income in the land to the north still remained and was irresistible.

Admittedly, certain other groups produced popular songs that express a rather enthusiastic and positive optimism about leaving their Old World for the benefits of the New. German Forty-Eighters, liberal Europeans, Irish exiles, Italians and Jews who both commended Columbus for his great discovery, and young male and female emigrants were all eager to escape the oppression at home and the burdensome traditional family rules and obligations for a freer life in America. Even the greatest victims of racial prejudice, the Chinese, describing their destination as *Gam Saan* (Gold Mountain), and the Mexicans, both looked forward to gaining great wealth from more-lucrative employment and finding a more stable economic and political order too.

Yet that pervasive optimism about the future was dimmed by a number of hardships emigrants encountered on their journey and particularly after their arrival. These were the abuse and mistreatment of minorities, especially of non-whites, by both individuals and local authorities; the inequity, discrimination, and corruption of the U.S. judicial system; and the excessive materialism and devastation inflicted on traditional cultural practices and gender roles.

Common too among the songs of many groups is the recounting of the difficulties that the newest emigrants, the "greenhorns," encountered upon arrival. Admittedly, their naïveté was the source of derision by both insiders and outsiders. Their innocence as newcomers was a source of lighthearted humor in the hands of ethnic vaudeville entertainers like Farfariello who made fun of their lack of sophistication in a new environment. But he and his counterparts in other groups also conveyed sympathetically the mental and psychic pain of the neophyte's initial adjustment.

A particular burden greenhorns bore may have caused the greatest disappointment and consequent suffering among immigrants in fact as well as in song. That was the weighty burden and responsibility they shouldered trying and occasionally failing to achieve their general goal of earning a sufficient living for both themselves and those left at home. The song repertoires among almost all groups are replete with realizations of the unexpected hardship and arduousness of the work and working conditions immigrants found. Except for the Scandinavians (excluding the Finns), attaining their objective of acquiring enough money from work was surprisingly difficult, whether successful or not. Thus, while many before arriving may have known of the type of work they were expected to do, what they found in addition were long hours and miserable working conditions.

While not expressed clearly in most songs, still commonly felt was a deep dis-appointment in not achieving what they had expected. The immigrants who came held extraordinarily high hopes for reaching their goal of finding freedom and prosperity, but soon enough many discovered that most of their hopes went un-fulfilled. Again, in some cases that deep disillusionment was inchoate in song, but one can better illustrate that frustration in the musical repertoire of two addi-tional ethnic groups. These two are valuable to include, for they existed at extreme opposites in their cultural adjustment in the United States. One had perhaps the easiest experiences in the transition, while the other one of the most difficult. These groups were the non-Irish British and the Japanese.

For example, two members of very different social classes in the former group, coincidentally the American "captain of industry" Andrew Carnegie and the labor leader Samuel Gompers, cited the very same song as influencing their two fami-lies' decision to leave the United Kingdom in the mid-1800s. That British tune heralded the nation across the Atlantic as the land of few restrictions and great opportunity:

> To the West, to the West, to the land of the free,
> Where the mighty Missouri rolls down to the sea,
> Where a man is a man even though he must toil,
> And the poorest may gather the fruits of the soil.
> Where children are blessings and he who hath most
> Has aid for his fortune and riches to boast,
> Where the young men exult and the aged may rest
> Away, far away to the land of the West![15]

That euphoria was similar to the vision of the destination conveyed by a Japanese emigrant song popular a half century later. It refers similarly to their buoyant hopes on the trip eastward. It recalls, in part, "Hawaii, Hawaii, like a dream so I came."[16]

But again, other considerations, such as the potential dangers of travel, ship-wrecks, bad weather, and the uncertainties of success, darkened these optimistic expectations in migration for those groups and the others. The Irish, Finns, Ital-ians, Mexicans, Chinese, Hungarians, and Poles, in particular, found that the work required of them in capitalist America was insecure and exploitative, so to their great dismay the anticipated economic improvement of "fortune and riches" was not assured and far less attainable than they had thought. That same Japanese song itself tells not only of that people's prior hopes but also of their disillusion-ment and misery in their job overseas. It concludes, "But my tears are flowing in the cane fields."[17]

Japanese sugar-cane workers in Hawaii, ca. 1910. Such immigrants were the major source of "*Hole, Hole, Bushi*" work songs in the Hawaiian Islands. (Courtesy Photographic Archives, Bishop Museum, Honolulu.)

The song is a lament of a wife who explains the stress that she, her spouse, and all agricultural workers were under. That burden was not only the physical one of laboring in the cane fields under a scorching sun, in thick dust, and suffering skin lacerations from handling the crop but also an emotional one. That included the burden of homeland responsibilities and a consequent sense of guilt for being away from loved ones. That was the lot of immigrant workers in other groups:

> "Send us money, send us money"
> Is the usual note from home.
> But how can I do it
> In this plight?
> My husband cuts the cane stalks
> And I strip [the sharp, needlelike] leaves
> [So] with sweat and tears we both work
> For our means.[18]

The issue of how to escape such misery for Japanese immigrant women presented them with a dilemma. One unpleasant alternative was to engage in prostitution; another was for both them and their men to find work on the less familiar Ameri-

can mainland; and a third was to give up and return to their homeland and an unknown future. They articulated this dilemma in song.[19] As one collector of these
musical vocals has expressed it, "Their troubled thoughts, aching hearts, and even
self-pity made their lives prosaic and without latitude."[20]

Add to all of these woes the problem for even the most successful, income-
saving immigrants of *all* the groups. One can expect that some may not have found
happiness even after achieving their economic goals. When they returned home,
some encountered a chorus of hostility from those left behind, who on occasion
criticized them for their new, Americanized ways. Even if they remained in the
United States and could bring over some relatives, they still suffered from guilt
about having left. Most always retained that family responsibility to protect the
welfare of those whom they had to leave behind. The Irish, Germans, and other
Europeans in particular rationalized their "desertions" by either promising to return or sending later for families. Even the younger emigrants, who were the most
eager to leave and seek release from Old World rules and duties, still continued
to shoulder them. It is no wonder that their songs and those of other newcomers
in America reflect, at least occasionally, a continued and enhanced malaise of nostalgia and homesickness.

If songs suggest an immigrant mentality in the past that was beset by both
unrealized hopes and duties, one might ask whether newcomers to America living
today, many of whom have fled for safety as refugees from oppressive homelands,
also retain any mixed feelings about leaving old-country habits and ties to their
ancestral past. Does that immigrant dilemma continue to show itself as an enduring inner struggle even when the very lives of contemporary involuntary arrivals
were threatened in their homeland? Some evidence, admittedly fragmentary and
anecdotal, does indeed suggest so.

For example, during the 1975–76 American bicentennial celebrations, an audio-
visual company interviewed what it believed were representative immigrants to
share their transnational experience in the early twentieth century. One of the
more important questions was, having lived so long in America, what connection,
if any, they felt with their native land, if they still identified as group members or
had changed their identity to "Americans."

While appreciative of the greater personal freedom and economic opportunity
one Greek elder found on this side of the Atlantic, he was still ambivalent about
the crossing. He expressed his condition metaphorically, concluding that his heart
was of two parts, each tied to the two countries. "You've got to love them both!"
he concluded. But the response indicates a yet unresolved emotional condition.

In another case in the series, a Russian Jewish woman who had immigrated
about 1911 expressed herself more pessimistically. She bemoaned that while
she had adjusted well materially to the New World, she would always remain

"Russian" in her heart. Americans, she said, lacked any aesthetic feeling and were simply too concerned with money and status.[21]

Those very same expressed American deficiencies were reconfirmed as an enduring conflict in the minds of contemporary immigrants as well a quarter century later. Take, for example, the case of recent Russian Jews who had left the economic and political horrors of the Soviet Union in the 1970s and 1980s. One might think escaping from that land of economic and political repression would have been a relief for those who had suffered materially and emotionally from discrimination. But despite the fact that their homeland during the Cold War and afterward into the twenty-first century continues to struggle mightily to provide an adequate living for its people, these "lucky" refugee-emigrants in America, the richest nation in the world, still seem to be having second thoughts about their move.

Evidence for that distress and the consequent controversy over that feeling erupted when a Russian-language newspaper in Brooklyn, New York, was recently embroiled in an argument among readers stemming from a letter that posed reservations about their life in the United States. The issue, surprisingly, was about whether America or Russia was the more desirable home. While most reacted with other letters that were "passionate paeans" to the New World's principal and richest democracy, a few did express misgivings that even the more enthusiastic may have felt. Outspoken dissenters echoed immigrant dissatisfaction that had been evident in the century past. They "bemoaned [America's] excessive materialism, the emptiness of its conversation . . . , [and its] inelegance" of dress. "Above all they lamented [its] . . . lack of . . . 'dukhovnost,' the spiritual dimension of life." The result was the realization of "a terrible emptiness inside."[22]

One unhappy woman, after six years in the United States, looked back on her coming as a mental dysfunction. It was like the attempted transplantation of "a flower that should live in black earth to sandy soil. It is still alive, but with each day it withers, and finally it stops blooming, and all that remains is a coarse stem."[23] Yet while suffering all that spiritual erosion and being torn psychologically, she ultimately and painfully decided *not* to go back. One might add that the musical evidence of such vocal misgivings among contemporary Middle Eastern and Southeast Asian immigrants reflects a similar pining to return to their roots and homelands.[24]

The immigrant songs, then, have suggested that historically, many others have labored under that same thorny dilemma. If all this is so, what it has meant for foreigners in the United States to be both ethnic and American must include considerable painful as well as hopeful sentiments. A number of other conclusions might be drawn from the ambivalence suggested by these songs and ballads since they question the ease of the Americanization process for immigrants—in fact, for *all* immigrants regardless of race. Musical expression also offers some premonition of how American culture may have affected the world at large now that our way of life has become so much more effectively exported. In any event, the whole process appears to have been, and continues to be, a more difficult one for the recipients than hitherto realized.

Finally, this excursion into song to illuminate the immigrant imagination may offer some greater insight into the current scholarly discussion over "transnationalism," the establishment of international networks of global migrants, a grassroots phenomenon that has become common in the present world. The significance of the global setting of peoples moving across national boundaries has increasingly drawn the attention of social scientists and historians. In a recent presidential address of the Organization of American Historians, a distinguished labor historian urged his listeners to recognize the importance of the mentality of the nation's people, many of whom were migrants traversing paths that led them to new cultures and new lands. Americanists, he emphasized, have until recently been loathe to place their stories in the international or transnational context that they deserve. Their subjects, while locally based both at home and abroad, not only constructed worldwide physical networks but also retained those contacts in an emotional framework. He urged his colleagues to accept the conclusion that "our investigation of America's past . . . must be informed by conceptual frameworks that include and integrate struggle and change at the local, national, and global levels."[25] That appeal should be accompanied with that of other scholars who pointed out that the arts are an avenue to that mentality. "[F]ashion, music, film . . . , visual arts," and hence song, "are some of the most conspicuous areas" of human activity in which the processes of syncretism and hybridization associated with transnationalism take place.[26]

Notes

1. Partisans in the debate over multiculturalism include such critics as Arthur Schlesinger Jr., *The Disuniting of America: Reflections on a Multicultural Society,* rev. ed. (New York: Norton, 1998); and David Hollinger, *Post-Ethnic America: Beyond Multiculturalism* (New York: Basic, 1995). Supporters include Gary Nash et al., *History on Trial: Culture Wars and the Teaching of the Past* (New York: Knopf, 1997).

2. Note the panel discussion concerning Gary Gerstle, "Liberty, Coercion, and the Making of Americans," *Journal of American History* 84 (Sept. 1997): 524–58 (esp. 525n4). See also Mae M. Ngae, "The Architecture of Race in American Immigration Law: A Reexamination of the Immigration Act of 1924," *Journal of American History* 86 (June 1999): 70; and Ewa Morawska, "In Defense of the Assimilation Model," *Journal of American Ethnic History* 13 (Winter 1994): esp. 76.

3. The pioneering article urging this group-by-group grassroots approach is Rudolph Vecoli, "Contadini in Chicago: A Critique of *The Uprooted,*" *Journal of American History* 51 (Dec. 1964): 404–17. I discuss the significance of this work in the context of American immigrant historiography in the conclusion. Gerstle's proper reference criticizing the Eurocentricity of most immigration historians does not invalidate the construction of ethnic associations among nonwhites. Gerstle, "Liberty, Coercion," 536, 548–50. The very existence of Chinatowns and Mexican barrios in U.S. cities harbored a complex of those groups' voluntary associations.

4. At the height of the ethnic revival in the late 1960s and 1970s, one historian did theorize about the degrees of ethnic affiliation, stressing the freedom of choice one has in America. Arthur Mann, *The One and the Many: Reflections on the American Identity* (Chicago: Univ. of Chicago Press, 1979), 169–72.

5. Margie McClain, *A Feeling for Life: Cultural Identity, Community, and the Arts* (Chicago: Urban Traditions, 1988), 12.

6. But while aware of folklife, he does not connect this activity to the immigrants' emotional sentiment. John Bodnar, *The Transplanted: A History of Immigrants in Urban America* (Bloomington: Indiana Univ. Press, 1985), 184–89. Note the absence or minimal reference to expressive culture in such recent standard texts as Maldwyn A. Jones, *American Immigration,* 2d ed. (Chicago: Univ. of Chicago Press, 1992); and Roger Daniels, *Coming to*

America (New York: HarperCollins, 1990); as well as the historiographical reviews of Ewa Morawska, "The Sociology and Historiography of Immigration," in *Immigration Reconsidered: History, Sociology, and Politics,* ed. Virginia Yans-McLaughlin (New York: Oxford Univ. Press, 1990), 187–238; and Russell A. Kazal, "Revisiting Assimilation: The Rise, Fall, and Reappraisal of a Concept in American Ethnic History," *American Historical Review* 100 (Apr. 1995): 437–71. Only Gerstle referred to the aesthetic in reference to the work of Werner Sollors, a literary scholar. "Liberty, Coercion," 541–43.

7. Examples of internal studies are Robert Orsi, *The Madonna of 115th Street: Faith and Community in Italian Harlem, 1880–1950* (New Haven: Yale Univ. Press, 1985), esp. 34; Kathleen Neils Conzen, "Ethnicity as Festive Culture: Nineteenth-Century German Americans on Parade," in *The Invention of Ethnicity,* ed. Werner Sollors (New York: Oxford Univ. Press, 1989), 44–76; and April Schultz, *Ethnicity on Parade: Inventing the Norwegian-American through Celebration* (Amherst: Univ. of Massachusetts Press, 1994), 123, 126, 132.

8. Clifford Geertz, *The Interpretation of Cultures* (New York: Basic, 1977), esp. 451; Victor Turner, *The Anthropology of Performance* (New York: PAJ, 1986), 23–24; Benedict Anderson, *Imagined Communities: Reflections on the Origins and the Spread of Nationalism* (London: Verso, 1983), 47, 49, 129 (where he stresses the "glue" of language). Besides the ethnic historians listed in note 9, some other examples of pioneering works on American festivity are Sean Wilentz, *Chants Democratic: New York City and the Rise of the American Working Class, 1788–1850* (New York: Oxford Univ. Press, 1984); and Susan Davis, *Parades and Power: Street Theatre in Nineteenth Century Philadelphia* (Philadelphia: Temple Univ. Press, 1986), 7, 177–79 nn11, 17 (acknowledging the influence of British historians E.P. Thompson and Eric Hobsbawm, the American folklorist Henry Glassie, and others).

9. Examples are Herbert Gutman, ed., *Work, Culture, and Society in Industrializing America* (New York: Vintage, 1977), 8–9; Kerby Miller, *Emigrants and Exiles: Ireland and the Irish Exodus to North America* (New York: Oxford Univ. Press, 1985); and Sidney Stahl Weinberg, *World of Our Mothers* (Chapel Hill: Univ. of North Carolina Press, 1988).

10. Anthony Seeger, "Whoever We Are Today, We Can Sing You a Song about It," in *Music and Black Ethnicity: The Caribbean and South America,* ed. Gerard H. Béhague (Miami: Univ. of Miami Press, 1994), 3. James P. Leary and Richard March refer to the neglect by *all* scholars. "Farm, Forest, and Factory: Songs of Midwestern Labor," in *Songs about Work: Essays in Occupational Culture for Richard Reuss,* ed. Archie Green (Bloomington: Indiana Univ. Folklore Institute No. 3, 1993), 254.

11. Sandra Blakeslee, "The Mystery of Music: How It Works on the Brain," *New York Times,* May 15, 1995; Susan D. Crafts et al., *My Music* (Middletown, Conn.: Wesleyan Univ. Press, 1993), xv; Charles Keil, "Music in Daily Life: Future Directions" (paper given at the Society of Ethnomusicologists and American Folklore Society joint conference, Milwaukee, Wis., Oct. 21, 1994), 5.

12. Steven Connor, *Postmodern Culture: An Introduction to Theories of the Contemporary* (Oxford: Basil Blackwell, 1989), 9–10, 16; George Lipsitz, *Time Passages: Collective Memory and American Popular Culture* (Minneapolis: Univ. of Minnesota Press, 1990), 134–35.

13. "Introduction: Ethnicity, Identity and Music," in *Ethnicity, Identity, and Music: The Musical Construction of Space,* ed. Martin Stokes (Providence, R.I.: Berg, 1994), 12.

14. Leonard B. Meyer, *Emotion and Meaning in Music* (Chicago: Univ. of Chicago Press, 1956), 261 and following.

15. Malcolm Budd, *Music and the Emotions: The Philosophical Theories* (London: Routledge and Kegan Paul, 1985), 149. Nicholas Tawa refers to that property of immigrant songs

in *A Sound of Strangers: Musical Culture, Acculturation, and the Post–Civil War Ethnic American* (Metuchen, N.J.: Scarecrow, 1982), 78.

16. W. Ray Crozier, "Music and Social Influence," in *The Social Psychology of Music*, ed. Adrian North (Oxford: Oxford Univ. Press, 1997), 74; Gordon C. Bruner III, "Music, Mood, and Marketing," *Journal of Marketing* 54 (Oct. 1990): 94.

17. Owe Ronstrom, "The Musician as Cultural Ethnic Broker," in *To Make the World Safe for Democracy: Towards an Understanding of Multi-Cultural Societies*, ed. Ake Daun et al. (Stockholm: Ethnology Institute, Stockholm Univ. Press, 1992), 163.

18. Anthony D. Smith, *The Ethnic Origins of Nations* (Oxford: Blackwell, 1986), 26, 49. "Music that is ethnic . . . reflects patterns of organization within the group and reveals the ways in which the group understands and maintains its identity." Philip V. Bohlman, "Old World Cultures in North America," in *Excursions in World Music*, ed. Bruno Nettl (Englewood Cliffs, N.J.: Prentice-Hall, 1992), 283.

19. Christopher Small, *Musicking: The Meanings of Performing and Listening* (Hanover, N.H.: Wesleyan Univ. Press, 1998), 185. Small refers also to George Lipsitz's comment in *Time Passages* (1990) that says that audiences in Western industrial societies come together and share "intimate and personal cultural moments with strangers" (39).

20. Theodore Reik, *The Haunting Melody: Psychoanalytical Experiences in Life and Music* (New York: Farrar, Straus, and Young, 1953), 90–91; Andreea Deciu Ritivio, *Yesterday's Self: Nostalgia and the Immigrant Identity* (Landham, Md.: Rowman and Littlefield, 2002), 1–21.

21. Simon Frith, "Towards an Aesthetic of Popular Music," in *Music and Society: The Politics of Composition, Performance, and Reception*, ed. Richard Leppert and Susan McClary (Cambridge: Cambridge Univ. Press, 1987), 140–44. While Frith was speaking about contemporary music, it seems plausible to apply it also to popular music of the past.

22. Reginald Byron, ed., *Music, Culture, and Experience: Selected Papers of John Blacking* (Chicago: Univ. of Chicago Press, 1995), 1.

23. Patricia S. Campbell, *Songs in Their Heads: Music and Its Meaning in Children's Lives* (New York: Oxford Univ. Press, 1998), 168–76.

24. Thomas Bail, "Topicalization and Collective Experience: On the Use of Folk Song as a Historical Source," in *The Press of Labor Migrants in Europe and North America, 1880s to 1930s*, ed. Christine Harzig and Dirk Hoerder (Bremen: Publications of the Labor Newspaper Preservation Project, 1985), 77.

25. Frances Hannett, "The Haunting Lyric: The Personal and Social Significance of American Popular Songs," *Psychoanalytical Quarterly* 33 (Apr. 1964): 237.

26. Anderson, *Imagined Communities*, 129, 132. Note a reference to the salience of political songs among labor socialists in nineteenth-century Germany that "embody symbolism, both literary and musical, that often reveal more about the emotional and intellectual texture of the movement than public speeches, newspaper articles, or party platforms." Vernon Lidtke, *The Alternative Culture: Socialist Labor in Imperial Germany* (New York: Oxford Univ. Press, 1985), 102. See also similar comments on song in other contexts in Laura Mason, *Singing the French Revolution: Popular Culture and Politics* (Ithaca, N.Y.: Cornell Univ. Press, 1996), 213, 220; and Simon P. Newman, *Parades and the Politics of the Street: Festive Culture in the Early American Republic* (Philadelphia: Univ. of Pennsylvania Press, 1997), chap. 5, 152 and throughout.

27. Simon Frith, "Why Do Songs Have Words?" in *Lost in Music: Culture, Style, and Musical Event*, ed. Avron Levine White (London: Routledge, 1987), 78–81.

28. A. L. Lloyd, *Folk Song in England* (New York: International, 1967), 368, 406–7. Note also the support for the methodology by the distinguished English social historian Samuel Raphael in his *Theatres of Memory,* vol. 1, *Past and Present in Contemporary Culture* (London: Verso, 1994), 11–12.

29. Roy Palmer, ed., *A Touch of the Times: Songs of Social Change, 1770–1914* (Baltimore: Penguin, 1974), 10–14, 18.

30. Lidtke, *Alternative Culture,* 102.

31. Alan P. Merriam, *The Anthropology of Music* (Evanston, Ill.: Northwestern Univ. Press, 1964), 190, 205–6.

32. Robert L. Wright, "Scandinavian, German, Irish, English, and Scottish Emigration Songs: Some Comparisons," in *Ballads and Ballad Research: Selected Papers of the International Conference on Nordic and Anglo-American Research . . . ,* ed. Patricia Conroy (Seattle: Univ. of Washington Press, 1978), 260.

33. Eric H. Erickson, *Childhood and Society,* 2d ed. (New York: Norton, 1963), 285–86. See also the long discussion and criticism of the "survivalists" in Stephen Stern, "Ethnic Folklore and the Folklore of Ethnicity," *Western Folklore* 36 (1977): 7–33; Seeger, "Whoever We Are Today," 4–12; and Gerhard Kubik, "Ethnicity, Cultural Identity, and the Psychology of Contact," in *Music and Black Ethnicity: The Caribbean and South America,* ed. Gerard H. Béhague (Miami: Univ. of Miami Press, 1994), 21–23. Anthony Giddens (*The Consequences of Modernity* [Stanford, Calif.: Stanford Univ. Press, 1990], 18–21) sees modernity as causing the wrenching displacement of place.

34. While the English and Scotch immigrants were numerous and possessed a rich musical tradition, other than among Mormons, it seems that few songs concerned their transit to America. James Leary, e-mail to author, Nov. 23, 2001.

35. Maldwyn A. Jones, *Destination America* (New York: Holt, Rinehart, and Winston, 1976), 25–42, 45; Edwin C. Guillet, *The Great Migration: The Atlantic Crossing by Sailing Ship since 1770* (Toronto: Univ. of Toronto Press, 1963), 85–90.

36. Robert Louis Stevenson, *The Amateur Emigrant* (London: Hogarth, 1892), 25, 32. See also observers in later years when ships had performing bands that permitted admission of steerage passengers. Guillet, *Great Migration,* 77; Edward Steiner, *On the Trail of the Immigrant* (New York: Revell, 1906), 43; Stephen Graham, *With the Poor Immigrants to America* (New York: Macmillan, 1914), 9, 34, 38. Music and dancing were apparently common at Ellis Island as well. Philip Taylor, *The Distant Magnet: European Emigration to the United States* (New York: Harper and Row, 1971), 166.

37. The best recent work on the saloon as a social institution is Madelon Powers, *Faces along the Bar: Lore and Order in the Workingman's Saloon, 1870–1920* (Chicago: Univ. of Chicago Press, 1998), 3, 6, 58–64, 191, 205. It is wise to note that saloon goers rather than performers often picked the tunes. Ibid., 205. See also William Kornbluh, *Blue Collar Community* (Chicago: Univ. of Chicago Press, 1974), 75–78; and James Leary, *Wisconsin Patchwork* (Madison: University of Wisconsin–Madison, 1987), 7–8. Leary includes house parties as ethnic venues.

1. The Irish

1. William H. A. Williams, "From Lost Land to Emerald Isle: Ireland and the Irish in American Sheet Music, 1800–1920," *Eire-Ireland* 26 (Spring 1991): 27. See also John Appel

and Selma Appel, *The Distorted Image: Stereotype and Caricature in American Popular Graphics, 1850–1922* (New York: Anti-Defamation League of B'nai B'rith, n.d.), slide 22 (from *Life,* Mar. 4, 1897).

2. John Moulden, comp., *Thousands Are Sailing: A Brief Song History of Irish Emigration* (Portrush, N. Ireland: Ulstersongs, 1994), 3.

3. Arnold Schrier, *Ireland and the American Emigration, 1850–1900* (Minneapolis: Univ. of Minnesota Press, 1958), 93. To avoid any confusion, I must restate that my criteria for song selection is their popularity or representativeness. Hence I include *both* broadsides and sheet music—more of the former as they emanated from the Irish working and peasant classes. Williams reminds us that some broadsides *became* sheet music for a wider audience, including even the middle class. William H. A. Williams, e-mail to author, Sept. 8, 1999.

4. Williams, "Lost Land to Emerald Isle," 23; Robert R. Grimes, *How Shall We Sing in a Foreign Land?: Music of Irish Catholic Immigrants in the Antebellum United States* (Notre Dame, Ind.: Univ. of Notre Dame Press, 1996), 3.

5. The standard work on Irish emigration is Kerby Miller, *Emigrants and Exiles: Ireland and the Irish Exodus to North America* (New York: Oxford Univ. Press, 1985); see esp. 536. For standard explanations of the influence of the potato famine on migration, see Lawrence McCaffrey, *The Irish Diaspora in America* (Bloomington: Indiana Univ. Press, 1975), 61; and Robert Scully, "The Irish and the 'Famine Exodus' of 1847," in *Cambridge Survey of World Migration,* ed. Robin Cohen (Cambridge: Cambridge Univ. Press, 1995), 81.

6. It is appropriate at this point to comment on a regrettable lacuna in recent Irish American historiography that substantiates my point of the continued neglect of songs as evidence of immigrant mentality. A recent general survey of that group's migration suggests that the recognition of Irish American expressive culture, no less than its integration in showing feeling, is still not fully accepted. While the author of this otherwise up-to-date synthesis acknowledges his admiration of the standard work by Kerby Miller, scholar Kevin Kenny still omits Irish immigrant songs that Miller used extensively. Kenny does allude to a related subject, the pervasive, negative stereotype of "Pat and Mike" performed in vaudeville, as well as the creative fiction on the group. But oddly his discussion sees them only as based on the Irish American distinctive penchant for alcohol. See Kenny, *The Irish American: A History* (London: Longman, 2000), 199–204.

A recent and valuable exception to the analyses of Irish American song is Mick Moloney's *Far from the Shamrock Shore: The Story of Irish American Immigration* (New York: Crown, 2002). Moloney is probably the leading authority on Irish American folk and popular song. However, like William Williams's book, his work is aimed at a general audience seeking a comprehensive story with musical stereotypes, commercial songs by non-Irish Tin Pan Alley writers for the American popular stage. We do list a few titles in common but rarely the same lyrics; hence our references lead to distinctive interpretations.

7. McCaffrey, *Irish Diaspora,* 60–68.

8. Moulden, *Thousands Are Sailing,* 6–7. Another version in Moulden substitutes the name "Canada" for "America." Still another version, found in *Delaney's Irish Song Book, No. 2* ([n.p., n.d], 1 in Box 271, Starr Music Collection, Lilly Library, Indiana University), published about the 1880s but popular much earlier, reads, "How sorry I am for to leave this green island / Whose cause I supported, both in peace and in war; / To live here in bondage, I ne'er could be happy, / The green fields of America are sweeter by far." I am grateful to Michael Gordon for this reference.

9. Schrier, *Ireland and the American Emigration,* 24, 42. Economic recessions did make correspondence less glowing.

10. Moulden, *Thousands Are Sailing,* 12–13. Moulden attests to the popularity of the song. John Moulden, e-mail to author, Jan. 16. 1999.

11. Identified by Miller, *Emigrants and Exiles,* 189. The full text is in Robert L. Wright, ed., *Irish Emigrant Ballads and Songs* (Bowling Green, Ohio: Bowling Green Univ. Popular Press, 1975), 177.

12. The several variations of the lyrics in folk tradition suggest its wide popularity. My sources are Edith Fowke, ed., *Traditional Singers and Songs from Ontario* (Hatboro, Pa.: Folklore Associates, 1965), 48–49; and Wright, *Irish Emigrant Ballads and Songs,* 52–63. Other versions and commentary are in Kerby Miller and Paul Wagner, *Out of Ireland: The Story of Irish Emigration to America* (Washington, D.C.: Elliott and Clark, 1994), 32, 107; Robert L. Wright, "Scandinavian, German, Irish Emigration Songs," in *Ballads and Ballad Research,* ed. Patrick Conroy (Seattle: Univ. of Washington Press, 1978), 262; McCaffrey, *Irish Diaspora,* 77; and Jerry Silverman, *Mel Bay Presents Songs of Ireland: 103 Favorite Irish and Irish-American Songs* (Pacific, Mo.: Mel Bay, 1991), 74. Bill Meek suspects that the song may have been composed in America. Meek, ed., *Songs of the Irish in America* (Skerries, Ireland: Gilbert Dalton, 1978), 60. See also the "ache of longing and loss and the bitter sense of exile" in Thomas F. Meager, *Inventing Irish in America: Generation, Class and Ethnic Identity in a New England City* (Notre Dame, Ind.: Univ. of Notre Dame Press, 2001), 30. James Leary lists the entire genre of nostalgic songs about "abandoned" homes among Croatian, Finnish, German, Hmong, Hollander, Italian, Norwegian, Polish, Slovak, Swedish, and Welsh groups in Wisconsin. Leary, "Leaving Skibbereen: Exile and Ethnicity . . . ," in *Wisconsin Folk Art: A Sesquicentennial Celebration,* ed. Robert Teske (Cedarburg, Wis.: Cedarburg Cultural Center, 1997), 49–50.

13. The fullest description and interpretation of the American wake is in Schrier, *Ireland and the American Emigration.* See also (for keening) Grimes, *How Shall We Sing,* 159; and (for the ritual's deep effect on the guilt-ridden exile's psychology) Miller, *Emigrants and Exiles,* 556–68.

14. Harriet Martineau, *Letters from Ireland* (London: John Chapman, 1852), 139–40.

15. From Moulden, *Thousands Are Sailing,* 4. The "tender" was a barge that took emigrants to the ship in the harbor.

16. Most of my information is from Schrier, *Ireland and the American Emigration* (88ff), and is further explained by Miller, *Emigrants and Exiles* (561). Miller stresses the political nature of the majority of these ballads.

17. Miller, *Emigrants and Exiles,* 563.

18. Leon B. Litwack, "The Psychology of Song: Songs and Hymns of Irish Migration," in *Religion and Identity,* ed. Patrick O'Sullivan (London: Leicester Univ. Press, 1996). The keening (wailing) tradition at an Irish wake is fully described in Seán Ó. Súilleabháin, *Irish Wake Amusements* (Cork: Mercier, 1967), 130–45.

19. William H. A. Williams, *'Twas only an Irishman's Dream: The Image of Ireland and the Irish in American Popular Song Lyrics, 1800–1920* (Urbana: Univ. of Illinois Press, 1996), 38.

20. *Delaney's Irish Song Book,* no. 4 (New York: Wm. M. Delaney, n.d.), 21. Dating the song is difficult, but from other pieces in the collection, it likely was known about 1865.

21. Kenneth Peacock, ed., *Songs of the Newfoundland Outports* (Ottawa: National Museum of Canada, 1965), 2:462–63; Wright, *Irish Emigrant Ballads and Songs,* 248–56.

22. From Gale Huntingdon and Lani Herrmann, eds., *Sam Henry's Songs of the People* (Athens: Univ. of Georgia Press, 1990), 190–91. The songs in this collection were taken from *Henry's Weekly* of the early 1920s.

23. Schrier, *Ireland and the American Emigration*, 97.

24. Elizabeth B. Greenleaf and Grace V. Mansfield, *Ballads and Sea Songs of Newfoundland* (Cambridge, Mass.: Harvard Univ. Press, 1933), 195–97.

25. Huntingdon and Herrmann, *Sam Henry's Songs*, 201.

26. Moulden, *Thousands Are Sailing*, 40–41.

27. Greenleaf and Mansfield, *Ballads*, 182–83, 195–97. See also, "My Charming Mary Neal" (1836) in Moulden, *Thousands Are Sailing*, 28. Kerby Miller discusses the horrible conditions on ships before 1840. *Emigrants and Exiles*, 252. The best work on the general subject is Edwin C. Guillet, *The Great Migration: The Atlantic Crossing by Sailing Ship since 1770* (Toronto: Univ. of Toronto Press, 1963), esp. 62. Interestingly, Robert Wright suggests that the ballads exaggerated the actual suffering of the emigrant crossing. *Irish Emigrant Ballads and Songs*, 10. The classic firsthand account of music in steerage is the 1879 crossing of Robert Louis Stevenson in his *The Amateur Emigrant* (London: Hogarth, 1892), 5–39.

28. Schrier, *Ireland and the American Emigration*, 99.

29. Rebecca S. Miller, "Irish Traditional and Popular Music in New York City: Identity and Social Change," in *The New York Irish*, ed. Ronald H. Bayor and Timothy J. Meager (Baltimore, Md.: Johns Hopkins Univ. Press, 1996), 483–84; "From Shore to Shore: Irish Traditional Music in New York City" (flyer for a video documentary) (Truckee, Calif.: Cherry Lane Productions, 1993); Laurence E. McCullough, "Irish Music in Chicago: An Ethnomusicological Study" (Ph.D. diss., University of Pittsburgh, 1978), 181; Michael Allen Gordon, "Studies in Irish and Irish-American Thought and Behavior in Gilded Age New York City" (Ph.D. diss., University of Rochester, 1977), xxvi.

30. Saloons certainly differed in social-class clientele and even in function. Here I am referring to the typical working-class establishments. Madelon Powers, *Faces along the Bar: Lore and Order in the Workingman's Saloon, 1870–1920* (Chicago: Univ. of Chicago Press, 1998), 6–11, 26, 190, 205.

31. These songs were probably initially popular in the late 1850s and early 1860s. Wright, *Irish Emigrant Ballads and Songs*, 523–26, 650–52; Gordon, "Irish and Irish-American Thought and Behavior in Gilded Age New York," xxxiii; Moulden, *Thousands Are Sailing*, 36; *The Variety Theatre Songster* (New York: New York Popular Publishing, [before 1900?]), 57; *Songbook*, no. 4, 22; *Henry De Marsan's New Comic and Sentimental Singers' Journal . . . No. 4* (New York: De Marsan, n.d.), 286. Richard Jensen takes the position, in a much extended and authoritative discussion, that despite their frequent reference to the phrase "No Irish Need Apply," immigrant workers in fact did not suffer much job discrimination. But he adds they did suffer political abuse and did *believe* that "the sign appeared in shops and factories in every large city, forcing them downward into the worst jobs." While he concludes that overall "Irish [American] is an American success story," he also asserts that psychologically the immigrants felt mistreated. Richard Jensen, "H-Ethnic: 'no Irish Need Apply' an urban legend," *H-Ethnic H-Net List* (Mar. 29, 2001).

32. Wright, *Irish Emigrant Ballads and Songs*, 525 (as published by H. De Marsan of New York). Another version is in Edith Fowke and Joe Glazer, *Songs of Work and Protest* (New York: Dover, 1973), 152–53. This evidence and Jensen, "No Irish Need Apply," seem to contradict the assertion of William Brooks that this version was unpopular in America. See William Brooks, "Progress and Protest in the Golden Age: Songs from the Civil War to the

Columbian Exposition," liner notes to *The Hand that Holds the Bread* (New World Record, NW267, 1978), 4. A scholarly disagreement over the pervasiveness of discrimination recently surfaced when another academic disagreed with Jensen over the authenticity of the phrase "no Irish need apply." For her the phrase was common in the late-nineteenth-century American press and represented discrimination that was "blatant" and "a fact of life for many Irish men and women." Maura Doherty, New York University, "No Irish Need Apply," *H-USA H-Net List* (Mar. 27, 2001), posted Mar. 28, 2001.

33. Kathleen O'Neil, "No Irish Need Apply," Item 009, Box 053, Lester Levy Collection of Sheet Music Online Catalog, the Johns Hopkins University, levysheetmusic.mse.jhu.edu, accessed Nov. 2001. Whatever its actual representativeness, the concern over labor exploitation among immigrants might be deduced from the publication of the song's sheet-music cover and a caption provided in Miller and Wagner, *Out of Ireland,* 56.

34. For a comprehensive account, see Norm Cohen, *Long Steel Rail: The Railroad in American Folksong* (Urbana: Univ. of Illinois Press, 1981), 553–59. See also *Songbook,* no. 4, 22; James J. Geller, *Famous Songs and Their Stories* (New York: Macaulay, 1931), 14–15; and Sigmund Spaeth, *A History of Popular Music in America* (New York: Random House, 1948), 244. Prominent New York Irish officials sang the song nostalgically in the early 1900s. E. J. Kahn, *The Merry Partners: The Age and Stage of Harrigan and Hart* (New York: Random House, 1955), 79–80. It was quite common for stage songs to continue folk themes. David Ingle, e-mail to author, February 17, 2000.

35. Cohen, *Long Steel Rail,* 554.

36. John Greenway, *American Folksongs of Protest* (Philadelphia: Univ. of Pennsylvania Press, 1953), 42–43; Greenleaf and Mansfield, *Ballads,* 123–24; McCaffrey, *Irish Diaspora,* 71, 77; David M. Emmons, *The Butte Irish: Class and Ethnicity in an American Mining Town, 1875–1925* (Urbana: Univ. of Illinois Press, 1989), 9, 25–26.

37. *Delaney's Irish Song Book,* no. 2.

38. David Roediger, *The Wages of Whiteness: Race and the Making of the American Working Class* (London: Verso, 1991), esp. 133–56. Robert Toll observes that the Irish were the most prominent minstrel stars of any immigrant group, hence seeking to distance themselves from close association with blacks. Toll, *Blacking Up: The Minstrel Show in Nineteenth Century America* (New York: Oxford Univ. Press, 1974), 175–76. Note too the uncomfortable relationship between both groups as described in Eric Lott, *Love and Theft: Blackface Minstrelsy and the American Working Class* (New York: Oxford Univ. Press, 1993), 95–96.

39. While the popularity of the song is unclear, it still expresses well-known Irish attitudes toward blacks. Lott, *Love and Theft,* 95–96; Silverman, *Songs of Ireland,* 78.

40. See, for example, Kenneth Moss, "St. Patrick's Day Celebrations and the Formation of Irish American Identity, 1845–75," *Journal of Social History* 29 (Fall 1995): 127, 134.

41. Ibid., 141.

42. For example, one of the better-known sponsors was the elitist Friendly Sons of St. Patrick in New York City. Kevin G. Kenny, " Religion and the Rise of Mass Immigration: The Irish Community of New York City, 1815–1840," *New York Irish History* 5 (1990–91): 30. See also Victor Greene, *American Immigrant Leaders, 1800–1910: Marginality and Identity* (Baltimore, Md.: Johns Hopkins Univ. Press, 1987), 19–27; and Moss, "St. Patrick's Day," 135–36.

43. Wayland D. Hand et al., "Songs of the Butte Miner," *Western Folklore* 9 (Jan. 1950): 7; Grimes, *How Shall We Sing,* 167.

44. *Delaney's Irish Songbook, No. 4,* 20.

45. Full lyrics are in Silverman, *Songs of Ireland,* 74. Its representativeness is shown in Wright, *Irish Emigrant Ballads and Songs,* 442–45.

46. Ellen Steckert, liner notes, *Songs of a New York Lumberjack,* ed. Kenneth S. Goldstein (Folkways Record, FA 2354, 1958).

47. Thomas N. Brown, *Irish-American Nationalism, 1870–1890* (Philadelphia: Lippincott, 1966), 24. Note Lawrence J. McCaffrey's reference to Irish Americans' "yearning for respectability" as their aim in the nineteenth and early twentieth centuries. McCaffrey, *The Irish Catholic Diaspora in America* (Washington, D.C.: Catholic Univ. Press, 1997), 171.

2. The Germans

1. John Jentz, Marquette University, e-mail to author, Jan. 31, 2000.

2. Walter D. Kamphoefner et al., eds., *News from the Land of Freedom: German Immigrants Write Home* (Ithaca, N.Y.: Cornell Univ. Press, 1991), 12. This source stresses the surprisingly large number of early-nineteenth-century arrivals who settled in cities. But those destinations might have been merely way stations for their ultimate goal of obtaining farmland in America.

3. John Jentz, e-mail to author, Jan. 31, 2000; Kathleen Conzen, "Ethnicity and Musical Culture among the Sauk, 1854–1920," in *Land without Nightingales: Music in the Making of German-America,* ed. Philip V. Bohlman and Otto Holzapfel (Madison, Wis.: Kade Institute, 2002), 36–39.

4. Lutz Rohrich, "German Emigrant Songs," in *Eagle in the New World: German Immigration to Texas and America,* ed. Theodore Gish and Richard Spuler (College Station: Texas A&M Univ. Press, 1986), 47.

5. Philip V. Bohlman, "Religious Music/Secular Music: The Press of the German American Church and Aesthetic Medium," in *The German American Press,* ed. Henry Geitz (Madison, Wis.: Max Kade Institute for German American Studies, 1992), 71.

6. Rohrich, "German Emigrant Songs"; Lutz Rohrich, "Auswandererschicksal in Lied," in *Der Grosse: Studien zur Amerika aus Wanderung,* ed. Peter Assion (Marburg, Germany: Jonas, 1985), esp. 102–5; Günther Moltmann, "German Emigrant Songs: The Politics and Images of Two Worlds, Old and New" (a paper in the author's possession, ca. 1990), 121; Moltmann, "Roots in Germany: Immigration and Acculturation of German-Americans," in *Eagle in the New World,* ed. Theodore Gish and Richard Spuler, 16.

7. A. B. Faust, *The German Element in the United States . . .* (New York: Steuben Society, 1927), 255. See also Edward C. Wolf, "Two Divergent Traditions of German-American Hymnody . . . ," *American Music* 3 (Fall 1985): 300–301; and Robert Rutherford Drummond, *Early German Music in Philadelphia* (New York: D. Appleton, 1910), 24.

8. Moltmann, "German Emigrant Songs," 116.

9. Ibid., 119.

10. Ibid., 118.

11. "Muss I denn zum Städtele N'Aus?" ("Must I Go Away from the Town?"), arranged by William Dressler and English translation by M. Barrett (Boston: Oliver Ditson [copyrighted by J. L. Peters], 1868). Copy in Box 233, Samuel De Vincent Collection, Smithsonian Institute, Washington, D.C.

12. Moltmann, "German Emigrant Songs, 122.

13. Ibid., 122–24.

14. Rohrich, "German Emigrant Songs," 65–66; Moltmann, "German Emigrant Songs," 118.

15. While these lyrics likely did attract emigrants, it is difficult to believe Lutz Rohrich's conclusion that they were taken as seriously as he claims. Rohrich, "German Emigrant Songs," 66–67. See also Moltmann, "German Emigrant Songs," 118.

16. Moltmann, "German Emigrant Songs, " 128–33.

17. Rohrich, "German Emigrant Songs," 52–53 (emphasis added). Moltmann states that later turn-of-the-century versions were less provocative. Moltmann, "German Emigrant Songs," 126.

18. Louis Pinck, *Verklingende Weisen: Lothringer Volksleider* (Metz: Lothringer Verlag, 1926), 159, 161.

19. Otto Holzapfel, "Lieder Deutscher Auswanderer: Ein Beitrag zur 200-Jahr-Feier der USA," *Bremisches Jahrbuch* 54 (1976): 17–18.

20. *Der Corner Grocer aus der Avenue A,* English text by John J. MacIntyre, in John Koegel, "Klein Deutschland: Adolph Philipp and German-American Musical Theatre in Turn-of-the-Century New York" (paper given at the Sonneck Society Meeting, Madison, Wis., Apr. 7, 1995).

21. William A. Owens, *Tell Me a Story, Sing Me a Song: A Texas Chronicle* (Austin: Univ. of Texas Press, 1983), 198–99.

22. Quoted without title in Michael Pupin, *From Immigrant to Inventor* (New York: Scribner, 1925), 35–36.

23. Leo Schelbert, "Glimpses of Ethnic Mentality: Six German Swiss Texts of Migration Related Folk Songs," in "Land without Nightingales: The Musical Culture of German Americans," ed. Philip Bohlman and Otto Holzapfel (manuscript in the author's possession), 148–49 and throughout. I am grateful to Philip Bohlman for his assistance.

24. Ibid., 165–69.

25. Rohrich, "Auswandererschicksal," 102–5.

26. Moltmann, "German Emigrant Songs," 121; Owens, *Tell Me a Story,* 199. Leo Schelbert refers to similar negative Swiss songs known as *Amerikalied.* Schelbert, "Glimpses of Ethnic Mentality," 163–64. See the general comment on *Bänkellieder,* or *Bänkelsgesangen,* in Rohrich, "Auswanderschicksal," 104–6, 108.

27. Rohrich, "Auswanderschicksal," 104–6, 108.

28. Note the conclusion in Moltmann, "Roots in Germany," 16.

29. James P. Leary and Richard March refer to spontaneous home singing among a German American farming family in 1870s Wisconsin. Leary and March, *Down Home Dairyland: A Listener's Guide* (Madison: Wisconsin Arts Board, 1996), 40. Kathleen Neils Conzen dwells on the group's unique or distinctive ethnic character in festivity. Conzen, "Ethnicity as Festive Culture: Nineteenth-Century German Americans on Parade," in *The Invention of Ethnicity,* ed. Werner Sollors (New York: Oxford Univ. Press, 1989), 48. And Heike Bungert is working on a study of ethnic festivals. Heike Bungert, University of Cologne, interview by author, Milwaukee, Wis., Oct. 5, 1999.

30. Madelon Powers, *Faces along the Bar: Lore and Order in the Workingman's Saloon, 1870–1920* (Chicago: Univ. of Chicago Press, 1998), esp. 3–11.

31. Note these upscale saloons in nationwide German colonies. See Klaus Ensslen, "German-American Working-Class Saloons in Chicago: The Social Function in an Ethnic and Class-Specific Cultural Context," in *German Workers' Culture in the United States,* ed.

Hartmut Keil (Washington, D.C.: Smithsonian Institution Press, 1988), 173–74; Stanley Nadel, *Little Germany: Ethnicity, Religion, and Class in New York City, 1845–1880* (Urbana: Univ. of Illinois Press, 1990), 104–7; Theodore Miller, "Milwaukee's German Cultural Heritage," *Milwaukee History* 10 (Autumn 1987): 96–99, 102; Philip Martin, liner notes to *Ach Ya!: Traditional German-American Music from Wisconsin* (Dodgeville, Wis.: Folklore Village Farm, 1985); Perry Duis, *The Saloon: Public Drinking in Chicago and Boston* (Urbana: Univ. of Illinois Press, 1983), 153–54; Royal Melendy, "The Saloon in Chicago," *American Journal of Sociology* 6 (Nov. 1900): 298–305; William F. Betterton, "Early Choral Groups," *Palimpsest* 45 (June 1964): 283; Lota M. Spell, "The Early German Contribution to Music in Texas," *American-German Review* 12 (Apr. 1946): 10; and Martha Fornell and Earl W. Fornell, "A Century of German Songs in Texas," *American-German Review* 24 (Oct.–Nov. 1957): 29.

32. Alan R. Burdette, "Ein Prosit der Gemütlichkeit: Heightened Experience and the Creation of Context in a German American Singing Society" (master's thesis, Indiana University, 1993), 5; Conzen, "Ethnicity as Festive Culture," 48–53.

33. This is also the conclusion of Heike Bungert. Bungert interview, Oct. 5, 1999.

34. Heike Bungert, e-mail to author, June 28, 2000. I am referring here to the formal German theater. German American clubs and *vereine* did often put on lighter-weight skits for entertainment. Unfortunately, evidence of this sort awaits further research.

35. Maxine Schwartz Seller, ed., *Ethnic Theater in the United States* (Westport, Conn.: Greenwood, 1983), 8.

36. Henry Marx, "Adolph Phillipp (1864–1936)," in *Germanica-Americana, 1976,* ed. Erich A. Albrecht and J. Anthony Burzle (Lawrence, Kans.: Max Kade Document and Research Center, 1976), 43–44; Philipp obituary, *New York Times,* July 31, 1936, 19.

37. Peter Conolly-Smith, "'Ersatz-Drama' and Ethnic (Self-)Parody: Adolph Philipp and the Decline of New York's German Language State, 1893–1918," in *Multilingual America: Transnationalism, Ethnicity, and the Languages of American Literature,* ed. Werner Sollors (New York: New York Univ. Press, 1998), 215–19. Philipp referred to the "greenhorns'" Dutch-English speech as "pidgin English." He modeled his musical comedies on the enormously popular vaudeville skits of Edward "Ned" Harrigan; one ran over eighteen hundred consecutive nights in Berlin. See "Ausverkauft is the Sign Every Night Where the German George Cohan Plays," *The (New York) World,* Mar. 2, 1913, M2; John Koegel, "Adolph Philipp," in *The New Grove Dictionary of American Music,* ed. H. Wiley Hitchcock and Stanley Sadie, 4 vols. (London: Macmillan, 1986), 3:556; and James L. Ford, "The German Stage in America," *Bookman* 20 (Nov. 1898): 242.

38. Conolly-Smith, "'Ersatz-Drama,'" 219.

39. Charles Hamm, *Yesterdays: Popular Song in America* (New York: Norton, 1979), 189. Others, without elaboration, also allude to this genre as enjoyed by later-generation German Americans. See Leary and March, *Downhome Dairyland,* 40; and Martin, liner notes to *Ach Ya!* If so, the criticism must have added to the immigrants' already uncomfortable psychic condition. Adolph Philipp, "A Remarkable Triple Identity," *The New York Dramatic Mirror* 74 (Nov. 20, 1915): 1.

40. Koegel, "Klein Deutschland."

41. Irving Paul Babow, "Secular Singing Societies of European Immigrant Groups in San Francisco," (Ph.D. diss., University of California, 1954), 236. Babow carefully asserts that his is only a local study, but other saengerfest programs and community singing suggest that his conclusions can be far more generally applied.

42. Irenaeus Stevenson, "The Sängerfest in Philadelphia," *Harper's Weekly* 41 (1897): 667; LaVern J. Rippley, *The German Americans* (Boston: Twayne, 1986), 133.

43. Hamm, *Yesterdays,* 189–191, 194. While Babow states that the singing societies almost exclusively offered folk songs, he later indicates that German and Austrian ensembles included works by their major eighteenth- and nineteenth-century classical composers. Babow, "Secular Singing Societies," 236, 292–94.

44. The only exception to this was a rare rendering from the *Heimat* genre. See *Souvenir, 15 Sängerfestes des Sängerbundes des Nordwesterns . . . Am 8 . . . 12 Juli, 1891 . . . Milwaukee, Wisconsin* (Milwaukee, 1891), 43–45; Germania Club, *Yearbook and Historical Review* (Chicago, 1940), 28–34; *Festordnung und Textbuch der New England Staaten für das Erste Saengerfest, Providence, Rhode Island, 26–30 Juni, 1866* (Providence, 1866); and Betterton, "Early Choral Groups," 287. For further corroboration regarding that song mixture, see Mary Sue Morrow, "Somewhere between Beer and Wagner: The Cultural and Musical Impact of German Männerchore in New York and New Orleans," in *Music and Culture in America, 1861–1918,* ed. Morrow (New York: Garland, 1998), 93; Suzanne G. Snyder, "The Indiana Männerchor: Contributions to a New Musicality in Midwestern Life," ibid., 114–18; *1853–1903 zur Erinnerung an das 50-jährige Jubilaum des Buffalo Sängerbund, den 19, 20, und 21 April 1903* (Buffalo, 1903), 8; *Baltimore and the Saengerfest. Official Program and Souvenir . . .* (Baltimore: Saengerfest Association, 1902 [1903]), app. 5; and a New York saengerfest reviewed in *The Song Messenger of the Northwest* 3 (Aug. 1865), 1.

45. "'I Remember,' by John E. Etterman, 'The Arion Society's Songs, Beer, and Friendship,'" Arion Singing Society File, Pratt Free Library, Baltimore.

46. "A Great Anniversary," *Baltimore Sun,* Oct. 1, 1880, 1. In 1890 Baltimore had 104,112 German-speaking residents, the tenth largest concentration in the country and one-quarter of the city's total population.

47. *Proceedings of the Maryland Historical Society . . . 150th Anniversary of the Settlement of Baltimore* (Baltimore: n.p. 1880), 57–78, 74.

48. *Fest Chore für die 20th National Sängerfest des Nordostlichen Sängerbundes* (New York, 1903), Germans in Baltimore File, Maryland Historical Society, Baltimore. See also *Baltimore and the Saengerfest. Official Program and Souvenir,* esp. app. 5. For other examples elsewhere of the dual role of *saengervereine* in combining traditional German and patriotic American songs on U.S. holidays, see *Festordnung und Textbuch der New England Staaten,* n.p.; William F. Betterton, "The Saengerfest of 1898," *Palimpsest* 45 (June 1964): 298; Rippley, *The German-Americans,* 132; Philip Bohlman, e-mail to author, Aug. 25, 1999; Fornell, "A Century of German Song," 29–30; *German Club of Chicago,* 23; David G. Detzen, *The Germans in Missouri, 1900–1918: Prohibition, Neutrality, and Assimilation* (Columbia: Univ. of Missouri Press, 1985), 132–33; and Judith B. Sorge, *San Antonio on Parade* (College Station: Texas A&M Press, 2003), ch. 6.

49. Quoted in Ann Bakajian Reagan, "Art Music in Milwaukee in the Late Nineteenth Century, 1850–1900" (Ph.D. diss., University of Wisconsin, Madison, 1980), 81.

50. Dieter Cunz, *The Maryland Germans: A History* (Princeton: Princeton Univ. Press, 1948), 246; Babow. "Secular Singing Societies," 238; Charles H. Meigel, "The Singing Germans of Baltimore," *Baltimore Sun,* Mar. 13, 1936, Germans in Baltimore File, Pratt Free Library, Baltimore; Stone, "Mid–19th Century American Beliefs in the Social Values of Music," 46.

51. Lidtke, *The Alternative Culture,* 102–5, 112, 114, 127, 135. Note the similar importance of singing societies in German American lives in Petra Lehmann, "Songs of the German

American Labor Movement," in *Land without Nightingales: The Musical Culture of German Americans,* ed. Philip Bohlman and Otto Holzapfel (manuscript in the author's possession), 407.

52. Lehmann, "Songs of the German American Labor Movement," 394.

53. Dieter Dowe, "The Workingman's Choral Movement in Germany before the First World War," *Journal of Contemporary History* 13 (Apr. 1978): 275, 289.

54. A similar group in New Orleans was less wealthy and included upper-class workers, but it also later developed elite pretensions. Morrow, "Somewhere between Beer and Wagner," 83–84. The Baltimore Männerchor grew similarly after its founding in 1856. Meigel, "Singing Germans." Note especially the uptown move and gentrification of two major New York societies. Peter J. D. Conolly-Smith, "The Translated Community: New York City's German-Language Press as Agent of Cultural Resistance and Integration, 1910–1918" (Ph.D. diss., Yale University, 1996), 63; Nadel, *Little Germany,* 114; and Foster, "Liederkrantz," 11.

55. Christine Heiss, "German Radicals in Industrial America: The Lehr- and Wehr-Verein in Gilded Age Chicago," in *German Workers in Industrial Chicago, 1850–1910,* ed. Hartmut Keil and John Jentz (DeKalb: Northern Illinois Univ. Press, 1983), 206–9, 213–14, 219–20.

56. From *Fackel,* June 3, 1883, quoted in Lehmann, "Songs of the German American Labor Movement," 17.

57. From *Fackel,* Apr. 1, 1883, quoted ibid., 25.

58. By 1890 two-thirds of all German Americans in the city were of working-class households. Ibid., 4, 17.

59. Heinz Ickstadt, "German Workers' Literature in Chicago—Old Forms in New Contexts," in *German Workers Culture in the United States,* ed. Hartmut Keil (Washington, D.C.: Smithsonian Institution Press, 1988), 214; Klaus Ensslen and Heinz Ickstadt, "German Working-Class Culture in Chicago: Continuity and Change in the Decade from 1900–1910," ibid., 237–45.

60. The particular source is the letters of Christian Kirst of Pittsburgh to his brothers, sisters, and daughter in Zusch, dated November 29, 1881, in Kamphoefner, *News from the Land of Freedom,* 471–74. His letter summarizes in most respects the ambivalence of others, such as farmers Wilhelm Stille (69–70, 72, 75, 85, 86, 88–89) and Christian Lenz (124, 126, 134) and workers Johann Carl Wilhelm Pritzlaff (305–7, 314), Martin Weitz (342–43, 347), Matthias Dorgathen (438, 425), and Ludwig Ditler (494, 498, 500). Ibid.

3. The Scandinavians and Finns

1. I follow the definition in Dorothy Burton Skardal, *The Divided Heart: Scandinavian Immigrant Experience through Literary Sources* (Lincoln: Univ. of Nebraska Press, 1974), 16–17. She excludes Icelanders and Finns; however, I refer to these two groups for reasons stated later in the chapter.

2. Rochelle Wright and Robert L. Wright, *Danish Emigrant Ballads and Songs* (Carbondale: Southern Illinois Univ. Press, 1983), 11; Anne-Charlotte Harvey, e-mail to author, April 6, 2000.

3. Jon Gjerde, *From Peasants to Farmers: The Migration from Balestrand, Norway, to the Upper Midwest* (New York: Cambridge Univ. Press, 1985), 116.

4. The term is commonly used in the literature. See Gjerde, *From Peasants to Farmers,* 116–17; and Albin Widen, "Scandinavian Folklore and Immigrant Ballads," *Bulletin of the American Institute of Swedish Arts, Literature, and Science* 2 (Jan.–Mar. 1947): 9.

5. Martin B. Ruud, "Norwegian Emigrant Songs," *Studies and Records* 2 (1927): 2–3.

6. Ibid., 123–25. Ruud indicates the attractiveness of American farming to Norwegians, while Ulf Beijbom indicates the same for Swedes. Beijbom, "Swedes," in Stephen Thernstrom, et al., eds., *Harvard Encyclopedia of American Ethnic Groups* (Cambridge: Harvard Univ. Press, 1980), 972.

7. Theodore C. Blegen and Martin B. Ruud, eds. and trans., *Norwegian Emigrant Songs and Ballads* (Minneapolis: Univ. of Minnesota Press, 1936), 7.

8. Ibid., 341–43. A slightly different version is in Ruud, "Norwegian Emigrant Songs," 4–5.

9. Basically from a translation of Skardal, *Divided Heart,* 273; and liner notes, *From Sweden to America: Emigrant-och immigrantvisor / Emigrant and Immigrant Songs,* record CAP 2011 (House of Emigrants, Växjo, Sweden: Caprice, n.d.). Some corrections made by Anne-Charlotte Harvey, e-mail communication to the author, Apr. 4, 2000. The song was in the oral tradition until collected by a folklorist in 1898. Anne Charlotte Harvey, *Return to Snoose Boulevard,* record Sp224 (Minneapolis: Olle I Skratthult Project, 1972). Other literary media refer to Sweden's "somber forests, snow-mantled peaks." Skardal, *Divided Heart,* 266.

10. Quoted in Ruud, "Norwegian Emigrant Songs," 4. Note also "The Emigrant's Lament" (1855), ibid., 15. On Rynning and his song, see also Theodore C. Blegen, *Norwegian Migration to America, 1825–1860* (Northfield, Minn.: Norwegian American Historical Association, 1931), 308–9.

11. Wright and Wright, *Danish Emigrant Ballads and Songs,* 10.

12. Quoted in Widen, "Scandinavian Folklore and Immigrant Ballads," 8.

13. Blegen and Ruud, *Norwegian Emigrant Songs and Ballads,* 187. For a thorough coverage of both the supportive and highly critical songs that came out of the Oleana experiment, see Hal Rammel, *Nowhere in America: The Big Rock Candy Mountain and Other Comic Utopias* (Champaign: Univ. of Illinois Press, 1996), 20. Rammel also offers a fascinating placement of this music in the European folk tradition of the "Poor Man's Paradise" and the role of America as utopia. See ibid., 12–15, 18–21.

14. Ruud, "Norwegian Emigrant Songs," 11–13.

15. Ibid., 14.

16. Einar Haugen, "Norwegian Emigrant Songs and Ballads," *Journal of American Folk-Lore* 51 (Jan.–Mar. 1938): 74–75.

17. The popularity of this song and "Vi sålde våra hemman (We Sold Our Homesteads)" are attested to by Robert L. Wright, *Swedish Emigrant Ballads* (Lincoln: Univ. of Nebraska Press, 1965), 19.

18. E. Gustav Johnson, "A Swedish Emigrant Ballad," *Scandinavian Studies* 20 (Nov. 1948): 196–97. Because he suffers so on the voyage, Johnson eventually gives up his quest at Castle Garden and returns home to Sweden, according to the quoted and reproduced song in Wright, *Swedish Emigrant Ballads,* 109.

19. A facsimile of the broadside with the original song text as published in Jan Jansson, *Utrag ur twenn* (Christinehamn, Sweden: Norman, 1854), is reproduced in Harvey, liner notes, *From Sweden to America,* 12. The English translation is in Widen, "Scandinavian

Folklore and Immigrant Ballads," 14–18. I am deeply grateful to Annike Holm of Milwaukee for her linguistic assistance.

20. Harvey, liner notes, *From Sweden to America,* 21. For more complete descriptions, see Anne-Charlotte Harvey, liner notes, *Memories of Snoose Boulevard: Songs of the Scandinavian Americans,* record Sp-223 (Minneapolis: Olle I Skratthult Project, 1972), 1.

21. Skardal, *Divided Heart,* 263–64, 314.

22. Quoted in Alan Swanson, *Literature and the Immigrant Community: The Case of Arthur Landfors* (Carbondale: Univ. of Southern Illinois Press, 1990), 50–52. See also Beijbom, "Swedes," 978.

23. Quoted in Carl G. Norman, *Emigratens sånger* (Emigrant Songbook) (Chicago: Excelsior, 1914), 11–13. A similar translation is in Nils Hasselmo, "Language in Exile," in *The Swedish Immigrant Community in Transition* (Rock Island, Ill.: Augustana Historical Society, 1963), 126.

24. From Theodore C. Grame, *America's Ethnic Music* (Tarpon Springs, Fla.: Cultural Maintenance Associates, 1976), 55–56.

25. Robert J. Buchkoe, in "Olle I Skratthult: Marquette Gem: Musical Treasure," *Marquette (Mich.) Monthly* 127 (May 1998), uses "anthem" in reference to the song "Hälsa dem Därhemma (Greet Those at Home)" for the Swedes, but it can be used for all three songs.

26. Harvey, liner notes, *Memories of Snoose Boulevard.*

27. I used the translation in Wright, *Swedish Emigrant Ballads,* 138–39.

28. Harvey, liner notes, *From Sweden to America,* 23.

29. Ibid. The spontaneous enthusiasm of the audience singing along with Harvey at the Snoose Boulevard Festival is obvious on the record.

30. Note also part of the appeal of the play and later musical was the "classic Swedish *nature* scenes" (emphasis added). Lars Furuland, "From Värmländingarne to Slavarna på Molokstorp: Swedish-American Ethnic Theatre in Chicago," in *Swedish-American Life in Chicago: Cultural Aspects of an Immigrant People, 1850–1930,* ed. Philip J. Anderson and Dag Blanck (Urbana: Univ. of Illinois Press, 1992), 139–41, 147.

31. Anne-Charlotte Harvey, "Swedish American Theatre," in *Ethnic Theater in the United States,* ed. Maxine Schwartz Seller (Westport, Conn.: Greenwood, 1983), 505–8.

32. See the many examples recorded by Peterson in Richard K. Spottswood's immense discography *Ethnic Music on Records,* 7 vols. (Champaign: Univ. of Illinois Press, 1990), 5:2715–18.

33. For more detail on the origins and activities of Peterson and the popularity of "Nikolina," see Victor Greene, *A Passion for Polka: Old Time Ethnic Music in America* (Berkeley: Univ. of California Press, 1992), 94–97.

34. Harvey, "Holy Yumpin' Yiminy: Scandinavian Immigrant Stereotypes in the Early Twentieth Century," in *Approaches to the American Musical,* ed., Robert Lawson-Peebles (Exeter: Exeter Univ. Press, 1996), 57.

35. Harvey, "My Name Is Yon Yonson, I Come from Wisconsin: Swedish American Types on the American Stage and Their Function in Assimilation/Ethnicization" (paper presented at Conference on Immigrant Cultures and Performing Arts, University of Minnesota, Mar. 1996), esp. 19–20. See also Maxine Schwartz Seller, ed., *Ethnic Theater in the United States* (Westport, Conn.: Greenwood, 1983), 8 (omitting the empathy for greenhorns).

36. A good example of a well-known immigrant song that satirizes the Swedish American dialect is Carl Bruce's "I Been a Swede from North Dakota" (ca. 1904). The English lyrics are in Harvey, liner notes, *From Sweden to America*, 14.

37. Kristin Hvidt, *Flight to America: The Social Background of 300,000 Danish Emigrants* (New York: Academic, 1975), 169–70; Dorothy Barton Skardal, "Danes," in Thernstrom, *Harvard Encyclopedia*, 281.

38. Wright and Wright, *Danish Emigrant Ballads and Songs*, 30–31.

39. Ibid., 193–96.

40. Ibid., 40–41.

41. Taken from William Hoglund, "Finns," in Thernstrom, *Harvard Encyclopedia*, 363–69.

42. Juha Niemela, "The Finnish American Musical Tradition," *Finnish Americana* (ca. 1990): 4 (offprint provided to the author). I am deeply grateful for Niemela's assistance and generosity.

43. Ibid., 14.

44. Blegen, *Norwegian Migration*, 312–13; Blegen and Ruud, *Norwegian Emigrant Songs*, 9. The principal labor leader in Norway was imprisoned around midcentury for urging workers to solve their economic problems by emigrating. Halvdan Koht, *The American Spirit in Europe: A Survey of Transatlantic Influences* (Philadelphia: Univ. of Pennsylvania Press, 1949), 74–75.

45. Aili Kolehmainen Johnson, "Finnish Labor Songs from Northern Michigan," *Michigan History* 31 (Sept. 1947): 332–33.

46. Hoglund, "Finns," 367.

47. While I cannot list the exact date of all the following songs, it is plausible to assume they represent the mentality of many workers around World War I, given not only the general class consciousness of Finnish workers but especially the bitter labor relations in the copper-mining country of the Upper Peninsula at that time. Note, for example, the songbook *Proletaarilauluja*, published in 1918 in Duluth; "Kaivantomiehen laulu" ("The Pitman's Song") of 1909; and "Kaukea tapaturma Kaivannossa" ("Terrible Accident in the Mine") of 1899, all in Simo Westerholm, comp. *Reisaavaisen laulu Ameriikkaan: Surtolais lauluja* (*The Traveler's Song in America*) (Kaustinen, Finland: Kansan musiikki-instituuti, 1983), 21, 27–28 (trans. Ivy Nevala and Juha Niemela). Note that early songsters of the temperance movement among the Finns supported the labor cause, for they included some of its songs. Juha Niemela, e-mail to author, Sept. 18, 1997.

48. Johnson, "Finnish Labor Songs," 338; William Hoglund, *Finnish Immigrants in America, 1880–1920* (Madison: Univ. of Wisconsin Press, 1960), 35.

49. Johnson, "Finnish Labor Songs," 339.

50. Niemela, " Finnish American Musical Tradition," 14.

51. Niemela e-mail, Sept. 18, 1997.

52. Westerholm, *Reisaavaisen*, 84. The song was likely extremely popular in the late 1920s. While Kylander was popular after 1922, I would contend that his compositions still reflected the group's working-class mentality.

53. Ibid., 65, 95, "Tiskarin Polkka," from the Columbia record 3169F, 1927.

54. From Juha Niemela, e-mail to author, Sept. 18, 1997, Jan. 28, 2000.

55. From Westerholm, *Reisaavasen*, 76–77.

56. Hoglund, *Finnish Immigrants*, 25–26.

57. Under the domination of the Swedes for most of the nineteenth century, the Norwegians and Finns, like the Germans, developed a strong male choral-singing-society movement that blossomed in the United States with nationalist songs. See Odd S. Lovoll, *A Century of Urban Life: The Norwegians in Chicago before 1930* (Urbana: Univ. of Illinois Press, 1988), especially 136, 253–55, 276–68, 307–8; Carl Hansen, "Northern Music in America, II. Norwegian," *American-Scandinavian Review* (Jan.–Feb. 1916): 42–43; and J. R. Christiansen, "The Urbanization of Immigrant Peasants: Can Music Help?" (paper presented at Immigration History Research Center Conference, University of Minnesota, 1996), 7–11. Christiansen dates the beginnings of these societies as early as the 1850s.

4. The Eastern European Jews

1. Compare a recent work that stresses the familiar reason that Jews felt empathy with other persecuted minorities because of their own persecution. Michael Alexander, *Jazz Age Jews* (Princeton: Princeton Univ. Press, 2001).

2. Arthur A. Goren, "Jews," in Thernstrom, *Harvard Encyclopedia*, 579.

3. For example, see Ruth Rubin, ed., *A Treasury of Jewish Folksong* (New York: Schocken, 1950); Rubin, *Voices of a People: The Story of Yiddish Folksong*, 2d ed. (New York: McGraw-Hill: 1973); Chana Gordon Mlotek, *Mir Trogn A Gezang!* 4th ed. (New York: Workmen's Circle, 1987); Jerry Silverman, comp., *The Yiddish Song Book* (New York: Stein and Day, 1983); Fred Somkin, "Zion's Harp by the East River: Jewish-American Popular Songs," *Perspectives in American History* 2 (1985): 183–220; Mark Slobin, *Tenement Songs: The Popular Music of Jewish Immigrants* (Urbana: Univ. of Illinois Press, 1982); and Irene Heskes, *Yiddish American Popular Songs, 1895–1950: A Catalog Based on the Lawrence Marwick Roster of Copyright Entries* (Washington, D.C.: Library of Congress, 1992).

4. Slobin, *Tenement Songs*, 123. See also Slobin's reluctance to generalize in ibid., 25. He does refer to a category, "The Family Tie," and a focus on "mother," though as a general theme among all American Jews rather than (as I see it) one that is distinctly Yiddish American. Ibid., 124–25.

5. Sol Gittleman, "Review of Lawrence H. Fuchs, *Beyond Patriarchy: Jewish Fathers and Families*," *H-Ethnic, H-Net Reviews*, May 2001, http://www.h-net.msu.edu/reviews/showrev.cgi?path=60591014227803.

6. Nathan Ausubel, ed., *A Treasury of Jewish Folklore: Stories, Traditions, Legends, Humor, Wisdom, and Folk Songs of the Jewish People* (New York: Crown, 1948), 653. Ausubel does refer to Palestinian songs that were sung by Zionists. Note the song distinction made between European and American Zionism in Slobin, *Tenement Songs*, 139–40.

7. He was referring specifically to sheet music. Slobin, *Tenement Songs*, 155.

8. Heskes, *Yiddish American Popular Songs*, xxiii; Slobin, *Tenement Songs*, 120.

9. A. Z. Idelsohn, *Thesaurus of Hebrew Oriental Melodies: The Folk Song of the East European Jews*, 10 vols. (Leipzig: Hofmeister, 1933), 9:x.

10. This is a modal pattern characterized by notes fluctuating quickly between both major and minor chords. For a fuller musical explanation, see Heskes, *Yiddish American Popular Songs*, xxiii.

11. Henry Sapoznik, *The Compleat Klezmer* (Cedarhurst, N.Y.: Tara, 1987), 8.

12. The most authoritative account appears to be Eleanor Gordon Mlotek, "America in East European Yiddish Folklore," in *The Field of Yiddish: Studies in Yiddish Language, Folklore, Literature,* ed. Uriel Weinreich (New York: Columbia Univ. Press, 1954), 181 and throughout.

13. See, for example, Reena Sigman Friedman, "Send Me My Husband Who Is in New York City: Husband Desertion in the American Jewish Immigrant Community, 1900–1926," *Jewish Social Studies* 44 (Winter 1982): 1, 4 (who states desertion was "a fact of life for numerous Jewish families" in the early 1900s); and Lloyd Fidkis, "Desertion in the American Jewish Family: The Work of the National Desertion Bureau in Cooperation with the Industrial Removal Office," *American Jewish History* 71 (Dec. 1981): 299.

14. From a 1913 Yiddish variation published in Warsaw and reprinted (among others) in Mlotek, "America," 181 and throughout. Note also Rubin, *Voices of a People,* 342, 344; and Rubin, "Yiddish Folksongs of Immigration and the Melting Pot," *New York Folklore Quarterly* 17 (Autumn 1951): 174–75

15. Charlotte Baum, Paula Hyman, and Sonya Michel, *The Jewish Woman in America* (New York: Dial, 1976), 116–18.

16. Mlotek, "America," 185. For the music and a variant, see Ruth Rubin, "Sholem Aleichem and Yiddish Folksongs," *Sing Out!* 9 (Winter 1959–60): 21–23.

17. Konrad Bercovici, *Around the World in New York* (New York: Century, 1924), 88, 93. See also Richard F. Shepherd and Vicki Gold Levi, *Live and Be Well: A Celebration of Yiddish Culture in America from the First Immigrants to the Second World War* (New York: Ballantine, 1982), 113; and Victor Greene, *A Passion for Polka: Old Time Ethnic Music in America* (Berkeley: Univ. of California Press, 1992), 62.

18. An excellent description and reminiscence of these Jewish "watering holes" is S. L. Blumenson, "Culture on Rutgers Square: The Fervent Days on East Broadway," *Commentary* 10 (July 1950): 65–74.

19. From a song by Gerson Rosenzweig in *Mesekheth Amerika* in Zosa Szajkowski, *An Illustrated Sourcebook of Russian Anti-Semitism* (New York: Ktav, 1980), 1:216. Note other work celebrating America by Louis Friedsell, "Yankeleh" (1904), which refers to the original exodus, "Moses led us out of Egyptian slavery. Here in America we are free," and "America" (1904) by Louis Gilrod and David Meyerowitz. Heskes, *Yiddish American Popular Songs,* 28.

20. Song 173, in Szajkowski, *An Illustrated Songbook,* vol. 2.

21. Both "Leben Zol Columbus" and "Mayn America" are dated in Heskes, *Yiddish American Popular Songs,* 103, 124. The Museum of Jewish Heritage of New York provided the author with a good translation of Rosenfeld's "Mayn America."

22. Slobin, *Tenement Songs,* 155.

23. Mlotek, *Mir Trogn,* 140–41.

24. Mario Maffi, *Gateway to the Promised Land: Ethnic Cultures of New York's Lower East Side* (New York: New York Univ. Press, 1995), 230–31. Some standard works are, among others, Nahma Sandrow, *Vagabond Stars: A World History of the Yiddish Theater* (New York: Harper and Row, 1977); and Irving Howe, *The World of Our Fathers* (New York: Harcourt, Brace, and Jovanovich, 1977), 460 and throughout.

25. Howe, *The World of Our Fathers,* 469.

26. Ibid., 484.

27. Reported in Sandrow, *Vagabond Stars,* 158.

28. Maffi, *Gateway,* 231.

29. Sandrow, *Vagabond Stars,* 116–23.

30. It was an *emigrant* drama, for the tragedy of the mother's passing justifies the hero's leaving Europe without any sense of guilt. Ibid., 116–23. Note also the synopsis of the plot in Maffi, *Gateway,* 232.

31. Heskes, *Yiddish American Popular Songs,* xxx, 69, 83, 192; Mlotek, "America," 191. Note the popularity of "A Brivele fun Rusland" in Ewa Morawska, "Changing Images of the Old Country in the Development of Ethnic Identity among East European Immigrants, 1880s–1930s: A Comparison of Jewish and Slavic Representatives," *Yivo Annual* 21 (1993): 280.

32. Heskes, *Yiddish American Popular Songs,* xxx, xxxii, 40; Slobin, *Tenement Songs,* 124.

33. Quoted from A. Z. Idelson, "The Folk Song of the East European Jews," *Thesaurus of Hebrew Oriental Melodies,* 10 vols. (Berlin: B. Harz, 1923–32), 119 (song 428); and Ausubel, *Treasury of Jewish Folklore,* 677–78, as cited in Mlotek, "America," 192.

34. Mlotek, "America," 192. See also Norman H. Warembud, comp., *Great Songs of the Yiddish Theater* (New York: J. and J. Kammen Music, 1875), 26–29. I am grateful to Paul Melrood for his translation.

35. S. L. Blumenson, "At the Tables Down at Schreibers: The Golden Age of Thomashefsky," *Commentary* 13 (Apr. 1952): 347.

36. Richard K. Spottswood, *Ethnic Music on Records: A Discography of Ethnic Recordings Produced in the United States, 1893 to 1941,* 7 vols. (Champaign: Univ. of Illinois Press, 1990), 3:1527.

37. Solomon Shmulewitz, "Ellis Island" (Hebrew Publishing, 1914). Songsheet in File 49, Box 5, Yiddish Song Collection, Yivo Archives, New York. Mark Slobin omits the second stanza, which dwells on the effect of immigrant rejection on the family. *Tenement Songs,* 155–56.

38. Liner notes, *Golden Land,* GL1001 (Warner Bros. Music, 1986); Chana and Joseph Mlotek, *Songs of Generations: New Pearls of Yiddish Songs* (New York: Workmen's Circle, 1990), 209.

39. Baum, Hyman, and Michel, *Jewish Women in America,* 74–75.

40. Aaron Kramer, "Four Yiddish Proletarian Poets: IV Poems of Joseph Borshover," *Jewish Life* 4 (Aug. 1950): 14–15. See also Rubin, *Treasury of Jewish Folksong,* 110–11.

41. For more information on Edelshtadt, see Aaron Kramer, "Four Yiddish Proletarian Poets: III Poems of David Edelshtadt," *Jewish Life* 4 (July 1950): 12–13; Howe, *World,* 420; and Howard Sachar, *A History of the Jews in America* (New York: Knopf, 1994), 207.

42. Howe, *World,* 421.

43. Aaron Kramer, "Four Yiddish Proletarian Poets: II Poems of Morris Rosenfeld," *Jewish Life* 4 (June 1950): 16–17; Paul Manseau, "Morris Rosenfeld," *Pakn Treger* 30 (Spring 1999): 42–44; Hutchins Hapgood, *The Spirit of the Ghetto,* ed. Moses Rischin (Cambridge: Harvard Univ. Press, 1967), 105.

44. Morris Rosenfeld, *The Teardrop Millionaire and Other Poems,* trans. Aaron Kramer (New York: Emma Lazarus Clubs of Manhattan, 1955), 5, 7, 9; Manseau, "Rosenfeld," 42–43. For a slightly different wording, see Rubin, "Yiddish Folksongs of Immigration," 178–79.

45. This translation is from a combination of sources; Rosenfeld, *Teardrop Millionaire,* 16–17; Pete Seeger and Bob Reiser, *Carry It On! A History in Song and Picture of the Work-*

ingmen and Women in America (New York: Simon and Schuster, 1985), 48–49; Morris Rosenfeld, *Songs of the Ghetto* (Upper Saddle River, N.J.: Literature House, 1976), 10–13 (1898 translation by Leo Wiener).

46. Aaron Kramer, "Four Yiddish Proletarian Poets: Poems of Morris Rosenfeld," 18; Rosenfeld, *Teardrop Millionaire*, 13.

47. For a review of these and other labor songs, see Slobin, *Tenement Songs*, 158–63.

48. Chana Mlotek to author, Mar. 21, 1996. Mlotek verifies Leiserowitz as the writer, but Prizant and Abe Schwartz are listed as lyricist and music composer in one copyright. The song's origins and its many variations are clarified in Henry Sapoznik, *Klezmer: Jewish Music from Old World to Our World* (New York: Schirmer, 1999), 99. The melody is from a Yiddish folksong. Note also "Who Wrote the Greeneh Kuzeenah?" *Jewish Daily Forward*, June 14, [?] (translated by Paul Melrood). Note also Norman H. Warembud, comp., *The New York Times Great Songs of the Yiddish Theater* (New York: Quadrangle, 1975), 45. See the entry for Leiserowitz in *Lexicon Fun Der Nayer Yidisher Literatur*, 8 vols. (New York: Altveltlekn Yidishn Kultur Kongres, 1963), 5:130.

49. Jerry Silverman, *Mel Bay's Immigrant Songbook* (Pacific, Mo.: Mel Bay, 1992), 220; Mlotek, *Mir Trogn*, 142–43; Warembud, *Great Songs of the Yiddish Theater*, 45; promotional appeal, Folder 114, Box 9, Yiddish Song Collection, Yivo Archives. Oddly, Mark Slobin omits the song in his work.

50. Sapoznik, *Klezmer*, 99–100. Sapoznik also suggests that "Di Grine Kusine" might have been a parody, a view I would challenge.

51. Mlotek, "America," 190. This translation is one of many versions by Chana Mlotek that she took from the A. Litvin Collection of the Yivo Institute. While citing the work in her article, Mlotek gives no indication of the song's central importance in the Jewish American repertoire, though she did so in her later work, *Mir Trogn*.

52. Heskes, *Yiddish American Popular Songs*, xxix, 181, 189–91. For some odd reason, Heskes refers to it as a "happy" tune. Spottswood, *Ethnic Music*, 3:1328, 1348, 1352, 1356, 1357, 1448, 1458, 1481.

53. Lebedeff's popularity and significance is noted in Mark Slobin, "Klezmer Music: An American Genre," *Yearbook for Traditional Music* 16 (1984): 36–37. See also Greene, *Passion for Polka*, 101–8.

54. Jonathan D. Sarna, "The Myth of No Return: Jewish Return Migration to Eastern Europe, 1881–1914," *American Jewish History* 71 (Dec. 1981): 256–67.

5. The Italians

1. John E. Zucchi, *The Little Slaves of the Harp: Italian Child Street Musicians in Nineteenth Century Paris, London, and New York* (Montreal: McGill-Queen's Univ. Press, 1992), 20–21.

2. The most convenient summaries are Humbert Nelli, "Italians," in Thernstrom, *Harvard Encyclopedia*, 545ff; Nelli, *From Immigrants to Ethnics: The Italian Americans* (New York: Oxford Univ. Press, 1983), esp. 19–18; and Rudolph Vecoli, "The Italian Diaspora, 1876–1976," in *The Cambridge Survey of World Migration*, ed. Robin Cohen (Cambridge: Cambridge Univ. Press, 1995), 114–22.

3. Luisa Del Guidice, ed., *Italian Traditional Song*, 2d ed. (Los Angeles: Istituto Italiano di Cultura, 1995), 3–4, 11, 45, 61. For the popularity of singing at both work and leisure,

see Luisa Del Guidice, "Italian Traditional Song in Toronto: From Autobiography to Advocacy," *Journal of Canadian Studies/Revue d'Etudes Canadiennes* 29 (Spring 1994): 84.

4. The reason for the neglect of scholars is likely the traditional mainstream indifference to this lower-class culture. This is especially true for the Italians. Note Del Guidice, *Italian Traditional Song,* 6; and liner notes of Anna L. Chairetakis, ed., *Calabria Bella, Dove T'hai Lasciate?* FES 34042 (New York: Folkways Records, 1979).

5. There were, for example, about one thousand performers on the streets of New York City in 1870. Zucchi, *Little Slaves of the Harp,* 20–23, 33–35, 39–40. See also Robert F. Foerster, *The Italian Emigration of Our Times* (Cambridge, Mass.: Harvard Univ. Press, 1919), 102–3.

6. Roberto Leydi, "Mama mia, dammi cento lire," in *Le Tradizioni Popolare in Italia: Canti e musiche popolari* (Milan, Italy: Electa, 1990), 115. Translations by Maria Bernocchi.

7. Regina D'Ariano and Roy D'Ariano, *Italo-American Ballads, Poems, Lyrics, and Melodies* (Parsons, W.Va.: McClain, 1976), xi.

8. Carla Bianco, *The Two Rosetos* (Bloomington: Indiana Univ. Press, 1979), 35–36.

9. Ibid., 36–37.

10. D'Ariano and D'Ariano, *Italo-American Ballads,* 157–59.

11. Ibid., 213–15, 220–22.

12. Bianco, *Two Rosetos,* 38–39.

13. Ibid., 38.

14. There appears to be a discrepancy in the texts of the work as provided in several translations. See Del Guidice, *Italian Traditional Song,* 68–71; Bianco, *Two Rosetos,* 37–38; and Leydi, "Mama Mia, dammi cento lire," *Revista Pirelli* 11–12 (1970): 158.

15. Leydi, "Mama Mia," *Revista Pirelli* 159.

16. Ibid.

17. Ibid.

18. Chairetakis, liner notes, *Calabria Bella.*

19. These verses are from "Le Canzoni degli emigranti," in Del Guidice, *Italian Traditional Song,* 71–73.

20. Leydi, "Mama mia," *Le Tradizione,* 114.

21. Bianco, *Two Rosetos,* 45.

22. The concept of "domus," the extended family home, was central to immigrant life. Robert Orsi, *The Madonna of 115th Street: Faith and Community in Italian Harlem, 1880–1950* (New Haven, Conn.: Yale Univ. Press, 1985), 24.

23. Bianco, *Two Rosetos,* 46–47 (emphasis added).

24. James P. Leary and Richard March, "Farm, Forest, and Factory: Songs of Midwestern Labor," in *Songs about Work: Essays in Occupational Culture for Richard A. Reuss,* ed. Archie Green (Bloomington: Indiana Univ. Press, 1993), 278.

25. Note the attention that is given to the matter in Michael La Sorte, *La Merica: Images of Italian Greenhorn Experience* (Philadelphia, Pa.: Temple Univ. Press, 1985), 159 and throughout. The problem for new arrivals in trying to express themselves is not unique to Italians and is the subject of study by many sociolinguists. But the topic still draws the attention of students of Italian immigrant adjustment. La Sorte offers a full explanation of the stages of development of the immigrant argot, from a regional dialect to an American immigrant speech, so it is unnecessary to review the process here.

26. Ibid., 159–67.

27. Ibid., 162.

28. Bianco, *Two Rosetos,* 39. Bianco says the song could have originated in America.

29. D'Ariano and D'Ariano, *Italo-American Ballads,* 81–84. The song was also popular in Campania in southern Italy.

30. Broughton Brandenburg, *Imported Americans: The Story of the Experiences of a Disguised American and His Wife Studying the Immigrant Question* (New York: Stokes, 1903), 175, 198–99.

31. Donna R. Gabaccia, *From Sicily to Elizabeth Street* (Albany: SUNY–Albany Press, 1984), 97.

32. Caroline Singer, "An Italian Sunday," *Century Magazine* 101 (Mar. 1921): 592.

33. For a description of the colorful neighborhood on the Lower East Side, see Konrad Bercovici, *Around the World in New York City* (New York: Century, 1924), 129.

34. Deanna Paoli Gumina, "Connazionali, Stenterello, and Farfariello: Italian Variety in San Francisco," *California Historical Quarterly* 54 (Spring 1975): 30; Salvatore Primeggia and Joseph A. Varacalli, "Southern Italian Comedy: Old to New World," in *Italian Americans in Transition,* ed. Joseph V. Scelsa et al. (New York: Center for Migration Studies, 1990), 245.

35. Emelise Aleandri, "The Italian American Theatre," in *Ethnic Theater in the United States,* ed. Maxine Schwartz Seller (Westport, Conn.: Greenwood, 1983), 240, 256–57.

36. Ibid., 253; Gumina, "Connazionali," 27–36; La Sorte, *La Merica,* 172; Primeggia and Varacalli, "Southern Italian Comedy," 141–42; Anna Maria Martellone, "The Formation of an Italian American Identity Through Popular Theatre," in *Multilingual America: Transnationalism, Ethnicity, and the Languages of American Literature,* ed. Werner Sollors (New York: New York Univ. Press, 1998), 240–42.

37. Primeggia and Varacalli, "Southern Italian Comedy," 243

38. A. Richard Sogliuzzo, "Notes for a History of Italian American Theatre in New York," *Theatre Survey* 14 (Nov. 1973), 60–62.

39. Ibid., 68.

40. I am deeply grateful to Nancy Carnevale for providing me with sections of her recent dissertation, "Living in Translation: Language and Italian Immigration in the United States, 1890–1945" (Ph.D. diss., Rutgers University, 2000). As is obvious, my observations here are heavily indebted to her research and her translations of Migliaccio's repertoire.

41. Del Guidice, "Italian Traditional Song in Toronto," 80.

42. Carnevale, "Living in Translation," 141.

43. Ibid., 141–43. For the complete texts, see Emelese Aleandri, "A History of Italian American Theatre, 1900–1919" (Ph.D. diss., New York University, 1984), 456, 458–59, 468–69. The popularity of "A Lengua 'Taliana" may be indicated by its becoming a Victor recording. While that did not happen until 1928, it is almost certain that Migliaccio performed the song earlier. See Richard K. Spottswood, *Ethnic Music on Records: A Discography of Ethnic Recordings Produced in the United States, 1893 to 1941,* 7 vols. (Champaign: Univ. of Illinois Press, 1990), 1:462.

44. Carnevale, "Living in Translation," 147.

45. Using other song examples, Carnevale admits that men also gain from this linguistic confusion, but women are the chief beneficiaries. Ibid., 149.

46. Aleandri, "Italian American Theatre," 468–69; "Lu Cafone Che Ragiona" ("The Peasant Clown Who Reasons"), in *Images: A Pictorial History of Italian Americans* (Staten Island, N.Y.: Center for Migration Studies, 1981), 136 (translation by Maria

Christina Bernocchi, Aug. 9, 2000). This very popular song was published in 1910 and recorded in New York on Victor in July 1916, according to Spottswood, *Ethnic Music,* 1:459.

47. Aleandri, "Italian American Theatre," 481; Spottswood, *Ethnic Music,* 1:459.

48. Unfortunately, the song, written by Frank Amodio and published by "E. Rossi," a well-known Italian bookstore owner on the Lower East Side, has no copyright date. But it is likely that the song appeared in the 1920s or early 1930s since Rossi's major activity was in that era. The interwar period was a time when Italian nationalism was reaching its peak in the United States, and the price of the song sheet was well within the reach of the ordinary worker. Lawrence Baldassaro, conversation with the author, June 4, 2001. Maria Bernocchi assisted with the translation.

6. The Poles and Hungarians

1. I would contend that the acronym used for these little-known, "silent" immigrants and their descendents, "PIGS" (Poles, Italians, Greeks, and Slavs) by Slovak American Michael Novak still exists as a negative stereotype in the minds of many non–East European Americans. Novak, *The Rise of the Unmeltable Ethnics: The New Political Force of the Seventies* (New York: Macmillan, 1972), 52–53. That image of a blue-collar *lumpenproletariat* remains.

2. John J. Bukowczyk, *And My Children Did Not Know Me: A History of the Polish Americans* (Bloomington: Indiana Univ. Press, 1987). Another succinct survey is James S. Pula, *Polish Americans: An Ethnic Community* (New York: Twayne, 1995). For the inclusion of eastern Europeans in an outstanding synthesis, see John Bodnar, *The Transplanted: A History of Immigrants in Urban America* (Bloomington: Indiana Univ. Press, 1987). For a similarly excellent work by a sociologist, see Ewa Morawska, *For Bread with Butter: The Life-worlds of East Central Europeans in Johnstown, Pennsylvania, 1890–1940* (New York: Cambridge Univ. Press, 1985).

3. See Leon T. Blaszczyk, "The Polish Singers' Movement in America," *Polish American Studies* 38 (Spring 1981): 51–53. This was probably true in the Polish German area of Poznania. Paula Savaglio, "Polka Bands and Choral Groups: The Musical Self-representation of Polish Americans in Detroit," *Ethnomusicology* 40 (Winter 1966): 37.

4. Stanislaus A. Blejwas, "Choral Nationalism: A History of the Polish Singers' Alliance in America, 1889–1999" (manuscript in author's possession), 11. I am grateful to Stanislaus Blejwas for supplying me with a copy of his unpublished manuscript.

5. Waclaw Kruszka, *A History of the Poles in America: A General History of the Polish Immigration in America,* pt. 1, ed. James S. Pula, trans. Krystyna Jankowska (Washington, D.C.: Catholic Univ. Press, 1993), 232–34.

6. Blaszczyk, "Polish Singers' Movement," 59; Blejwas, "Choral Nationalism," 11.

7. Blejwas shows that gratitude at a celebration put on by St. Paul–area Polish parishes on the group's constitution day in 1899. Blejwas, "Choral Nationalism," 143.

8. Polonia is the Polish American community. On the significance of these statues in creating a Polish American identity, see Victor Greene, *Immigrant Leaders: Marginality and Identity* (Baltimore, Md.: Johns Hopkins Univ. Press, 1987), 106, 114–16, 121, 142; and Pula, *Polish Americans,* 2, 59. A similar symbol of the transformation for Hungarian Americans is the 1902 Cleveland statue for their nationalist hero, Lajos Kossuth, *with song.* See

Zoltan Fejos, "Three Faces of the National Hero Statues of Kossuth in the United States," *The Hungarian Quarterly* 40 (Winter 1999): 108–12.

9. Morawska, *For Bread with Butter,* 67, 71. See also the comment of an observer of the motivation of Russian Poles, Wladydslaw Orkan, *Listy Ze Wsi* (*Letters from the Village*), 2 vols. (Warszawa: Gebethnera and Wolff, 1925), 1:119–20.

10. Wincenty Witos, *Moje Wspomnienia* (*My Memoirs*) (Paris: Institut Literacki, 1964), 187–88.

11. Pula, *Polish Americans,* 18.

12. Note the tripartite social distinctions made between German Poles at the top and Galician (Austrian) Poles at the bottom in ibid., 22. For the appeal of individual freedom, especially to women, see Thaddeus C. Radzialowski, " Family, Women and Gender: The Polish Experience," in *Polish Americans and Their History: Community, Culture, and Politics,* ed. John J. Bukowczyk (Pittsburgh: Univ. of Pittsburgh Press, 1996), 68.

13. Witold Kula et al., comp. *Writing Home: Immigrants in Brazil and the United States, 1890–1891,* trans. Josephine Witulich (New York: Columbia Univ. Press, 1986), passim. Most came from the Russian sector near the Prussian border. Two later memoirs apparently describe the ship passage as more upsetting, especially due to storms and seasickness; but that concern too was mixed with and contributed to their uncertainty about achieving their goal. *Pamiętniki Emigrantów, Stany Zjednoczone,* 2 vols. (Warszawa: Kiazka i Wiedza, 1977), 1:80, 286.

14. Most of the song expresses the emigrant's painful departure, involving much prayer, weeping, and an aching heart over leaving his homeland. He takes the train to Hamburg and onboard ship there he fears he will drown, a death made worse as he will not have the proper religious rites. To his relief, his fervent prayers to the Holy Virgin are answered as he does arrive safely in New York. But the anxiety remains as he enters that strange city, desperately seeking relatives. From Jonas Balys, ed., *Lietuvi Dainos Amerikoje: Pasakojamosios Dainos ir Baladas* (*Lithuanian Folksongs in America: Narrative Songs and Ballads*) (Boston: Lithuanian Encyclopedia, 1958), xxv, 190–91, 294. I am grateful to Rev. William Wolkovich for his help in translation.

15. *Pamiętniki Emigrantów,* 2:414.

16. Quoted in Morawska, *For Bread with Butter,* 78.

17. Quoted in ibid., 77–78.

18. Ibid., 68, 72.

19. Thaddeus Gromada, e-mail to author, June 29, 1999. See also Gromada, "The Tatra Eagle: A Source for the Study of Goral Immigration," *Tatranski Orzeł* (*The Tatran Eagle*) 51 (1998–94): 2; and Gromada, "Polish Tatra Highlander Folk Music and Dance Ensembles in America," *Tatranski Orzeł* (*The Tatran Eagle*) 48 (Spring 1995): 6.

20. Gromada e-mail, June 29, 1999. "Góralu, Czy ci nie Żal" appears to have been sung on both sides of the Atlantic, as was a similar piece, "Zrobił Góral Krzyż Na Czole," which was recorded in Chicago in October 1974. See Richard K. Spottswood, liner notes, *Folk Music in America: Songs of Migration and Immigration,* LBC 6, (1977), 6:6–7, cited in Deborah Anders Silverman, *Polish American Folklore* (Urbana: Univ. of Illinois Press, 2000), 111–12.

21. *Pamiętniki Emigrantów,* 1:136.

22. Orkan, *Listy,* 122.

23. One song that I hesitate offering as evidence is "Jak Jechałem z Ameryki" ("When I Journeyed from America") because I cannot confirm its date any more precisely than

pre–World War II. It was known in the 1930s in northern New Jersey and Detroit and thus may simply have been a response to the Great Depression rather than a commentary on life in the early years of mass immigration. It is the lament of a foundry worker who after three years finally returns to his home and family around Kraków. But the reception is painful as a result of his long absence, for his children consider him a stranger and flee. Harrier Pawlowska, ed., *Merrily We Sing* (Detroit, Mich.: Wayne State Univ. Press, 1983), xxii–xxiii, 154–55. See also Bukowczyk, *My Children Did Not Know Me,* v.

24. The song is fully described and analyzed in Waclaw Kruszka, *A History of the Poles in America to 1908,* ed. James Pula, trans. Krystyna Jankowski (Washington, D.C.: Catholic Univ. of America Press, 1993), 303–5. Its importance is supported in A. Bartosz, "65 Lat Służ by Dla Polonia (65 Years Service for Polonia)," in *(Stevens Point, Wis.) Gwiazda Polarna,* Paż dziernika [Oct.] 27, 1973; and Karen Majewski, letter to the author, Orchard Lake, Mich., Jan. 28, 1997 (who refers to the evaluation of Francis Bolek in *Who's Who in America* [New York: Harbinger House, 1939]).

25. Translation from Karen Majewski, e-mail to the author, Jan. 7, 1997.

26. The *kuplet* as an informal, narrative song of humor and satire is not precisely the same as the strophic couplet in English. I shall therefore use the Polish term here to recognize the difference. See the discussion in Barbara Szydłowska-Ceglowa and Wojciech Chojnacki, *Polski Wujek Sam: Kuplety Polski w Ameryce (Polish Uncle Sam: Polish* Kuplety *in America)* (Warszawa: Polonia, 1989), 29–32, 42.

27. The *kuplety* were often written by actors or performers who sold their compositions in the various cabarets and vaudeville theaters in which they performed. Mary Cygan, "Inventing Polonia: Notions of Polish American Identity, 1870–1990," *Prospects: An Annual of American Cultural Studies* 23 (1998): 224.

28. Barbara Szydłowska-Ceglowa, letter to author, June 20, 1996.

29. Szydłowska-Ceglowa and Chojnacki, *Polski Wujek Sam,* 41.

30. Ibid., 41–42.

31. Ibid., 36–37. I acknowledge with appreciation the translation assistance of Dr. Basia Kowalska of Lublin, Poland. There is undoubtedly a bias in this collection in favor of the songs from the large industrial cities especially the number that had to do with life in Chicago. But the emphasis is justifiable as I will explain below.

32. Ibid.

33. Ibid., 36–37, 168–69.

34. Ibid., 149.

35. From a 1909 publication in the satirical journal *Bicz Bozy* (The Divine Whip), with similar criticisms in 1915. "I Jeszcze Coś" ("One More Thing") and "Tuzin 'Wielkości' Amerykanskich" ("A Thousand American Majorities"), in Szydłowska-Ceglowa and Chojnacki, *Polski Wujek Sam,* 58, 142–43, 249–52.

36. Ibid., 101–3. This song was most popular around World War I.

37. Pawlowska, *Merrily We Sing,* 157–58.

38. From a collection published in the mid-1920s in Milwaukee. Note too the discussion and compare the male complaint over the new female self-confidence in Szydłowska-Ceglowa and Chojnacki with the spirited song of the young women traveling Chicago and Ohio in 1905 "to service . . . matrimony" and "a fine life." Szydłowska-Ceglowa and Chojnacki, *Polski Wujek Sam,* 34–35, 213–14; Edward Steiner, *On the Trail of the Immigrant* (New York: Revell, 1906), 44.

39. The word refers to a bench in front of an old-country cottage where people would engage in conversation. Szydłowska-Ceglowa and Chojnacki, *Polski Wujek Sam*, 70.

40. A "basic survival orientation" and "a positive wish," according to Ewa Morawska; a "peasant fatalism, reinforced by a dolorous . . . Polish Roman Catholism," according to John Bukowczyk. I am basing my synthesis here on the succinct review in Pula, *Polish Americans*, 47–53.

41. Paula Benkhart, "Hungarians," in Thernstrom, *Harvard Encyclopedia*, 464–65; Andrew Vazsonyi, "The 'Cicisbeo' and the Magnificent Cuckold: Boardinghouse Life and Lore in Immigrant Communities," *Journal of American Folklore* 91 (Apr.–June 1978): 641–42, 652; Jozsef Gellén, "Immigrant Experience in Hungarian American Poetry before 1945: A Preliminary Assessment," *Acta Scientiarium Hungaricae* 20, nos. 1–2 (1978): 81–83.

42. Benkhart, "Hungarians," 466–67; Gellén, "Immigrant Experience," 82, 84.

43. Geza Hoffman, *Csonka Munkásosztály Az Amerikai Magyarság* (*Mutilated Working Class: The American Hungarians*) (Budapest: Hungarian Economic Society, 1911), 229–30. I am grateful to Judit Szathmari for her help with translations.

44. Helen Ware, "The American-Hungarian Folk Song," *The Musical Quarterly* 11 (1916): 437, 440; Nicholas Tawa, *A Sound of Strangers: Musical Culture, Acculturation, and the Post–Civil War Ethnic American* (Metuchen, N.J.: Scarecrow, 1982), 292.

45. James P. Leary and Richard March, "Farm, Forest, and Factory: Songs of Midwestern Labor," in *Songs about Work*, 278. The song, with a 1941 copyright, is listed also in John S. Nieminski, comp. and ed., *Latest Polish Radio Song Book* (Chicago: Sajewski, 1943).

46. An imprecise but still suggestive percentage of re-emigrants shows a much greater rate for Hungarians. Nearly two-thirds of the number of Magyars who came between 1899 and 1924 returned (63.9 percent), while only two-fifths (39.6 percent) of Poles. Included, however, is the minority going back for visits. See table 2, based on government statistics, in S. Thernstrom, *Harvard Encyclopedia*, 1036. The theme pervading all Hungarian immigrant writing is one of "longing for [the] homeland." Gellén, "Immigrant Experience," 84.

47. Maria G. Y. Kormendi, *Elindultunk Idegenbe . . . : Amerikai Magyar Munkádalok* (We Set Out for a Foreign Land . . . : Hungarian-American Workers Songs) (Budapest: Zenemukiaido, 1965), 13, 69. Translations by Edith Moravsik.

48. Zoltan Fejos, *A Chicagói Magyarok Két Nemzedéke, 1890–1940* (*Two Generations of Hungarians in Chicago, 1890–1940*) (Budapest: Kozep-Europa, 1993), 109, 238.

49. "Ha Bemegyek A Salonos Urnal (When I Drop in on the Saloonkeeper)," in Kormendi, *Elindultunk*, 43.

50. Ware refers to a South Bend fiddler and singer, Adam Pista, who was a traveling bard popular for such melancholy ballads. Ware, "American-Hungarian Folk Song," 435–37, 439–40. The poet Kemény also refers to a mine as flowerless, "a dark, prison cell," and "an open grave." Gellén, "Immigrant Experience," 90, 96.

51. From Jan Brzoza, *Powrót z Ameryki* (*Return from America*) (Warszawa: Ludowa Spoldzielnia Wydawnica, 1966), supplied and translated in Karen Majewski, letter to the author, Orchard Lake, Michigan, January 28, 1997. A similar lament about the death of a Slovak immigrant steelworker, which pervaded the Pittsburgh district was the 1910 song "He Lies in the American Land." Slovaks, like many Poles and Hungarians, took jobs in heavy industry and readily composed songs about their difficult, everyday working life.

Another, also from McKeesport, does not refer to color, simply the burial of a worker in a mill accident and the posthumous arrival of his wife and children, who grieve over his grave. Pete Seeger and Bob Reiser, *Carry It On! A History in Song and Picture of the Workingmen and Women in America* (New York: Simon and Schuster, 1985), 81, cited with background in Theodore C. Gramm, *America's Ethnic Music* (Tarpon Springs, Fla.: By the author, 1976), 21, 68–69.

52. A good, succinct summary of the active participation of Polish immigrant workers in labor unrest is Pula, *Polish Americans*, 48–53.

53. See Victor Greene, *Slavic Community on Strike: Immigrant Labor in Pennsylvania Anthracite* (Notre Dame, Ind.: Univ. of Notre Dame Press, 1968), 199–203.

54. George Korson, *Minstrels of the Mine Patch* (Philadelphia: Univ. of Pennsylvania Press, 1938), 235–36; Korson, liner notes, *Songs and Ballads of the Anthracite Miners*, CD 1502 (Cambridge, Mass.: Rounder Records, 1997), 11–12.

55. These immigrants did sing socialist songs, as evidenced by at least one Polish American songbook in the possession of Karen Majewski, St. Mary's College Archives, Orchard Lake, Michigan. But I could not determine the extent of its popularity in sources nor where and when the pieces were sung. On the occasional appeal of socialism among immigrants, see Bukowczyk, *My Children Did Not Know Me*, 73; Pula, *Polish Americans*, 78; and Donald Pienkos, "Politics, Religion and Change in Polish Milwaukee," *Wisconsin Magazine of History* 61 (Spring 1978): 194–95.

56. The songs are from Károly Cserepes, "Kivándorlas/Emigration: Fejezetek a Nagy Kivándorlás történetéböl/Pages of the Great Emigration Story (1896–1914)" SLPX 18153 (Budapest: Hungaraton Records, 1989). It is important also to note that the record cover refers to the well-known Hungarian motto that reflects the sense of marginality and emotional dilemma of travelers: "To emigrate is sad / To return is no joy, either."

57. For immigrant feeling and the enigma over the ethnic relationship to the rise of the new Poland, see Victor Greene, *For God and Country: The Rise of Polish and Lithuanian Ethnic Consciousness in America* (Madison, Wis.: Society Press, 1975), 69–73; Pula, *Polish Americans*, esp. 54; and Bukowczyk, *My Children Did Not Know Me*, 51, 56.

58. Szydłowska-Czeglowa and Chojnacki, *Polski Wujek Sam*, 183.

59. It may be instructive to note that one of the two most popular songs Bohemian immigrants in Milwaukee sang at home was "Kde Domov Muj?" ("Where Is My Home?"), which also speaks of the "paradise" of meadows, brooks, fountains, forests, gardens, and mountains. It later became the Czech national anthem. Herbert W. Kuhm, "Milwaukee's Early Bohemians *Ze Zaslych Dob*—From Times Past," *Milwaukee History* 18 (Autumn–Winter 1995): 91; translated in Geogiana Dolejsi, *Sokol Minnesota Sings: Songs of Czechoslovakia* (St. Paul: Sokol Minnesota, 1993), 1–2.

7. The Chinese

1. "Still noticeably lacking in the literature are studies that rely primarily on the voices of Asian immigrants and their American born offspring. . . . [W]e must recover their voices." K. Scott Wong and Sucheng Chan, eds., *Claiming America: Constructing Chinese American Identities during the Exclusion Era* (Philadelphia, Pa.: Temple Univ. Press, 1998), vii–viii.

2. Marlon Kau Hom, "Some Cantonese Folksongs on the American Experience," *Western Folklore* 42 (Apr. 1983): 126–39; Hom, *Songs of Gold Mountain: Cantonese Rhymes from San Francisco Chinatown* (Berkeley: Univ. of California Press, 1987); Su de San Zheng, "From Toison to New York: Muk Yu Songs in Folk Tradition," *Chinoperl Papers* 16 (1992–93); Sude San Zheng, "Immigrant Music and Transnational Discourse: Chinese American Music Culture in New York City" (Ph.D. diss., Wesleyan University, 1993); Madeline Yuanyin Hsu, *Dreaming of Gold, Dreaming of Home: Transnationalism and Migration between the United States and South China* (Stanford, Calif.: Stanford Univ. Press, 2000); Him Mark Lai, Genny Lim, and Judy Yung, *Island: Poetry and History of Chinese Immigrants on Angel Island, 1910–1940* (1980; reprint, Seattle: Univ. of Washington Press, 1991). I include the interviews and especially the famous wall poems there as well as their form, which according to Susan Cheng of Music from China, is consonant with the song lyrics. Susan Cheng, e-mail to author and telephone conversation with the author, New York City, June 15, 2000.

3. Su de San Zheng, "Music and Migration: Chinese American Traditional Music in New York City," *The World of Music* 32 (1990): 52.

4. Thomas Chin et al., eds., *A History of Chinese in California* (San Francisco: Chinese Historical Society of America, 1969), 20. Chin shows 82 percent of the Chinese immigrants from Sze Yup and nearby districts in 1876 and 1928. See also Him Mark Lai, "Chinese," in Thernstrom, *Harvard Encyclopedia*, 218.

5. Another term for America was *Fakei* (Land of the Flowery Flag). Hom, *Songs of Gold Mountain*, 5–8; Zheng, "Toison to New York," 39–42; Lai, "Chinese," 218–19, 223. The enduring power of the passion and dream of making money in the United States, both before and after Exclusion, to support the family and relatives back home, especially compared to political and economic instability in China, is well covered in Hsu, *Dreaming of Gold*, 3, 16, 27, 54.

6. Qui Huanxing, *A Cultural Tour across China*, trans. Harry J. Huang (Beijing: New World, 1993), 380. The Guangdong population consisted of two peoples in the mid-1800s: the Punti, who were older settlers, and the Hakka, who had arrived in waves in the fourteenth and seventeenth centuries. The latter lived east of Canton and likely made up most of the emigrants going to America. Tin-Yuke Char, comp. and ed., *The Sandalwood Mountains: Readings and Stories of the Early Chinese in Hawaii* (Honolulu: Univ. of Hawaii Press, 1975), 22–24.

7. Robert Lee, "Singing to Remember: Uncle Ng Makes His Mark," *Artspiral* 6 (Summer 1992): 5.

8. See the succinct explanation of the *muk-yu* tradition in Hom, *Songs of Gold Mountain*, 47–48. Hom also notes their extraordinary popularity in San Francisco Chinatown. Additional information comes from Su de San Zheng, "Taishan Muyu in America: An Unknown Treasure," *Music from China Newsletter* 2 (Summer 1996): 1, 4; Zheng, "Immigrant Music," 53; and Lee "Singing to Remember," 5–7; Marlon K. Hom, "A Muk-Yu from Gold Mountain," in *Chinese America: History and Perspectives, 1989* (San Francisco: Chinese Historical Society of America, 1989), 15–16. See also Leung Pui Chee, "Mu-Yu-Shu: An Examination of Their Contents and How They Have Been Kept Extant and Studied," *Journal of Oriental Studies* 14 (July 1976): 85.

9. Bell Yung, *Cantonese Opera: Performance as Creative Process* (New York: Cambridge Univ. Press, 1989), 8, 12–13, 18; Nora Yeh, "The Tradition of Yue Ju Cantonese Opera," *Folklife Center News* 20 (Spring 1998): 10.

10. Ronald William Riddle, "Chinatown's Music: A History and Ethnography of Music and Musical Drama in San Francisco's Chinese Community" (Ph.D. diss., University of Illinois, 1976), 11, 104–10, 124, 229. Riddle stresses the segregation and isolation of the group in everyday life, including its musical activity, after the initial honeymoon period of Anglo-American acceptance.

11. Hom, "Some Cantonese Folksongs," 128 (from a 1929 Toishan collection).

12. Ibid., 135; Hom, *Songs of Gold Mountain*, 40, 64.

13. Quoted in Hom, "Some Cantonese Folksongs," 135. Obviously, the not uncommon absence of husbands of even ten years or more placed an unbelievable hardship on the women who shouldered the family responsibilities and their own moral code. Judy Yung, *Unbound Feet: A Social History of Chinese Women in San Francisco* (Berkeley: Univ. of California Press, 1993), 20.

14. From Char, *Sandalwood Mountains*, 67. On the pain from the long stay abroad, see also Theodore C. Grame, *America's Ethnic Music* (Tarpon Springs, Fla.: Cultural Maintenance Associates, 1976).

15. The collection belongs to an old folksinger known as Uncle Ng from the Toishan region. He was born in 1910; sang *muk-yu,* including emigrant songs that were known in his village as a youth; and continued his singing in New York City at least until 1993 (perhaps later). Zheng, "Immigrant Music," 257–61.

16. Chinn, *History of the Chinese in California,* 16.

17. I use the translation in Zheng, "Immigrant Music," 46–47.

18. Ibid., 47–52.

19. Ibid., 48.

20. Ibid., 48, 49

21. Ibid., 50, 51.

22. Hom, *Songs of Gold Mountain,* 60.

23. Him Mark Lai, "Chinese Language Bibliographic Project," *Amerasia Journal* 5 (1978): 104.

24. Quoted from Kai-yu Hsu, trans. and ed., *Twentieth Century Chinese Poetry: An Anthology* (New York: Doubleday, 1963), 51–52. Wen I-to was a leader of a school known as the Crescent Poets, who among other principles felt a "noble sympathy with one's fellow man" to achieve truth and beauty. Ibid., xxiv, xxvi. See also Wen I-to, *Red Candle: Selected Poems,* trans. Tao-Tao Sanders (London: Jonathan Cape, 1972), 10, 50–51; and Wen Yiduo, *Selected Poetry and Prose,* ed. Catherine Yi-Yu Cho Woo (Beijing: Panda, 1990). Woo indirectly suggests the poem was written in America in 1922 or 1923. The complete poem set to music, probably by Karl Korte, is in Korte, *Songs of Wen I-to: High Voice and Piano* (New York: E. C. Schirmer, 1973), 2, 9–17. A court case of a Westerner's "harassment" of two laundrymen in New York around 1886 is described in R. David Arkush and Leo O. Lee, eds., *Land without Ghosts: Chinese Impressions of America from the Nineteenth Century to the Present* (Berkeley: Univ. of California Press, 1989), 73–74.

25. Note the description of "Ed" in Maxine Hong Kingston, *China Men* (New York: Knopf, 1980), 63.

26. Hsu, *Dreaming of Gold,* 92. Strangely, her work pays little attention to the subject of the psychological effect of majority discrimination.

27. Paul Siu, *The Chinese Laundryman: A Study of Social Isolation* (New York: New York Univ. Press, 1987), 113, 116. The statement was taken late in the immigration period, the 1930s, and the respondent still preferred America to China. Yet Siu uses this confession

to generalize that immigrants as a whole considered laundry work or labor in a chop-suey house as a "dog's life" and "slave labor." Ibid., 120.

28. A. Ying, comp., *Huagong Jinyue Wenxue Ji* (*A Collection of Literature against the United States Treaty Excluding Chinese Labor*) (Shanghai: 1962), 677–78. I am grateful to Emily Hill for her translation.

29. Ibid.

30. Among others, good summaries of the depredations and the legal history of the anti-Chinese movement are Diane Mei Lin Mark and Ginger Chih, *A Place Called Chinese America* (Dubuque, Iowa: Kendall, Hunt, 1982), 36–41; and Henry Shih-Shan Tsai, *The Chinese Experience in America* (Bloomington: Indiana Univ. Press, 1986), 57–75.

31. An excellent survey analysis of the minor judicial successes of the Chinese in moderating the corpus of discriminatory state and federal laws is Charles J. McClain, *In Search of Equality: The Chinese Struggle against Discrimination in the Nineteenth Century* (Berkeley: Univ. of California Press, 1994), esp. 277–83.

32. Lucy E. Salyer, *Laws Harsh as Tigers: Chinese Immigrants and the Shaping of Modern Immigration Law* (Chapel Hill: Univ. of North Carolina Press, 1995), 163.

33. W. A. P. Martin, *The Awakening of China* (New York: Doubleday, 1907), 253–54.

34. Tsai, *Chinese Experience,* 78. See also Him Mark Lai, "Island of Immortals: Chinese Immigrants and the Angel Island Station," *California History* 57 (Spring 1978): 89–90. Lai says that the boycott was partly successful in relaxing some minor restrictions. The spirited role of San Francisco Chinese Americans in initiating, supporting, and wanting the boycott to continue even after it ended is described in Delber K. McKee, "The Chinese Boycott of 1905–1906 Reconsidered: The Role of Chinese Americans," *Pacific Historical Review* 55 (May 1986): 174–89. For a summary, see Silas K. C. Geneson, "Cry Not in Vain: The Boycott of 1905," *Chinese America, History and Perspectives* 11 (1997): 27–45 (esp. 40). Geneson cites the support of immigrant sojourners who had returned to China. These actions, along with later immigrant songs and poems explained below, support my contention of widespread dissatisfaction.

35. Lai, "Island of Immortals," 90–92; Yumei Sun, "San Francisco's *Chung Sai Tat Po* and the Transformation of Chinese Consciousness, 1900–1920," in *Print Culture in a Diverse America,* ed. James P. Danky and Wayne A. Wiegand (Urbana: Univ. of Illinois Press, 1998), 90–91. Lucy Salyer refers to the boycott's effect in mobilizing and unifying Chinese Americans. Salyer, *Laws Harsh as Tigers,* 167.

36. Jack Chen, "American Chinese Opera, Chinese American Reality," *East Wind* 5 (Spring–Summer 1986): 15–16.

37. Wei Hua Zhang, "The Musical Activities of the Chinese American Communities in the San Francisco Bay Area: A Social and Cultural Study" (Ph.D. diss., University of California, Berkeley, 1994), 32–34. Note also Chen, "American Chinese Opera," 15.

38. Lai, "Chinese Language," 104. The libretto in the *Young China* newspaper is in the Asian American Collection, Ethnic Studies Library, University of California, Berkeley. I am grateful to my translator, Xiaphong Shi, for her efforts and her own judgment concerning the popularity of the opera. Xiaphong Shi, e-mail to author, April 11, 1999.

39. This account is likely the last part of the opera, episodes 32–67 in the newspaper. The date of the work is sometime during the Qin Dynasty, so prior to 1911, when the republic began. Characteristically, the American doctor is given a Chinese name, Dr. Gao. Xiaphong Shi observes that it is likely based on a true event. Shi e-mail, April 11, 1999.

40. Wilt Idema and Lloyd Haft, *A Guide to Chinese Literature* (Ann Arbor: Center for Chinese Studies, University of Michigan, 1997), 238.

41. From Him Mark Lai, "The Angel Island Immigration Station," *Bridge: An Asian American Perspective* (Apr. 1977): 7.

42. Lai, Lim, and Yung, *Island.*

43. Ibid., 93. Immigration officials allowed some to bypass further examination on the island and go directly ashore while others who were suspected as entering illegally were detained. But Connie Young Yu quotes a 1914 arrival who says everyone was detained. Yu, "Rediscovered Voices: Chinese Immigrants and Angel Island," *Amerasia Journal* 4 (1977): 125–26. Him Mark Lai omits any mention of immigrants bypassing island review. Except for the few who had influence and were able to avoid processing, all were examined and detained from a few hours to years. Lai, "Angel Island Immigration Station," 5.

44. Cheng e-mail, June 15, 2000. The performance in song of one representative Angel Island wall inscription is on cassette, "Chinese Sojourner Stranded on Angel Island," pt. 1 (New York: Music from China, 1985). This poem includes instructions for musical performance, possibly a typical condition. Yea-Fen Chen, conversation with author, August 3, 2000. I thank Yea-Fen Chen for her translation.

45. Quoted in Yu, "Rediscovered Voices," 123. Hom has translated a series of immigrant songs that express bitter criticism of treatment on the island and other complaints found in *Jinshan ge ji* (Songs of Gold Mountain), collected and published in San Francisco in 1911, along with other sources. Note in particular the anonymous and untitled work of an Angel Island inmate in Hom, "Some Cantonese Folksongs," 132.

46. Quoted in Emma Gee, "Translation: Poems of Angel Island," *Amerasia Journal* 9 (Fall–Winter 1982): 86. Unfortunately, I am unable to date this poem, but it certainly repeats much of the immigrant dissatisfaction expressed in the pre-1930 era.

8. The Mexicans

1. The major sources for this chapter are Manuel Gamio, "The Songs of the Immigrant," chap. 7 in *Mexican Immigration to the United States: A Study of Human Migration and Settlement* (Chicago: Univ. of Chicago Press, 1930) (from interviewees around 1926–27); Paul S. Taylor, "Songs of the Mexican Migration," *Puro Mexicano*, ed. J. Frank Dobie (Austin: Texas Folklore Society, 1935), 221–45; Américo Paredes, *A Texas-Mexican Cancionero: Folksongs of the Lower Border* (Urbana: Univ. of Illinois Press, 1976) (and other works); and Maria Herrera-Sobek, *Northward Bound: The Mexican Immigrant Experience in Ballad and Song* (Bloomington: Indiana Univ. Press, 1993). Herrera-Sobek's stated purposes are to present a reference work of songs from which future scholars could draw and prove to them that Mexican immigrants were "aware of their role in history." Ibid., xii–xiii.

2. From Carolyn Jung, "San Jose Bands' Rhythms Transcend Borders," *San Jose Mercury News,* Mar. 5, 1994, 10, as cited in George Lipsitz, *Dangerous Crossroads: Popular Music, Postmodernism, and the Poetics of Place* (London: Verso, 1994), 132.

3. Matt S. Meier and Feliciano Rivera, *Mexican Americans–American Mexicans: From Conquistadors to Chicanos* (New York: Hill and Wang, 1993), 234.

4. These ballads are indeed distinctive in the Mexican case since few works among all the other groups refer to specific folk leaders. The Chinese, for example, traditionally es-

chew such a pantheon. The epic poem of military exploits is absent in their literature since they are a people who have condemned war. Wilt Idema and Lloyd Haft, *A Guide to Chinese Literature* (Ann Arbor: Center for Chinese Studies, University of Michigan, 1997), 116.

5. See Robert W. Johannsen, *To the Halls of the Montezumas: The Mexican War in the American Imagination* (New York: Oxford Univ. Press, 1985), 164–70.

6. Dime novels of the mid-1800s portrayal of "the average Mexican [was] a man of brutal insensitivity." Cecil Robinson, *Mexico and the Hispanic Heritage Southwest in American Literature* (Tucson: Univ. of Arizona Press, 1977), 60.

7. From Gamio, *Mexican Immigration,* 17.

8. Ibid., 2, 5, 38.

9. The most authoritative explanation is Américo Paredes, "The Mexican *Corrido:* Its Rise and Fall," in *Madstones and Twisters,* ed. Mody C. Boatright, et al. (Dallas: Southern Methodist Univ. Press, 1958), 91, 95.

10. Nellie Foster, "The Corrido: A Mexican Culture Trait Persisting in Southern California" (master's thesis, University of Southern California, 1939), 7; Arthur L. Campa, *The Spanish Folksong of the Southwest* (Albuquerque: University of New Mexico Bulletin, 1933), 5. George Sánchez identifies the *corrido* as particularly popular and an expression of the masses in the Los Angeles area in the era of heightened Mexican nationalism from 1910 to 1940. Sánchez, *Becoming Mexican American: Ethnicity, Culture, and Identity in Chicano Los Angeles, 1900–1945* (New York: Oxford Univ. Press, 1993), 177–78. I see the genre as having greater chronological and cultural significance.

11. John Holmes McDowell, "The *Corrido* of Greater Mexico as Discourse, Music, and Event," in *"And Other Neighborly Names": Social Process and Cultural Image in Texas Folklore,* ed. Richard Bauman and Roger D. Abrahams (Austin: Univ. of Texas Press, 1981), 47, 50. For the *corrido* as a "rich source" for public opinion in the *pueblo* in general and about the United States, see Merle E. Simmons, *The Mexican Corrido as a Source for Interpretive Study of Modern Mexico (1879–1950)* (Bloomington: Indiana Univ. Press, 1969), 37, 459–60.

12. Maria Herrera-Sobek, *The Mexican Corrido: A Feminist Analysis* (Bloomington: Indiana Univ. Press, 1990), 117.

13. See Campa, *Spanish Folksong,* 5–10, 33; and Arthur L. Campa, *Spanish Folk Poetry in New Mexico* (Albuquerque: Univ. of New Mexico Press, 1946), 18–19.

14. Paredes, *Texas-Mexican Cancionero,* xviii–xxii.

15. Taylor, "Songs of the Mexican Migration," 221.

16. Bruno Nettl, *Folk Music in the United States* (Detroit, Mich.: Wayne State Univ. Press, 1976), 104–5.

17. Taylor, "Songs of the Mexican Migration," 238–39. Note the continuing condemnation of emigrants as traitors in Ilan Stavans, *The Hispanic Condition: Reflections on Culture and Identity in America* (New York: HarperCollins, 1995), 22,

18. Taylor, "Songs of the Mexican Migration," 222–23. The lyrics refer to the Republic of Mexico, which was established after the 1910 revolution.

19. Ibid., 241–45.

20. Note Alfred L. Campa, "Comparing Mexican and American Cultures" in Mario T. Garcia, *Mexican Americans: Leadership, Ideology, and Identity, 1930–1960* (New Haven, Conn.: Yale Univ. Press, 1989), 286–88.

21. Gregory Rodriguez, "Taking the Oath: Why We Need a Revisionist History of Latinos in America," *Los Angeles Times,* Aug. 20, 2000, as reprinted in *H-Ethnic* e-mail, August 24, 2000.

22. Paredes, *Texas-Mexican Cancionero,* 154, 161–62. I am combining several versions.

23. Ibid., 25–26. Herrera-Sobek, "Working and Traveling on the Railroad," chap. 2 in *Northward Bound,* 41–48. A review of examples listed in that chapter supports my generalization about the lack of protest in song.

24. As translated in Philip Sonnichsen, liner notes, *Corridos and Tragedias de la Fontera,* CD 7019–7020 (El Cerrito, Calif.: Folklyric/Arhoolie Records, 1994), 53–59.

25. Paul Schuster Taylor, *An American-Mexican Frontier: Nueces County, Texas* (Chapel Hill: Univ. of North Carolina Press, 1934), 143–46.

26. Foster, "The Corrido," 168–71. The song was recorded in 1926. Manuel Peña, "Notes toward an Interpretation of California-Mexican Music," in *From the Inside Out: Perpectives on Mexican and Mexican-American Folk Art,* ed. Karana Hattersley-Drayton et al. (San Francisco: Mexican Museum, 1989), 67. Manuel Gamio lists other songs in which workers blame the labor contractor for the arduous conditions of working on the railroad or in the beet field. Gamio, *Mexican Immigration,* 84–88.

27. Gamio, *Mexican Immigration,* 129 and throughout; Paredes, *Texas-Mexican Cancionero,* 153–60; Herrera-Sobek, *Northward Bound,* 108, 117, 121.

28. It was collected about 1927 and appears in Gamio, *Mexican Immigration,* 93–94.

29. Ibid., 89. Maria Herrera-Sobek has taken examples from Américo Paredes and a 1924 Mexican publication. Herrera-Sobek, *Northward Bound,* 106–7. The criticism seems to date back to the nineteenth century, according to another satirical song, "Americanas y Mexicanas" ("American Women and Mexican Women"), in Campa, *Spanish Folk Poetry,* 215. When Americans first came to New Mexico, it tells the incoming Anglo women to "have [their men] . . . take you back home" because of their thin figures, modern stoves, cowboy hats, promiscuity, factory employment, and their "put on make-up."

30. All of the last three ballads are in Foster, "The Corrido," 45, 152–59. Foster writes that several of them were recorded.

31. A relevant additional work, "Desde Mexico He Venido" ("From Mexico I Have Come"), that appeared early in the 1890s criticizes *both* American and Mexican American husbands for allowing wives the kind of freedom they enjoyed in the new land. Paredes, *Texas-Mexican Cancionero,* 154.

32. Manuel Peña, *Música Tejana: The Cultural Economy of Artistic Transformation* (College Station: Texas A&M Univ. Press, 1999), 14–24, 40 and throughout. Peña also asserts the powerful musical influence that the south Texas *corrido* concerning intercultural conflict had over the entire Southwest border region.

33. I thank my colleague James Leary for referring to the continuation of such songs into the 1960s and 1970s, as evidenced in the records issued by Chris Strachwitz of Arhoolie Records, El Cerrito, California.

34. Paredes, *Texas-Mexican Cancionero,* xviii. The author speaks of the Texas Mexican only, but the comment can be applied to immigrant Mexicans in the entire borderland region. See also Américo Paredes, *"With His Pistol in His Hand": A Border Ballad and Its Hero* (Austin: Univ. of Texas Press, 1975), 150.

35. Paredes, "Mexican *Corrido,*" 98. The guerilla war was carried on during the conflict as well against the American army of Zachary Taylor. Philip Sonnichsen lists other guerillas who found their way into the *corrido* repertoire for opposing Taylor's army. Sonnichsen, liner notes, *Corridos,* 25. One should remember, though, that not all Mexicans were opposed to the Anglo-American conquest of the Southwest in the post-1848 era. Paredes, *Texas-Mexican Cancionero,* 22.

36. Sonnichsen, liner notes, *Corridos,* 38-39; Stavans, *Hispanic Condition,* 66; Peña, "Notes toward an Interpretive History," 67. Murrieta was known as California's most famous bandit among the Anglo-American reading public from the seven dime novels of Joseph E. Badger published by Beadle and Adams in the 1870s and early 1880s. Daryl James, *The Dime Novel Western* (Bowling Green, Ohio: Bowling Green State Univ. Press, 1978), 91-93. The ballad was recorded twice in 1934 by Los Madrugadores and Hermanos Sanchez. Richard K. Spottswood, *Ethnic Music on Records: A Discography of Ethnic Recordings Produced in the United States, 1893 to 1941,* 7 vols. (Urbana: Univ. of Illinois Press, 1990), 4:2046.

37. Paredes, *Texas-Mexican Cancionero,* 22-23.

38. Ibid., 27, 47-48; Paredes, "Mexican *Corrido,*" 104; Paredes, "*With His Pistol in His Hand,*" 25.

39. Paredes, *Texas-Mexican Cancionero,* 30.

40. Américo Paredes offers the most thorough account, comparing the history and legend of the ballad in "*With His Pistol in His Hand.*"

41. One can find the many variants and texts in many works. The one I use here is the translation in Stavans, *Hispanic Condition,* 142-43. Another is in Sonnichsen, liner notes, *Corridos,* 30-33,

42. Paredes, *Texas-Mexican Cancionero,* 32-34, 71-73.

43. Friedrich Katz, *The Life and Time of Pancho Villa,* (Stanford, Calif.: Stanford Univ. Press, 1998), 793.

44. Foster, "The Corrido," 37-38, 90-93; Katz, *The Life and Times of Pancho Villa,* 793; Paredes, *Texas-Mexican Cancionero,* 39-40; Paredes, "Mexican *Corrido,*" 101.

45. Paredes, "*With His Pistol in His Hand,*" 150. Paredes refers to the Mexican epithet for the Rangers as "ham eaters" in *Texas-Mexican Cancionero,* 39-40.

46. Ibid., 90-91. Note a variant entitled "La Punitiva" in Foster, "The Corrido," 90-93. Another, "Corrido de Pancho Villa," was recorded in San Antonio in April 1934. Spottswood, *Ethnic Music,* 4:1630.

47. For the full lyrics to the recording of "La Punitiva" made on July 16, 1929, by Luis Hernandez y Leonardo Sifuentes in El Paso, see Guillermo E. Hernandez, *The Mexican Revolution: Corridos about the Heroes and Events, 1910-1920, and Beyond!* See also liner notes, CD 7041-7044 (El Cerrito, Calif.: Folklyric/Arhoolie Records,1996), 74.

48. Katz, *Pancho Villa,* 793. John Rutherford states that the Columbus, New Mexico, raid and the ensuing Punitive Expedition were in the eyes of the Mexican public "reassertions of Mexican machismo against an iniquitous foe, and therefore of deep patriotic significance." Rutherford, *Mexican Society during the Revolution: A Literary Approach* (Oxford: Clarendon, 1971), 163. See also the discussion in Simmons, *Mexican Corrido,* 263. Thus it is logical to assume that the story of these events also affected Mexican immigrants.

49. Examples are "Contrabandistas Tequileros" and "*Corrido* de los Bootleggers," in Sonnichsen, liner notes, *Corridos,* 104-15. For others who viewed the conflict between smugglers and border officials as continued cultural conflict, see the discussion in Paredes, *Texas-Mexican Cancionero,* 42-44.

50. Gamio, *Mexican Immigration,* 146-47; Hernandez, *Mexican Revolution,* 9.

51. Placing the social distress simply on the vagaries of economic conditions are the songs "La Crisis" ("The Crisis"), "Efectos de la Crisis" ("Effects of the Crisis"), "El Paisano Repatriado" ("The Repatriated Countryman"), "Los Desocupados" ("The Unemployed"),

and two entitled "Los Repatriados" ("The Repatriated"). Those songs blaming U.S. authorities for unfair and cruel treatment are "La Crisis Actual" ("The Present Crisis"), "Adios Paisanos" ("Good-Bye Countrymen"), "Adios Estados Unidos" ("Good-Bye, United States"), "Corrido de la Emigración" ("*Corrido* of the Immigration Officers"), and "El Deportado" ("The Deported One"). See Foster, "The Corrido," 171, 175–78, 180–96; and Taylor, "Songs of the Mexican Migration," 225–26, 232–35.

52. Leo Grebler, Joan W. Moore, and Ralph C. Guzman, *The Mexican American People* (New York: Free Press, 1970), 525.

53. Taylor, "Songs of the Mexican Migration," 224–26; Sonnichsen, liner notes, *Corridos,* 42–46; Manuel Peña, e-mail to the author, July 24, 2000; Foster, "The Corrido," 23, 48–49, 112, 117, 180. Many lines are repeated for emphasis in Sonnichsen. Foster refers to its popularity and its Vocalion Recording (no. 8287, 1929–30). From Richard K. Spottswood, comp., *Ethnic Music on Records,* 7 vols. (Urbana: Univ. of Illinois Press, 1990), 4:1664.

54. The ballads are in Sonnichsen, liner notes, *Corridos,* 59–66, 82–99,121–28, 138–43; and Foster, "The Corrido," 23, 39.

55. Philip Sonnichsen, "Los Madrugadores: Early Spanish Radio in California," *La Luz* (June 1977): 15. Sonnichsen graciously provided additional evidence of the overwhelming devotion of the radio listeners at the time. Sonnichsen, telephone conversation with the author, Aug. 7, 2000.

56. The "Corrido de Pedro González" appeared during his trial and, likely because of its inflammatory nature, the recording by Los Madrugadores was withdrawn almost immediately in 1934. González served six years of his sentence and was then deported to Mexico. See Chris Strachwitz and Zac Salem, liner notes, *Pedro J. González and Los Madrugadores, . . . 1931–37,* CD 7035 (El Cerrito, Calif.: Folklyric/Arhoolie Records, 2000), 7. See also the interview and video, "Ballad of an Unsung Hero" (San Diego: Cinewest, 1983); Philip Sonnichsen, e-mail to author, Aug. 10, 2000. George Sánchez refers to González as one of two musicians who "served an important role in redefining Mexican culture in an American urban environment." Sánchez, *Becoming Mexican American,* 187,

57. Meier and Rivera, *Mexican Americans–American Mexicans,* 233.

58. Sánchez, *Becoming Mexican American,* 274.

Conclusion

1. Note the justification for review in Ewa Morawska, "In Defense of the Assimilation Model," *Journal of American Ethnic History* 13 (Winter 1994): 76.

2. Oscar Handlin, *The Uprooted,* (New York: Dunlap, 1951).

3. Rudolph Vecoli, "Contadini in Chicago: A Critique of *The Uprooted,*" *Journal of American History* 51 (Dec. 1964): 404–17. Vecoli's article had a notable influence on later works. For example, see Roy Rosenzwieg, *Eight Hours for What We Will: Leisure in an Industrial City, 1870–1920* (New York: Cambridge Univ. Press, 1983), 1–5; and Lizabeth Cohen, *Making a New Deal: Industrial Workers in Chicago, 1919–1939* (New York: Cambridge Univ. Press, 1990), 1–9, 361–68. A good recent assessment of Vecoli's work is John Bukowczyk, "Homage to the Contadini: The Influence of Rudolph J. Vecoli on Immigration and Ethnic History," *Italiana Americana* 20 (Summer 2002): 125–34.

4. Handlin commented on criticisms and omissions in a later edition. See *The Uprooted: The Epic Story of the Great Migrations That Made the American People*, 2d ed. (Boston: Atlantic, Little, Brown, 1973), chap. 14. The historiographical survey that reviews criticisms is in Russell A. Kazal, "Revisiting Assimilation: The Rise, Fall, and Reappraisal of a Concept in American Ethnic History," *American Historical Review* 100 (Apr. 1995): esp. 438, 446–48, 452–53.

5. The foremost exponent of this position is David R. Roediger, especially in his *The Wages of Whiteness: Race and the Making of the American Working Class* (London: Verso, 1991).

6. The pioneer globalist was Frank Thistlethwaite with his address at the 11th Congress of Historical Sciences in Stockholm. See his "Migration Overseas in the Nineteenth and Twentieth Centuries," in *A Century of European Migrations,* ed. Rudolph Vecoli and Suzanne Sinke (Urbana: Univ. of Illinois Press, 1991), 17–49

7. Morawska, "In Defense of the Assimilation Model," 82–86.

8. John Bodnar shows how powerful interests distorted ethnic memory construction in his *Remaking America: Public Memory, Commemoration, and Patriotism in the Twentieth Century* (Princeton, N.J.: Princeton University Press, 1992), 42 and throughout.

9. Matthew Frye Jacobson, *Special Sorrows: The Diasporic Imagination of Irish, Polish, and Jewish Immigrants in the United States* (Cambridge, Mass.: Harvard Univ. Press, 1995), 10, 219–20.

10. See the "insurrection favorites" among the Poles on their Constitution Day, "Poland Has Not Perished," ibid., 78.

11. Ibid., 81.

12. Michael Kammen, "Introduction," in *The Past Before Us: Contemporary Historical Writing in the United States* (Ithaca, N.Y.: Cornell Univ. Press, 1980), 20, 39 (emphasis added). Note Gary Gerstle's synthesis of the clash between civic and racial nationalisms in *American Crucible: Race and Nation in the Twentieth Century* (Princeton, N.J.: Princeton Univ. Press, 2001).

13. Robert V. Merton, *Sociological Ambivalence and Other Essays* (New York: Free Press, 1976), 6–7.

14. Ibid., 12. Note Ewa Morawska, "The Immigrants Pictured and Unpictured in the *Pittsburgh Survey: Social Science and Social Reform in the Early Twentieth Century,* ed. Maurine W. Greenwald and Margo Anderson (Pittsburgh: Univ. of Pittsburgh Press, 1996), 234. A much more elaborate discussion of their tensions is Morawska, "Sociological Ambivalence: The Case of East European Peasant-Immigrant Workers in America, 1880s–1930s," *Qualitative Sociology* 10 (Fall 1987): 225–50.

15. I was unable to find a title for this song. It is mentioned in Samuel Gompers's autobiography as one of two popular tunes sung in his boyhood days by English workers. See Gompers, *Seventy Years of Life and Labor,* 2 vols. ([1925]; reprint, New York: Augustus Kelley, 1967), 1:19. For the Carnegies, it was a "well-known emigrant ballad [Andrew's] father sang." Quoted in Maldwyn Jones, *Destination America* (New York: Holt, Rinehart, and Winston, 1976), 15.

16. Quoted in Ronald Takaki, *A Distant Mirror: A History of Multicultural America* (Boston: Little, Brown, 1993), 254.

17. Ibid.

18. Quoted in Eileen H. Tamura, "Japanese," in *A Nation of Peoples: A Sourcebook of America's Multicultural Heritage,* ed. Elliott Barkan (Westport, Conn.: Greenwood, 1999),

320. "Hole Hole Bushi," cane-worker labor songs, originated in Hawaii among women workers but were apparently also sung in Seattle and likely in rural California too. Kazuo Ito, *Issei: A History of Japanese Immigrants in North America*, trans. Shinichiro Nakamura and Jean S. Gerard (Seattle, Wash.: Japanese Community Service, 1973), 23; Franklin S. Odo, e-mail to author, Aug. 14, 2000; Akemi Kikumura, e-mail to author, Aug. 28, 2000. For songs about the dashed "Hawaiian dream," see Franklin S. Odo and Harry Minoru Urata, "Hole, Hole, Bushi: Songs of Hawaii's Japanese Immigrants in Hawaii," in *Hawaii Mana* (Hawaii: Elepaio, 1981), 71; Susan Miyo Asai, "Transformations of Traditions: Three Generations of Japanese American Music Making," *Musical Quarterly* 79 (Fall 1995): 431; Ronald Takaki, *Pau Hana: Plantation Life and Labor in Hawaii* (Honolulu: Univ. of Hawaii Press, 1983), 59, 89, 125, 178; and Gary Y. Okihiro, *Cane Fires: The Anti-Japanese Movement in Hawaii, 1865–1945* (Philadelphia, Pa.: Temple Univ. Press, 1991), 30, 34–35.

19. "Hole-Hole Bushi: The Only Song of the Japanese in Hawaii," *The Hawaii Herald*, Feb. 2, 1973, 4.

20. Yukuo Uyehara, "The Horehore-Bushi: A Type of Japanese Folksong Developed and Sung among Early Immigrants in Hawaii," *Social Process in Hawaii* 28 (1981): 119.

21. Interviews of Sam Fortosis and Nina Goodenov, in *They Chose America: Conversations with Immigrants*, vols. 1, 2 (New York: Visual Education, 1975), audio cassettes.

22. The following is taken from Alison Smale, "Their Hearts Belong to Mother Russia: Some Emigres Go Home after Finding American Life Mercenary and Shallow," *New York Times*, Aug. 22, 2000, A21. For the appeal of the homeland's "simple life," where "children can know their neighbors," to Vietnamese returnees, see Seth Mydans, "Former Refugees See Opportunities in Vietnam," *New York Times*, Dec. 5, 1994, A1, A8.

23. Smale, "Their Hearts Belong to Mother Russia," A21.

24. From Anne Rasmussen, liner notes, and performance of "Wakef 'Ala Shat Baher" ("Standing on the Shore"), in *The Music of Arab Americans: A Retrospective Collection* CD 1122 (Cambridge, Mass.: Rounder Records, 1997); Amy Catlin, liner notes, and performance of "Tsaaj Ntsaws-Tsi Teb Tsaws Chaw" ("Refugee Song"), in Baua Xou Mus, *The Music of the Hmong People of Laos*, CD 446 (El Cerrito, Calif.: Arhoolie, 1995); music of Wisconsin Asians, in James Leary, *Wisconsin Folklore* (Madison: Univ. of Wisconsin Press, 1998), 303; and Wang Chou Vang, untitled song (recorded by James Leary), in *In Tune with Tradition*, ed. Robert Teske (Cedarburg, Wis.: Cedarburg Cultural Center, 1990). I am grateful to James Leary for these last two references.

25. David Montgomery, "Racism, Immigrants, and Political Reform," *Journal of American History* 87 (Mar. 2001): 1274 (revised version of an address before the Organization of American Historians, St. Louis, April 2000).

26. Steven Vertovec and Robin Cohen, "Introduction," in *Migration, Diasporas, and Transnationalism*, ed. Vertovec and Cohen (Cheltenham, U.K.: Edgar Elgar, 1999), xxiii (internally referencing Stuart Hall, "Cultural Identity and Diaspora").

Selected Bibliography

Collections

Arion Singing Society File, Pratt Free Public Library, Baltimore, Maryland. PFPL.
Asian American Collection (in Chinese). Ethnic Studies Library, University of California Library, Berkeley, California. AAC.
De Vincent Song Collection, Museum of American History, Smithsonian Institution, Washington, D.C. DSC.
Music Collection, Yivo Institute, New York, New York. MCYI.
In Stambler Collection, Yivo Institute, New York, New York. SCYI.
Star Collection, Lilly Library, Indiana University, Bloomington, Indiana. SCLL.

Primary Sources

"Adolph Philipp: A Remarkable Triple Identity." *The New York Dramatic Mirror* 74 (November 20, 1915): 1.
"Ausverkautt Is the Sign Every Night Where the German George Cohen Plays." *The World,* March 2, 1913.
Beijbom. Ulf. Liner notes to *From Sweden to America,* 1981. Caprice Record CAP 2011.
Bianco, Carla. *The Two Rosetos.* Bloomington: Indiana Univ. Press, 1979.
Brzoźa, Jan. *Powrot z America (Return from America).* Warsaw, Poland: Ludowa Spółdzielnia Wydawnica, 1966.
D'Ariano, Regina, and Roy D'Ariano. *Italo-American Ballads, Poems, Lyrics, and Melodies.* Parsons, W.V.: McClain, 1976.
Delaney's Irish Song Book, nos. 2 and 4. New York: Wm. Delaney, n.d. SCLL.
Del Guidice, Luisa, ed. *Italian Traditional Song.* 2d ed. Los Angeles: Istituto Italiano de Cultura, 1995.
De Marsan's New Comic and Sentimental Singers' Journal . . . No. 4. New York: De Marsan, n.d.
1853–1903 Zur Erinnerung an das 50-jährige Jubiläum des Buffalo Sängerbund . . . (Buffalo, 1903). PFPL.

Fackel, April 1 and June 3, 1883 (German Workers' Newspaper, Chicago) from Petra Lehman, "Songs of the German American Labor Movement." Paper in "Land Without Nightingales." Mss. in author's possession.

Festordnung und Textbuch der New England Staaten für . . . Erste Saengerfest, Providence, Rhode Island, 26–30 Juni 1866 (Providence, 1866). PFPL.

Ford, James L. "The German Stage in America." *Bookman* 20 (November 1898): 1.

"Foreign Record Field." *Columbia Record* 12 (May 1914). In Pekka Gronow, ed. *Studies in Scandinavian-American Discography 2.* Helsinki: Finnish Institute of Recorded Sound, 1977. 10.

Foster, Nellie. "The Corrido: A Mexican Culture Trait Persisting in Southern California." Master's thesis. University of Southern California, 1939.

Fowke, Edith, ed. *Traditional Singers and Songs from Ontario.* Hatboro, Penn.: Folklore Associates, 1965.

Gamio, Manuel. *Mexican Immigration to the United States: A Study of Human Migration and Settlement.* Chicago: Univ. of Chicago Press, 1930.

Gee, Emma. "Translation: Poems of Angel Island." *Amerasia Journal* 9 (Fall–Winter, 1982): 83–88.

Gompers, Samuel. *Seventy Years of Life and Labor.* New York: Augustus Kelley, 1925. Reprint, 1967.

Graham, Stephen. *With the Poor Immigrants to America.* New York: Macmillan, 1914.

"A Great Anniversary." *Baltimore Sun,* October 1, 1880.

"*Heimathlied*" in John Koegel, "Klein Deutschland: Adolph Philipp and German-American Musical Theatre in Turn-of-the-Century New York." Paper presented at the Sonnick Society Meeting, Madison, Wisconsin, April 7, 1995.

Henninghausen, L. P. "The German Day in Baltimore, Oct. 6, 1891." *Annual Reports, Society for the History of the Germans in Baltimore* 5(1891): 41–72

Hoffman, Geza. *Csonka Munkásosztály Az Amerikai Magyarság (Mutilated Working Class: The American Hungarians).* Budapest: Hungarian Economic Society, 1911.

"Hole-Hole Bushi: The Only Song of the Japanese in Hawaii." *The Hawaii Herald,* February 2, 1973.

Huntingdon, Gale, and Lani Henderson, eds. *Sam Henry's Songs of the People.* Athens: Univ. of Georgia Press, 1990.

Jang, Leung Sin. "A Laundryman Sings the Blues." *Chinese America: History and Perspectives* 5 (1991): 10.

Kamphoefner, Walter, et al., eds. *News from the Land of Freedom: German Immigrants Write Home.* Ithaca, N.Y.: Cornell Univ. Press, 1991.

Korson, George. Liner notes, "Me Johnny Mitchell Man." On *Songs and Ballads of the Anthracite Miners,* 1947. Rounder Records CD 1502.

Lei, Hua Qiao Xue. "Blood and Tears of an Overseas Chinese." Serialized articles dating from February 26, 1911, to April 10, 1911, in *Young* China (San Francisco Chinese language newspaper). AAC.

Levin, Neil. *Songs of the American Jewish Experience.* New York: Jewish Board of Education, 1976.

Leydi, Roberto. "Mama mia, dammi cento lire." In *Le Tradizione Popolare in Italia: Canti e musiche popolare. (Popular Tradition in Italy: Songs and Popular Music.)* Milan: Electa, 1990.

Martin, Philip. *Ach Ya!: Traditional German-American Music from Wisconsin*. Dodgeville: Folklore Village Farm. 1985.

Martineau, Harriet. *Letters from Ireland*. London: John Chapman, 1852.

Meigel, Charles H. "The Singing Germans of Baltimore." *Baltimore Sun*, March 13, 1936. Germans in Baltimore File, PFPL

Milwaukee County Historical Society. *Souvenir: 15 Sängerfestes des Sängerbundes des Nordwesterns . . . Am 8 . . . 12 Juli, 1891*. (Milwaukee: Milwaukee County Historical Society, 1891).

Mlotek, Eleanor Gordon. *Mir Trogn a Gezang!* 4th ed. New York: Workmen's Circle, 1987.

Mlotek, Zalmen, and Moishe Rosenfeld. Liner notes to *Songs from the Golden Land*, [n.d.]. Warner Bros. Music record-tape 001.

Mouldon, John, comp. *Thousands Are Sailing: A Brief Song History of Irish Emigration*. Portrush, Northern Ireland: Ulstersongs, 1994.

"Muss I Denn Zum Stadtele N'Aus" ("Must I Then Go Away from the Town"). Box 233, DSC.

Norman, Carl G. *Emigratens sånger (Emigrant Song Book)*. Chicago: Excelsior, 1914.

Pawlowska, Helen. *Merrily We Sing: 105 Polish Folksongs*. Detroit: Wayne State Univ. Press, 1983.

Peacock, Kenneth, ed. *Songs of the Newfoundland Outports*. Ottawa: National Museum of Canada, 1965.

Proceedings of the Maryland Historical Society . . . 150th Anniversary of the Settlement of Baltimore. Baltimore: Maryland Historical Society, 1880.

Proletaarilauluja Songbook. Duluth: [n.p.], 1918.

Pupin, Michael. *From Immigrant to Inventor*. New York: Scribner's, 1925.

Quaife, Milton M., ed. *An English Settler in Pioneer Wisconsin: The Letters of Edwin Bottomley, 1842–1850*. Madison: The Society, 1918.

Rattermann, H. M. "Anfänge und Entwicklung des Musik und des Gesanges in den Vereinigten Staaten. . . ." *Deutsche-Amerikanische Geschichts Geschichtsblätter* 12 (1912): 327–80.

Rosenfeld, Morris. *The Teardrop Millionaire and Other Poems*. Trans. Aaron Kramer. New York: Emma Lazarus Clubs of Manhattan, 1955.

Rubin, Rose, ed. *A Treasury of Jewish Folksong*. New York: Schocken, 1950.

———. "Sholem Aleichem and Yiddish Folksongs," *Sing Out* 9 (Winter 1959–60): 21–26.

Smale, Alison. "Their Hearts Belong to Mother Russia: Some Emigrants Go Home after Finding American Life Mercenary and Shallow." *New York Times*, August 22, 2000.

Smulevitz, Solomon. "Der Brivele der Mamen." Sheet Music Song, 1921. Box 3, folder 29, MCYI.

Spottswood, Richard. *Ethnic Music on Records: A Discography of Ethnic Recordings Produced in the United States, 1893 to 1942*. 7 vols. Urbana: Univ. of Illinois Press, 1990.

Stambler, B-H. Liner notes to *Aaron Lebedeff Sings Rumania, Rumania and Other Yiddish Theater Favorites*, 1968(?). Collector's Guild Record 631.

Steiner, Edward. *On the Trail of the Immigrant*. New York: Revell, 1906.

Stephenson, E. Irenaeus. The Sängerfest in Philadelphia." *Harper's Weekly* 41 (1897): 667.

Stephenson, Robert Louis. *The Amateur Emigrant*. London: Hogarth, 1892, 1984.

Strachwitz, Chris, and Zac Salem. Liner notes to *Pedro J. Gonzalez and Los Madrugadores . . . 1931–37*, 2000. Arhoolie CD 7035m.

Szajkowski, Zosa. *An Illustrated Sourcebook of Russian Anti-Semitism.* 2 vols. New York: Ktav, 1980.

Szydłowska-Ceglowa, Barbara, and Wojciech Chojnacki, comps. *Polski Wujek Sam: Kuplety Polski w Ameryce (Polish Uncle Sam: Polish* Kuplety *in America).* Warsaw, Poland: Polonia, 1989.

Taylor, Paul S. "Songs of the Mexican Migration." In *Puro Mexicano,* ed. J. Frank Dobie, 221–41. Austin: Texas Folk-Lore Society, 1935.

Thigpen, Kenneth A. *Folklore and the Ethnicity Factor in the Lives of Romanian-Americans.* Reprint. New York: Arno, 1980.

Ware, Helen. "The American-Hungarian Folk-Song." *The Musical Quarterly* 2 (July 1916): 434–41

Wen I-to. *Red Candle: Selected Poems.* Trans. Tao-Tao Sanders. London: Jonathan Cape, 1972.

Westerholm, Simo, comp. *Reisaavaisen laulu Amerikkaan . . . (The Traveler's Song in America).* Kaustinen: Kansan musiikki-instituuti, 1983.

Wright, Robert L, ed. *Irish Emigrant Ballads and Songs.* Bowling Green, Ohio: Bowling Green Univ. Popular Press, 1975.

———. *Swedish Emigrant Ballads.* Lincoln: Univ. of Nebraska Press, 1965.

Wright, Rochelle, and Robert L. Wright. *Danish Emigrant Ballads and Songs.* Carbondale: Southern Illinois Univ. Press, 1983.

Ying, A., comp. *Huagong Jinjue Wenxue Ji.* Shanghai: [n.p.], 1962. Collection of literature against the U.S. treaty excluding Chinese labor.

Secondary Works

Anderson, Benedict. *Imagined Communities: Reflections on the Origins and the Spread of Nationalism.* London: Verso, 1983.

Alexander, Michael. *Jazz Age Jews.* Princeton, N.J.: Princeton Univ. Press, 2001.

Appel, John, and Selma Appel. *The Distorted Image: Stereotype and Caricature in American Popular Graphics, 1850–1922.* Slide set with booklet. New York: Anti-Defamation League of B'nai B'rith, 1973.

Ausubel, Nathan, ed. *A Treasury of Jewish Folklore: Stories, Traditions, Legends, Humor, Wisdom, and Folk Songs of the Jewish People.* New York: Crown, 1948.

Babow, Irving Paul. "Secular Singing Societies of European Immigrant Groups in San Francisco." Ph.D. dissertation, University of California, 1954.

Bail, Thomas. "Topicalization and Collective Experience: Selected Papers of John Blacking." In *The Press of Labor Migrants in Europe and North America, 1880s to 1930s,* ed. Christine Harzig and Dirk Hoerder. Bremen, Germany: Publications of the Labor Newspaper Preservation Project, 1985.

Betterton, William F. "The Sangerfest of 1898." *Palimpsest* 45 (June 1964): 293–300.

Blakeslee, Sandra. "The Mystery of Music: How It Works on the Brain." *New York Times,* May 15, 1995.

Blegen, Theodore C., and Martin C. Ruud, eds. *Norwegian Emigrant Songs and Ballads.* Minneapolis: Univ. of Minnesota Press, 1936.

Blejwas, Stanislaus. "'To Sing Out the Future of Our Beloved Fatherland': Choral Nationalism and the Polish Singers' Alliance, 1889–1939." *Journal of American Ethnic History* 19 (Fall 1999): 3–25.

Blue, Howard C. "Conclusion: The Pageantry of Difference: The Psychological Development and Creative Expression of Racial and Ethnic Identity." In *Racial and Ethnic Identity: Psychological Development and Creative Expression,* ed. Herbert W. Harris, 223–32. New York: Routledge, 1995.

Blumenson, S. L. "Culture on Rutgers Square: The Fervent Days on East Broadway." *Commentary* 10 (July 1950): 65–74.

———. "The Golden Age of Tomashefsky: At the Tables Down at Schreibers." *Commentary* 13 (April 1952): 344–51.

Bohlman, Philip V. "Old World Cultures in North America." In *Excursions in World Music,* ed. Bruno Nettl, 278–324. Englewood Cliffs, N.J.: Prentice-Hall, 1992.

Brooks, William. Liner note, "Progress and Protest in the Golden Age: Songs of the Civil War to the Columbian Exposition." *The Hand that Holds the Bread,* 1978. New World Record, NW267.

Brown, Thomas N. *Irish American Nationalism.* Philadelphia, Pa.: Lippincott, 1966.

Bruner, Gordon C. III. "Music, Mood, and Marketing." *Journal of Marketing* 54 (October 1990): 94–104.

Buckhoe, Robert J. "Olle i Stratthult, Marquette Gem, National Treasure. *Marquette Monthly,* no. 127 (May 1998): 8–11.

Budd, Malcolm. *Music and the Emotions: The Philosophical Theories.* London: Routledge and Kegan Paul, 1985.

Burdette, Alan R. "Ein Prosit Der Gemütlichkeit: Heightened Experience and the Creation of Context in a German American Singing Society." Master's thesis, Indiana University, 1993.

Byington, Margaret F. *Homestead: The Households of a Mill Town.* Pittsburgh, Pa.: Center for International Studies and Russell Sage Foundation, 1910, 1974.

Byron, Reginald, ed. *Music, Culture, and Experience: Selected Papers of John Blacking.* Chicago: Univ. of Chicago Press, 1995.

Campa, Arthur L. *Spanish Folk Poetry in New Mexico.* Albuquerque: Univ. of New Mexico Press, 1946.

Campbell, Patricia S. *Songs in Their Heads: Music and Its Meaning in Children's Lives.* New York: Oxford Univ. Press, 1998.

Carnevale, Nancy. "Living in Translation: Language and Italian Immigration in the United States, 1890–1945." Ph.D. dissertation, Rutgers University, 2000.

Cautela, Giuseppe. "The Italian Theatre in New York." *The American Mercury* 12 (September 1927): 106–12.

Clark, Christopher. "Mentalité and the Nature of Consciousness." In *Encyclopedia of American Social History,* 3 vols., ed. Mary Kupiec Cayton, et al., 1:387–95. New York: Scribner, 1993.

Cohen, Norm. *Long Steel Rail: The Railroad in American Folksong.* Urbana: Univ. of Illinois Press, 1981.

Connor, Steven. *Postmodern Culture: An Introduction to Theories of the Contemporary.* Oxford, U.K.: Basil Blackwell, 1989.

Conolly-Smith, Peter. "Ersatz-Drama and Ethnic (Self-) Parody: Adolph Philipp and the Decline of New York's German Language Stage, 1893–1918." In *Multilingual America: Transnationalism, Ethnicity and the Languages of American Literature,* ed. Werner Sollors, 215–39. New York: New York Univ. Press, 1998.

Conzen, Kathleen Neils. "Ethnicity as Festive Culture: Nineteenth-Century German Americans on Parade." In *The Invention of Tradition,* ed. Werner Sollors, 44–76. New York: Oxford Univ. Press, 1989.

Crafts, Susan, et al. *My Music.* Middletown: Wesleyan Univ. Press, 1993

Crozier, W. Ray. "Music and Social Influence." In *The Social Psychology of Music,* ed. Adrian North, 67–83. Oxford, U.K.: Oxford Univ. Press, 1997.

Cygan, Mary. "Inventing Polonia: Notions of Polish American Identity, 1870–1990." *Prospects: An Annual of American Cultural Studies* 23 (1998): 209–46.

Davis, Fred. *Yearning for Yesterday: A Sociology of Nostalgia.* New York: Free Press, 1979.

Davis, Susan. *Parades and Power: Street Theatre in Nineteenth Century Philadelphia.* Philadelphia, Pa.: Temple Univ. Press, 1986.

Del Guidice, Luisa, ed. "Italian Traditional Song in Toronto: From Autobiography to Advocacy." *Journal of Canadian Studies/Revue d'Études Canadiennes* 29 (Spring 1994): 74–89

———. *Studies in Italian American Folklore.* Logan: Utah State Univ. Press, 1993.

Drummond, Robert Rutherford. *Early German Music in Philadelphia.* New York: Appleton, 1910.

Emmons, David. *The Butte Irish: Class and Ethnicity in an American Mining Town, 1875–1925.* Urbana: Univ. of Illinois Press, 1989.

Ensslen, Klaus, and Heinz Ickstadt. "German Working Class Culture in Chicago: Continuity and Change in the Decade from 1900–1910." In *German Workers in Industrial Chicago, 1850–1910: A Comparative Perspective,* ed. Hartmut Keil and John Jentz, 236–52. DeKalb: Northern Illinois Univ. Press, 1983.

Erickson, Eric. *Childhood and Society.* 2d ed. New York: Norton, 1963.

Fejos, Zoltan. *A Chicagoi Magyarok Ket Nemzedske, 1890–1940 (Two Generations of Hungarians in Chicago, 1890–1940): Preservation and Transformation of an Ethnic Heritage.* Budapest, Hungary: Kozep Europa Intezet, 1993.

Fornell, Earl W., and Martha Fornell. "A Century of German Song in Texas." *American German Review* 24 (Oct.–Nov. 1957): 29–31.

Friedman, Reena Sigman. "Send Me My Husband Who Is in New York City: Husband Desertion in the American Jewish Immigrant Community, 1900–1926." *Jewish Social Studies* 44 (Winter 1982): 1–18.

Frith, Simon. "Towards an Aesthetic of Popular Music." In *Music and Society: The Politics of Composition, Performance, and Reception,* ed. Richard Leppert and Susan McClary, 77–106. Cambridge, U.K.: Cambridge Univ. Press, 1987.

———. "Why Do Songs Have Words?" In *Lost in Music: Culture, Style, and Musical Event,* ed. Avron Levine White. London: Routledge and Kegan Paul, 1987.

Furuland, Lars. "From Värmlandingarna to Slavarna på Molokstorp: Swedish American Ethnic Theater in Chicago." In *Swedish-American Life in Chicago: Cultural and Urban Aspects of an Immigrant People, 1850–1930,* ed. Philip J. Anderson and Da Blanck, 133–49. Urbana: Univ. of Illinois Press, 1992.

Geertz, Clifford. *The Interpretation of Cultures.* New York: Basic, 1977.

Gellén, József. "Immigrant Experience in Hungarian American Poetry before 1945 (a Preliminary Assessment)." *Acta Scientiarum Hungaricae* 20, nos. 1 and 2 (1978): 81–97.

Geller, James J. *Famous Songs and Their Stories.* New York: Macauley, 1931.

Geneson, Silas K. C. "Cry Not in Vain: The Boycott of 1905." *Chinese America* 11 (1997): 27–45.

Gerstle, Gary. "Liberty, Coercion, and the Making of Americans." *Journal of American History* 84 (September 1997): 524–28.

Giddens, Anthony. *The Consequences of Modernity*. Stanford, Calif.: Stanford Univ. Press, 1990.

Glen, Susan A. *Daughters of the Shtetl: Life and Labor in the Immigrant Generation*. Ithaca, N.Y.: Cornell Univ. Press, 1990.

Gordon, Michael Allen. "Studies in Irish and Irish American Thought and Behavior in Gilded Age New York City." Ph.D. dissertation, University of Rochester, 1977.

Greene, Victor. *Passion for Polka: Old Time Ethnic Music in America*. Berkeley: Univ. of California Press, 1992.

———. *American Immigrant Leaders, 1800–1910*. Baltimore: Johns Hopkins Univ. Press, 1987.

Greenway, John. *American Folksongs of Protest*. Philadelphia: Univ. of Pennsylvania Press, 1953.

Grimes, Robert. *How Shall We Sing in a Foreign Land?: Music of Irish Catholic Immigrants in the Antebellum United States*. Notre Dame, Ind.: Univ. of Notre Dame Press, 1996.

Gromada, Thaddeus. "Polish Tatra Highlander Folk Music and Dance Ensembles in America." *Tatranski Orzeł* 48 (Spring 1995): 2, 6–8.

Guillet Edwin C. *The Great Migration: The Atlantic Crossing by Sailing Ship Since 1770*. Toronto: Univ. of Toronto Press, 1963.

Gutman, Herbert, ed. *Work, Culture, and Society in Industrializing America*. New York: Vintage, 1977.

Hamm, Charles. *Yesterdays: Popular Song in America*. New York: Norton, 1979.

Hand, Wayland D. et al. "Songs of the Butte Miner." *Western Folklore* 9 (January 1950): 1–49.

Hanes-Harvey, Anne Charlotte. "My Name is Yon Yonson, I Came from Wisconsin; Immigrant Types on the American Stage and their Function in Assimilation/Ethnicization." Paper presented at the Immigration History Research Center, University of Minnesota, March 1996.

Hannett, Frances. "The Haunting Lyric: The Personal and Social Significance of American Popular Songs." *Psychoanalytical Quarterly* 33 (April 1964): 226–69.

Harvey, Anne Charlotte. "Swedish American Theatre." In *Ethnic Theatre in the United States,* ed. Maxine Schwartz Seller, 491–512. Westport, Conn.: Greenwood, 1983.

Heiss, Christine. "German Radicals in Industrial America: The Lehr- and Wehr-Vereine in Gilded Age Chicago." In *German Workers in Industrial Chicago, 1850–1910*, ed. Hartmut Keil and John Jentz, 206–35. Dekalb: Northern Illinois Univ. Press, 1983.

Herrera-Sobek, María. *Northward Bound: The Mexican Immigrant Experience in Ballad and Song*. Bloomington: Indiana Univ. Press, 1993.

Heskes, Irene. "Music as Social History." *American Music* 2 (Winter 1984): 73–87.

———. *Yiddish-American Popular Songs, 1895–1950: A Catalog Based on the Lawrence Marwick Roster of Copyright Entries*. Washington, D.C.: Library of Congress, 1992.

Hollinger, David. *Post Ethnic America: Beyond Multiculturalism*. New York: Basic, 1995.

Hom, Marlon Kau. *Songs of Gold Mountain: Cantonese Rhymes from San Francisco Chinatown*. Berkeley: Univ. of California Press, 1983.

Hsu, Madeline Yuan-yin. *Dreaming of Gold, Dreaming of Home: Transnationalism and Migration Between the United States and South China*. Stanford, Calif.: Stanford Univ. Press, 2000.

Huntingdon, Gale and Hermann, Lani, eds. *Sam Henry's Songs of the People.* Athens: Univ. of Georgia Press, 1990.

Idelson, A. Z. *Thesaurus of Hebrew Oriental Melodies: The Folk Song of the East European Jews.* 10 vols. Leipzig, Germany: Hofmeister, 1933.

Jacobson, Matthew Frye. *Special Sorrows: The Diasporic Imagination of Irish, Polish, and Jewish Immigrants in the United States.* Cambridge, Mass.: Harvard Univ. Press, 1995.

Johnson, Aili Kolehmainen. "Finnish Labor Songs from Northern Michigan." *Michigan Folklore* 31 (September 1947): 331–43.

Kahn, E. J. *The Merry Partners: The Age and Stage of Harrigan and Hart.* New York: Random House, 1955.

Katz, Friedrich. *The Life and Times of Pancho Villa.* Stanford, Calif.: Stanford Univ. Press, 1998.

Katzman, Jacob. *Song of the Golden Land: The Jewish Immigrants' Experience in America as Reflected in their Music.* New York: Touro College, 1985,

Kazal, Russell A. "Revisiting Assimilation: The Rise, Fall, and Reappraisal of a Concept in American Ethnic History." *American Historical Review* 100 (April 1995): 437–71.

Keil, Charles. "Music in Daily Life: Future Directions." Paper presented at American Anthropological Association meeting, Milwaukee, October 21, 1994.

Keil, Hartmut, ed. *German Workers' Culture in the United States.* Washington, D.C., Smithsonian Institution Press, 1988.

Kenny, Kevin. *The Irish American: A History.* London: Longman, 2000.

———. "Religion and the Rise of Mass Immigration: The Irish Community of New York City, 1815–1840." *New York Irish History* 5 (1990–91): 29–38.

Koegel, John. "Klein Deutschland: Adolph Philipp and German-American Musical Theatre in Turn-of-the-Century New York." Paper presented at Sonneck Society Meeting, Madison, Wisconsin, April 7, 1995.

———. "Adolph Philipp." In *The New Grove Dictionary of American Music,* 4 vols., edited by H. Wiley Hitchcock and Stanley Sadie (London: Macmillan, 1986), 3:556.

Kornbluh, William. *Blue Collar Community.* Chicago: Univ. of Chicago Press, 1998.

Kormendi, Maria G. Y. *Elindultunk Idegenbe . . . Amerikai Magyar Munkádalok (We Set Out for a Foreign Land . . . Hungarian Workers Songs).* Budapest, Hungary: Zenemukiaido, 1965.

Korson, George. *Minstrels of the Mine Patch.* Philadelphia: Univ. of Pennsylvania Press, 1938.

Kramer, Aaron. "Four Yiddish Proletarian Poets: Two Poems of Morris Rosenfield." *Jewish Life* 4 (June 1950): 16–19.

Kubik, Gerhard. "Ethnicity, Cultural Identity and the Psychology of Contact." In *Music and Black Ethnicity,* edited by Gerard H. Béhague (Miami, Fla.: Univ. of Miami Press, 1994), 21–23.

La Sorte, Michael. *La Merica: Images of the Italian Greenhorn Experience.* Philadelphia, Pa.: Temple Univ. Press, 1985.

Lai, Him Mark, et al. *Island: Poetry and History of Chinese Immigrants on Angel Island, 1910–1940.* Seattle: Univ. of Washington Press, 1980, 1991.

Leary, James. "Leaving Skibbereen: Exile and Ethnicity in Wisconsin Folklore." In *Wisconsin Folk Art: A Sesquicentennial Celebration,* ed. Robert Teske, 49–50. Cedarburg, Wis.: Cedarburg Cultural Center, 1997.

———. *Wisconsin Patchwork.* Madison: Univ. of Wisconsin Board of Regents, 1987.

———, and Richard March. "Farm, Forest, and Factory: Songs of Midwestern Labor." In *Songs about Work: Essays in Occupational Culture for Richard A. Reuss,* ed. Archie Green, 253–86. Bloomington: Indiana Univ. Press, 1994.

———. *Downhome Dairyland: A Listener's Guide.* Madison: Wisconsin Arts Board, 1996.

Lee, Robert. "Singing to Remember: Uncle Ng Makes His Mark." *Artspiral* 6 (Summer 1992): 5–7.

Leung, Chun-kin. "Notes on Cantonese Opera in North America." *Chinoperl Papers* 7 (1977): 9–21.

Lidtke, Vernon. *The Alternative Culture: Socialist Labor in Imperial Germany.* New York: Oxford Univ. Press, 1985.

Lipsitz, George. *Time Passages: Collective Memory and American Popular Culture.* Minneapolis: Univ. of Minnesota Press, 1990.

———. *Dangerous Crossroads: Popular Music, Postmodernism, and the Poetics of Place.* London: Verso, 1994.

Litwak, Leon B. "The Psychology of Song: Songs and Hymns of Irish Migration." In *Religion and Identity,* vol. 5, ed. Patrick O'Sullivan, 70–89. Leicester, U.K.: Leicester Univ. Press, 1996.

Lloyd, A. L. *Folk Song in England.* New York: International, 1967.

Lornell, Kip, and Anne K. Rasmussen, eds. *Musics of Multicultural America: A Study of Twelve Musical Communities.* New York: Schirmer, 1997.

Lott, Eric. *Love and Theft: Blackface Minstrelsy and the American Working Class.* New York: Oxford Univ. Press, 1993.

Lovoll, Odd. *A Century of Urban Life: The Norwegians in Chicago before 1930.* Urbana: Univ. of Illinois Press, 1988.

Lull, James. "Popular Music and Communication: An Introduction." In *Popular Music and Communication,* 2d ed., ed. James Lull, 1–32. Newbury Park, Calif.: Sage, 1992.

Lyons, Sean. "Fighting Words: A Historian Challenges the 'No Irish" Myth." *Boston Globe,* March 16, 2003.

MacDonald, John Holmes. "The Corrido of Greater Mexico as Discourse, Music and Event." In *"And Other Neighborly Games": Social Process and Culture Image in Texas Folklore,* ed. Richard Baumann and Roger Abrahams, 41–75. Austin: Univ. of Texas Press, 1981.

Mann, Arthur. *The One and the Many: Reflections on the American Identity.* Chicago: Univ. of Chicago Press, 1979

Martellone, Anna Maria. "The Formation of an Italian American Identity through Popular Theatre." In *Multilingual America: Transnationalism, Ethnicity, and the Languages of American Literature,* ed. Werner Sollors, 240–45. New York: New York Univ. Press, 1998.

Marx, Henry. "Adolph Philipp (1864–1936)." In *Germanic-American, 1976,* ed. Erich A. Albrecht and J. Anthony Burzle, 43–47. Lawrence, Kans.: Max Kade Document Center and Research Center, 1976.

Mason, Laura. *Singing the French Revolution: Popular Culture and Politics.* Ithaca, N.Y.: Cornell Univ. Press, 1996,

McCaffrey, Lawrence. *The Irish Catholic Diaspora in America.* Washington, D.C.: Catholic Univ. Press, 1997.

———. *The Irish Diaspora in America.* Bloomington: Indiana Univ. Press, 1975.

McClain, Margie. *A Feeling for Life: Cultural Identity, Community and the Arts.* Chicago: Urban Traditions, 1988.

McCullough, Laurence E. "Irish Music in Chicago: An Ethnomusicological Study." Ph.D. dissertation, University of Pittsburgh, 1978.

Meager, Thomas. *Inventing Irish in America: Generation, Class, and Ethnic Identity in a New England City.* Notre Dame, Ind.: Univ. of Notre Dame Press, 2001.

Meek, Bill, ed. *Songs of the Irish in America.* Skerries, Ireland: Gillbert Dalton, 1978.

Meigel, Charles H. "The Singing Germans of Baltimore." *Baltimore Sun,* March 13, 1936. PFPL.

Merriam, Alan P. *The Anthropology of Music.* Evanston, Ill.: Northwestern Univ. Press, 1964.

Merton, Robert V. *Sociological Ambivalence and Other Essays.* New York: Free Press, 1976.

Meyer, Leonard B. *Emotion and Meaning in Music.* Chicago: Univ. of Chicago Press, 1956.

Miller, Kerby. *Emigrants and Exiles: Ireland and the Irish Exodus to North America.* New York: Oxford Univ. Press, 1985.

———, and Paul Wagner. *Out of Ireland: The Story of Irish Emigration to America.* Washington, D.C.: Elliot and Clark, 1994.

Miller, Rebecca S. "Irish Traditional and Popular Music in New York City: Identity and Social Change." In *The New York Irish,* ed. Ronald Bayor and Timothy J. Meager, 481–507. Baltimore, Md.: Johns Hopkins University, 1996.

Mlotek, Eleanor Gordon. "America in East European Yiddish Folksong." In *The Field of Yiddish: Studies in Yiddish Language, Folklore, Literature,* ed. Uriel Weinreich, 179–195. New York: Columbia Univ. Press, 1954.

Moloney, Mark. *Far from the Shamrock Shore: The Story of Irish American Immigration.* New York: Crown, 2002.

Moltmann, Günter. "Roots in Germany: Immigration and Acculturation of German Americans." In *Eagle in the New World: German Immigration to Texas and America,* ed. Theodore Gish and Richard Spuler, 3–25. College Station: Texas A&M Univ. Press, 1986.

Morawska, Ewa. "Changing Images of the Old Country in the Development of Ethnic Identity Among East European Immigrants, 1880s–1930s: A Comparison of Jewish and Slavic Representatives." *Yivo Annual* 21(1993): 273–341.

———. *For Bread with Butter: Life-Worlds of East Central Europeans in Johnstown, Penn., 1890–1940.* Cambridge: Cambridge Univ. Press, 1985.

———. "The Immigrants Pictured and Unpictured in the *Pittsburgh Survey.*" In *Pittsburgh Surveyed: Social Science and Social Reference in the Early 20th Century,* ed. Maurine W. Greenwald and Margo Anderson, 221–41. Pittsburgh, Pa.: Univ. of Pittsburgh Press, 1996.

———. "In Defense of the Assimilation Model." *Journal of American Ethnic History* 13 (Winter 1994): 76.

———. "Sociological Ambivalence: The Case of East European-Immigrant Workers in America, 1880s-1930s." *Qualitative Sociology* 10 (Fall 1987): 225–50.

———. "The Sociology and Historiography of Immigration." In *Immigration Reconsidered: History, Sociology, and Politics,* ed. Virginia Yans-McLaughlin, 187–238 New York: Oxford Univ. Press, 1990.

Moss, Kenneth. "St. Patrick's Day Celebrations and the Formation of Irish American Identity." *Journal of Social History* 29 (Fall 1995): 125–48.

Nadel, Stanley. *Little Germany: Ethnicity, Religion, and Class in New York City, 1845–1880.* Urbana: Univ. of Illinois Press, 1990.

Nash, Gary, et al. *History on Trial: Culture Wars and the Teaching of the Past.* New York: Knopf, 1997.

Newman, Simon. *Parades and the Politics of the Street: Festive Culture in the Early American Republic.* Philadelphia: Univ. of Pennsylvania Press, 1997.

Newton, Christopher. "Farfariello: The Immigrant Butterfly on Stage." Paper given at Immigration History Research Center Conference, University of Minnesota, March 1995.

Ngae, Mae M. "The Architecture of Race in American Immigration Law: A Reconsideration." *Journal of American History* 86 (June 1999): 67–92.

Nusbaum, Philip. Liner notes to *Norwegian-American Music From Minnesota: Old Time and Traditional Favorites,* 1989. Minnesota Historical Society Record.

Odo, Franklin, and Harry Minoru Urata, "Hole, Hole, Bushi: Songs of Hawaii's Japanese Immigrants." *Hawaii Mana* 6 (Hawaii: Elepaio, 1981), 69–75.

———, and Kazuto Sinoto. *A Pictorial History of the Japanese in Hawai'i, 1885–1924.* Honolulu, Hawaii: Bishop Museum Press, 1985.

Orsi, Robert. *The Madonna of 115th Street: Faith and Community in Italian Harlem, 1880–1950.* New Haven, Conn.: Yale Univ. Press, 1985.

Owen, William A. *Tell Me a Story, Sing Me a Song: A Texas Chronicle.* Austin: Univ. of Texas Press, 1983.

Palmer, Roy, ed. *A Touch of the Times: Songs of Social Change, 1770–1914.* Baltimore, Md.: Penguin, 1974.

Paredes, Américo. *A Texas-Mexican Cancionera: Folksongs of the Lower Border.* Urbana: Univ. of Illinois Press, 1976.

———. *'With a Pistol in His Hand": A Border Ballad and its Hero.* Austin: Univ. of Texas Press, 1975

Peña, Manuel. *Música Tejana: The Cultural Economy of Artistic Transformation.* College Station: Texas A&M Univ. Press, 1999.

———. "Notes toward an Interpretive History of California-Mexican Music." In *From the Inside Out: Perspectives on Mexican and Mexican–American Folk Art,* ed. Karana Hattersley-Drayton, et al., 64–73. San Francisco: Mexican Museum, 1989.

Pinck, Louis. *Verklingende Weisen: Lothringer Volkslieder.* Metz, Germany: Lothringer Verlag, 1926.

Powers, Madelon. *Faces along the Bar: Lore and Order in the Workingman's Saloon, 1870–1920.* Chicago: Univ. of Chicago Press, 1998.

Primeggia, Salvatore, and Joseph A. Varacalli. "Southern Italian Comedy: Old to New World." In *Italian Americans in Transition,* ed. Joseph V. Scelsa, et al., 241–52. Staten Island, N.Y.: American Italian Historical Association, 1990.

Raphael, Samuel. *Theatres of Memoir.* Vol. 1: *Past and Present in Contemporary Culture.* London: Verso, 1994.

Reik, Theodore. *The Haunting Melody: Psychoanalyitical Experiences in Life and Music.* New York: Farrar, Strauss, and Young, 1953.

Roediger, David. *The Wages of Whiteness: Race and the Making of the American Working Class.* London: Verso, 1991.

Riddle, Ronald William. *Flowing Streams: Music in the Life of San Francisco's Chinese.* Westport, Conn.: Greenwood, 1983.

Röhrich, Lutz. "Auswandererschicksal in Lied." In *Der Grosse: Studien Zur Amerika aus wandererung,* ed. Peter Assion, 71–110. Marburg, Germany: Jonas, 1985.

———. "German Immigrant Songs." In *Eagle in the New World: German Immigration to Texas and America,* ed. Theodore Gish and Richard Spuler, 47–84. College Station: Texas A&M Univ. Press, 1986.

Romeyn, Esther. "Worlds in between Worlds: Italian Americans and Farfariello: Their Comic Double." Ph.D. dissertation, University of Minnesota, 1990.

Ronstrom, Owe. "The Musician as Cultural Ethnic Broker." In *To Make the World Safe For Democracy: Towards an Understanding of Multi-Cultural Societies,* ed. Åke Daun, et al., 163–69. Stockholm: Ethnology Institute, Stockholm Univ. Press, 1992.

Rubin, Ruth. *Voices of a People: The Story of Jewish Folksong.* New York: Schocken, 1950.

———. "Yiddish Folksongs in New York City." *New York Folklore Quarterly* 2 (February 1946): 15–23.

Sandrow, Nahma. *Vagabond Stars: A World History of the Yiddish Theater.* New York: Harper and Row, 1977.

Sarna, Jonathan. "The Myth of No Return: Jewish Return Migration to Eastern Europe, 1881–1914." *American Jewish History* 71 (December 1981): 256–68.

Schelbert, Leo. "Glimpses of Ethnic Mentality: Six German Swiss Texts of Migration Related Folk Songs." In *Land without Nightingales: The Musical Culture of German Americans,* ed. Philip V. Bohlman and Otto Holzapfel. Mss. in author's possession. Later revision published in Bohlman and Holzapfel, *Land without Nightingales: Music in the Making of German America.* Madison: Kade Institute for German American Studies, University of Wisconsin–Madison, 2002.

Schlesinger, Arthur Jr. *The Disuniting of America: Reflections on a Multicultural Society.* Rev. ed. New York: Norton, 1998.

Schrier, Arnold. *Ireland and the American Emigration, 1850–1900.* Minneapolis: Univ. of Minnesota Press, 1958.

Schultz, April. *Ethnicity on Parade: Inventing the Norwegian-American through Celebration.* Amherst: Univ. of Massachusetts Press, 1994.

Scully, Robert. "The Irish and the 'Famine Exodus' of 1847." In *Cambridge Survey of World Migration,* ed. Robin Cohen, 80–84. Cambridge, U.K.: Cambridge Univ. Press, 1995.

Seeger, Anthony. "Whoever We Are Today, We Can Sing You a Song About it." In *Music and Black Ethnicity: The Caribbean and South America,* ed. Gerard H. Bèhague. Miami: Univ. of Miami Press, 1994.

Silverman, Deborah Anders. *Polish American Folklore.* Urbana: Univ. of Illinois Press, 2000.

Simmons, Merle, E. *The Mexican Corrido as a Source for Interpretive Study of Modern Mexico.* Bloomington: Indiana Univ. Press, 1969.

Skardal, Dorothy Burton. *The Divided Heart: Scandinavian Immigrant Experience Through Literary Sources.* Lincoln: Univ. of Nebraska Press, 1974,

Slobin, Mark. "A Survey of Early Jewish American Sheet Music, (1898–1921)." In *Working Papers in Yiddish and East European Studies* (New York: YIVO, 1976).

———. *Tenement Songs: The Popular Songs of Jewish Immigrants.* Urbana: Univ. of Illinois Press, 1982.

Small, Christopher. *Musicking: The Meanings of Performing and Listening.* Hanover, N.H.: Wesleyan Univ. Press. 1998.

Smith, Anthony. *The Ethnic Origins of Nations.* Oxford. U.K.: Blackwell, 1986.

Somkin, Fred. "Zion's Harp By the East River: Jewish-American Popular Songs in Colum-
    bus's Golden Land, 1900–1914." *Perpectives in American History* 29 (1985): 183–220.
Spaeth, Sigmund. *A History of Popular Music in America*. New York: Random House,
    1948.
Stavans, Ilan. *The Hispanic Condition: Reflections on Culture and Identity in America*. New
    York: HarperCollins, 1995.
Stern, Stephen, and John Allan Cicala, eds. *Creative Ethnicity: Symbols and Strategies of
    Contemporary Ethnic Life*. Logan: Utah State Univ. Press, 1991.
————. "Ethnic Folklore and the Folklore of Ethnicity." *Western Folklore* 36 (1977):
    7–33.
Stokes, Martin. "Introduction: Ethnicity, Identity, and Music." In *Ethnicity, Identity, and
    Music: The Musical Construction of Space*, edited by Martin Stokes (Providence, R.I.:
    Berg, 1994), 1–27.
Stone, James H. "Mid-Nineteenth Century American Beliefs in the Social Value of Music."
    Musical Quarterly 43 (January 1957): 38–49.
Súilleabháin, Seán Ó. *Irish Wake Amusements*. Cork, Ireland: Mercier Press, 1967.
Tawa, Nicolas. *A Sound of Strangers: Musical Culture, Acculturation, and the Post-Civil War
    Ethnic American*. Metuchen, N.J.: Scarecrow Press, 1982.
Swanson, Alan. *Literature and the Immigrant Community: The Case of Arthur Landfors*.
    Carbondale: Southern Illinois Univ. Press, 1990.
Taylor, Philip. *The Distant Magnet: European Emigration to the United States*. New York:
    Harper and Row, 1971.
Toll, Robert. *Blacking Up: The Minstrel Show in Nineteenth Century America*. New York:
    Oxford Univ. Press, 1974.
Tsai, Henry Shih-Shan. *China and Overseas Chinese in the United States, 1868–1911*. Fayette-
    ville: Univ. of Arkansas Press, 1983.
Turner, Victor. *The Anthropology of Performance*. New York: PAJ, 1986.
Vazsonyi, Andrew. " The 'Cicisbeo' and the Magnificent Cuckold: Boardinghouse Life and
    Lore in Immigrant Communities." *Journal of American Folklore* 91 (April–June 1978):
    641–56.
Vecoli, Rudy. "Contadini in Chicago: A Critique of *The Uprooted*." *Journal of American
    History* 51 (December 1964): 404–17.
Ware, Helen. "The American-Hungarian Folk Song" *The Musical Quarterly* 2 (July 1916):
    434–41.
Weinberg, Sidney Stahl. *World of Our Mothers*. Chapel Hill: Univ. of North Carolina Press,
    1988.
Widen, Albin. "Scandinavian Folklore and Immigrant Ballads," *Bulletin of the American
    Institute of Swedish Arts, Literature, and Science* 2 (January–March 1947): 2–44.
Wilentz, Sean. *Chants Democratic: New York City and the Rise of the American Working
    Class, 1788–1850*. New York: Oxford Univ. Press, 1984
Williams, William H. A. "From Lost Land to Emerald Isle: Ireland and the Irish in Ameri-
    can Sheet Music." *Eire-Ireland* 26 (Spring 1991): 19–45.
————. '*Twas Only an Irishman's Dream: The Image of Ireland and the Irish in American
    Popular Song Lyrics, 1800–1920*. Urbana: Univ. of Illinios Press, 1996.
Wolf, Edward C. "Two Divergent Traditions of German-American Hymnody. . . ." *Ameri-
    can Music* 3 (Fall 1985): 299–312.

Wright, Rochelle, and Robert L. Wright. *Danish Emigrant Ballads and Songs.* Carbondale: Southern Illinois Univ. Press, 1983.

Wright, Robert L. "Scandinavian, German, Irish, English, and Scottish Emigration Songs: Some Comparisons." In *Ballads and Ballad Research: Selected Papers of the International Conference on Nordic and Anglo-American Ballad Research,* ed. Patricia Conroy, 259–88. Seattle: Univ. of Washington Press, 1978.

Zheng, Su de San. "Immigrant Music and Transnational Discourse: Chinese American Music Culture in New York City." PhD dissertation, Wesleyan University, 1993.

Zucchi, John E. *The Little Slaves of the Harp: Italian Street Child Street Musicians in Nineteenth Century Paris, London, and New York.* Montreal: McGill-Queen's Univ. Press, 1992.

Recordings

Brooks, William. "Progress and Protest in the Golden Age: Songs from the Civil War to the Columbian Exposition," 1978. *The Hand that Holds the Bread,* New World NW267.

Chairetakis, Anna L., ed. *Calabria Bella, Dove T'hai Lasciate?* 1979. Folkways Records, FES 34042.

Corridos and Tragedias de la Frontera: Mexican American Border Music, 1994. Liner notes by Philip Sonnichsen. CD Edition. Arhoolie/Folklyric Records, 7019/7020.

Cserepes, Károly. *Kivándorlás/Emigration: Fejezetek a Nagy Kivándorlás történetéböl (Pages of the Great Emigration Story),* 1989. Hungaraton SLPX 18153.

Fortis, Sam, and Nina Goodenov. Interviews in *They Chose America,* 1975. Vols. 1 and 2. Audio cassettes. Visual Education Corporation.

Harvey, Anne Charlotte. *Return to Snoose Boulevard,* 1972. Phonograph record. Olle I Skratthult Project, Sp 224.

———. *Memories of Snoose Boulevard: Songs of the Scandinavian Americans,* 1972. Stereo Album. Olle I Stratthult Project, SP-223.

Martin, Phil. Liner notes to *Across the Fields: Traditional Norwegian American Music From Wisconsin,* 1982. Folklore Village Farm Record.

Spottswood, Richard. *Folk Music in America: Songs of Migration and Immigration,* 1977. Vol. 6. Recordings LBC 6.

———, ed. *Folk Music in America: Dance Music, Reels, Polkas, and More,* 1977. Vol. 4. Recording LBC 4.

Stechert, Ellen. Liner notes to *Songs of a New York Lumberjack,* 1958. Folkways Record, FA 2354.

Index